The Persian Gulf After the Cold War

THE PERSIAN GULF AFTER THE COLD WAR

Edited by M. E. AHRARI
and JAMES H. NOYES

Westport, Connecticut
London

Library of Congress Cataloging-in-Publication Data

The Persian Gulf After the Cold War / edited by M. E. Ahrari and James
  H. Noyes.
        p.   cm.
  Includes bibliographical references and index.
  ISBN 0–275–94457–3 (alk. paper)
  1. Persian Gulf Region—Politics and government. I. Ahrari,
Mohammed E. II. Noyes, James H.
DS326.P44   1993
953.05'3—dc20   93–13535

British Library Cataloguing in Publication Data is available.

Copyright © 1993 by M. E. Ahrari and James H. Noyes

All rights reserved. No portion of this book may be
reproduced, by any process or technique, without the
express written consent of the publisher.

Library of Congress Catalog Card Number: 93–13535
ISBN: 0–275–94457–3

First published in 1993

Praeger Publishers, 88 Post Road West, Westport, CT 06881
An imprint of Greenwood Publishing Group, Inc.

Printed in the United States of America

The paper used in this book complies with the
Permanent Paper Standard issued by the National
Information Standards Organization (Z39.48–1984).

10 9 8 7 6 5 4 3 2 1

For my father, for teaching me to love and reason, and for Charles T. Goodsell, another great teacher, a scholar, and a friend. For teachers like them I am reminded of Henry Brooks Adams' observation: "A teacher affects eternity; he can never tell where his influence stops."

M. E. Ahrari

And for George Lenczowski, from a beneficiary of his extraordinary scholarship and friendship over 40 years.

James H. Noyes

Contents

Tables and Figures ix
Acknowledgments xi
Maps xiii

    Introduction: Background and Overview 1
        M. E. Ahrari and James H. Noyes

I The Outside Powers and the Persian Gulf

1 Policies of the United States and the Commonwealth of Independent States: A Post–Cold War Perspective 21
    James H. Noyes

2 The Persian Gulf: A European Challenge to U.S. Hegemony? 48
    Leon T. Hadar

II Dominant Indigenous Players

3 Iran in the Post–Cold War Persian Gulf Order 81
    M. E. Ahrari

4 Iraq and the Post–Cold War Order 99
    Ahmad Hashim

5 The Saudi Role in the New Middle East Order 125
    Joseph Twinam

III Strategic Issues and Prospects

6 Gulf Oil: Geo-Economic and Geo-Strategic Realities in the Post–Cold War and Post–Gulf War Era 149
   David Winterford and Robert E. Looney

7 Arms Race in the Persian Gulf: The Post–Cold War Dynamics 172
   M. E. Ahrari

8 The Gulf Cooperation Council: Prospects for Collective Security 197
   Kenneth Katzman

   Conclusion: Regional Outlook 221
   M. E. Ahrari and James H. Noyes

Appendix A: The Proliferation of Chemical Weapons in the Middle East and Its Implications 233
Appendix B: The Proliferation of Ballistic Missiles in Selected Middle Eastern Countries 234
Selected Bibliography 235
Index 237
About the Editors and Contributors 241

Tables and Figures

TABLES

7.1 Military Expenditures (MILEX) in Constant Dollars and
as Percentage of GNP: Selected Middle Eastern Countries   176
7.2 Military Expenditures (MILEX), GNP, and Percentages of
MILEX in Relation to GNP: Iran and Saudi Arabia   178
7.3 Percentage of Each Supplier's Agreement Value in the
Middle East, 1983–90   182
7.4 Ballistic Missile, Chemical/Biological, and Nuclear
Capabilities in Selected Middle Eastern Countries   185

FIGURES

7.1 Arms Transfer Agreements, 1984–90, with the Near East   182
7.2 Arms Deliveries to Iran and Iraq Collectively, 1983–90   183

Acknowledgments

For an author and one of the editors of a project of this nature, the most pleasant task is to acknowledge those who have either directly or indirectly affected it. The foremost among those are two individuals who took time to read my own chapter on the arms race, Major General Peter Robinson, commandant of my own institution, and Brad Roberts, editor of *Washington Quarterly*. My colleague Armin Ludwig has been more than generous with his time in providing four maps for this volume (as he has been in furnishing numerous other maps for me in my teaching assignments).

I have always regarded librarians to be a special breed of people who have so much patience with and interest in research projects of their clients. I do not know whether I would have been able to finish any project without their incessant help. Sue Goodman, Middle East Bibliographer at the Air University Library, is one such person. She conducted tedious and time-consuming research for me on a number of topics, and frequently on short notice. I also wish to thank Shirley Laseter, Chief of the Reference Branch; Terry Hawkins, Bibliographer of Strategic Defenses; and Ruth Griffin of the Inter-library Loans Section of the same library for their help. Annie Robinson and Kenosha Toles provided timely secretarial assistance.

Writers also get their encouragement from their families and friends. Of course, my immediate family has always remained a source of love, affection, and encouragement, despite the physical distance that has kept us apart. I also wish to acknowledge two friends, Judy Robbins and Richard ("Dicky") Walsh, who made a lot of difference in the whacky world of an intellectual. I especially thank them for their forbearance.

M. E. Ahrari

Maps

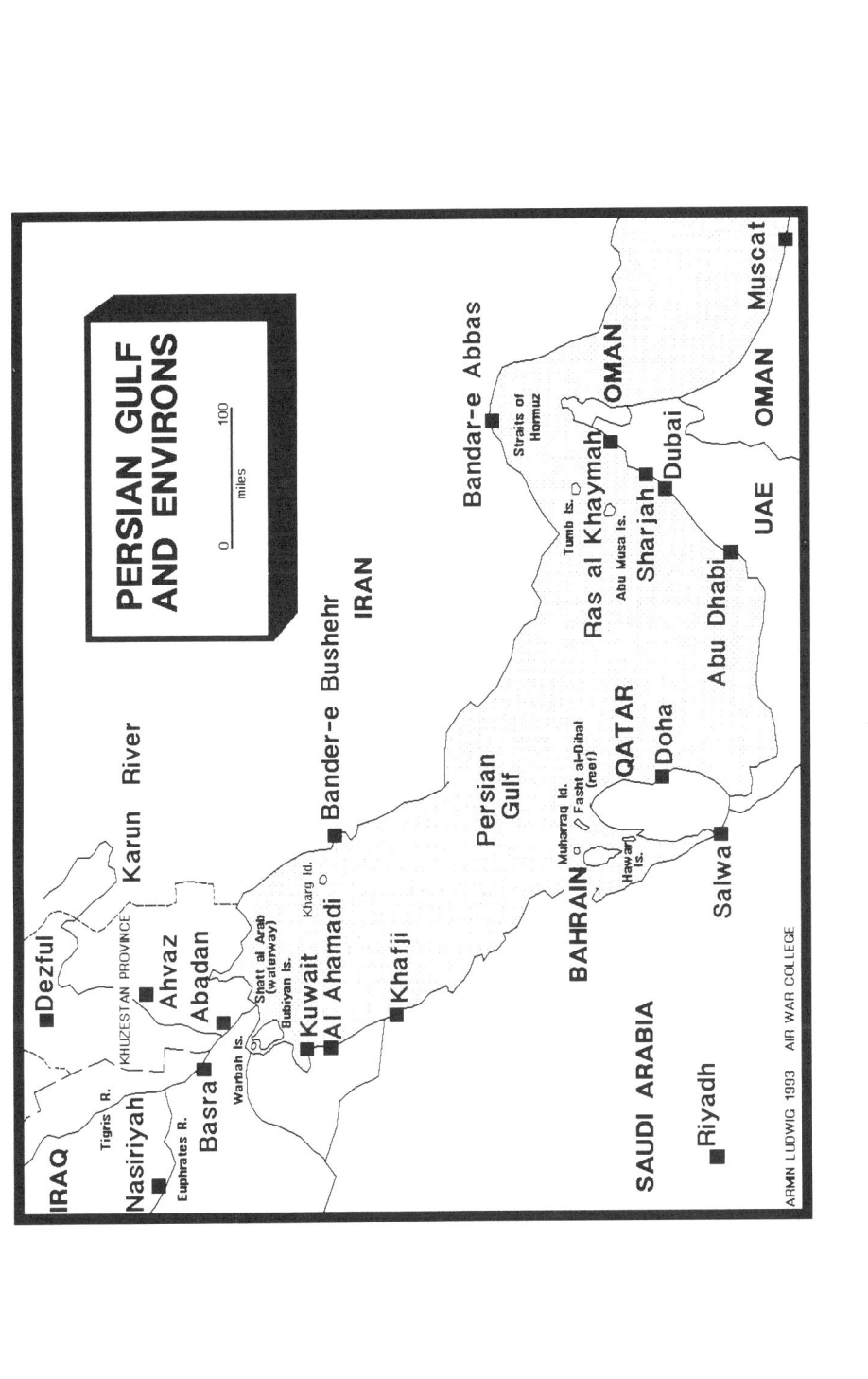

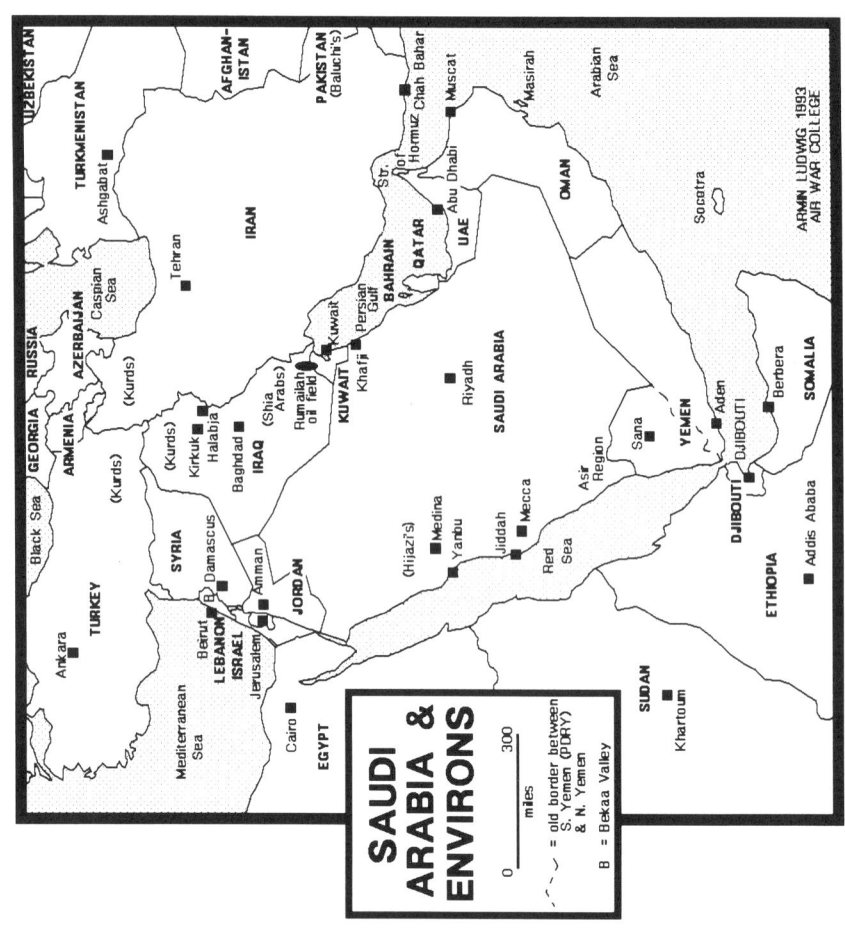

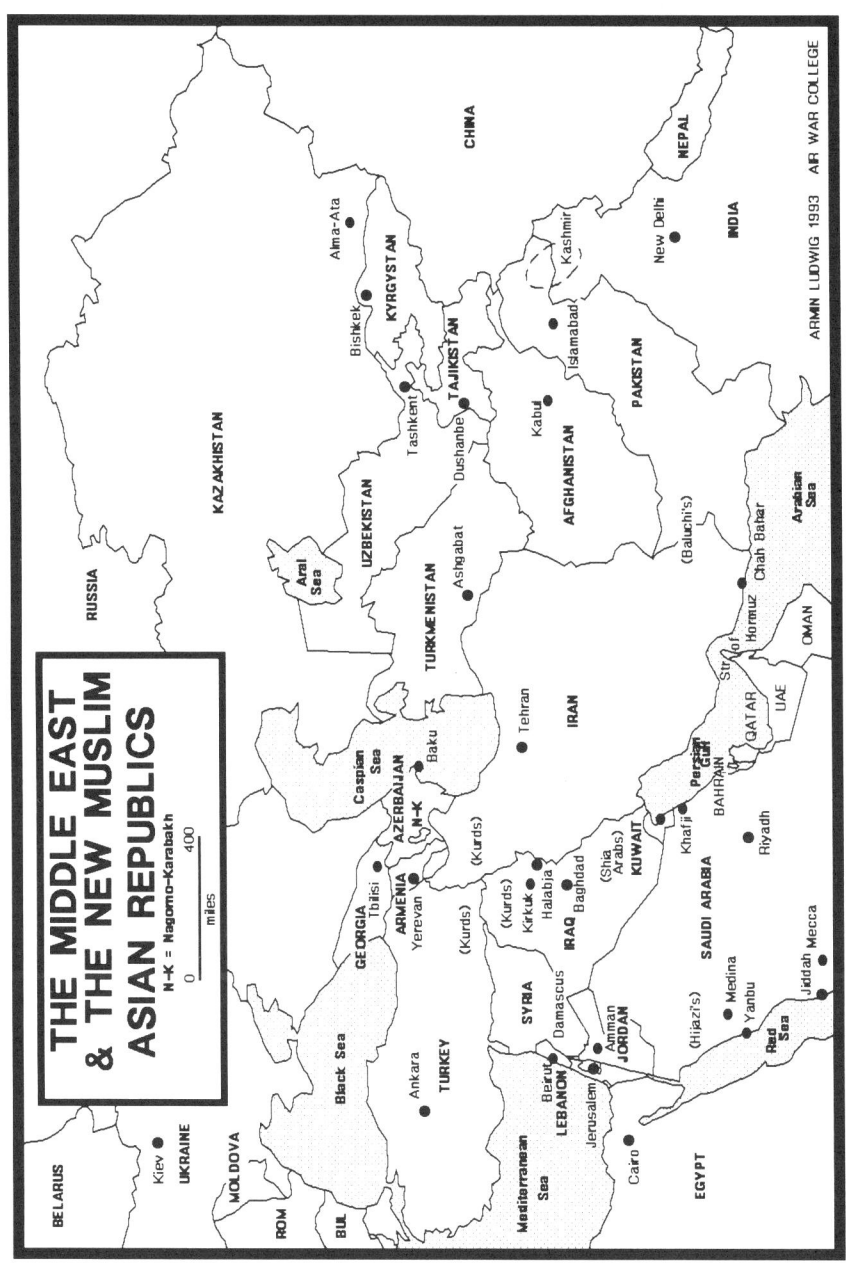

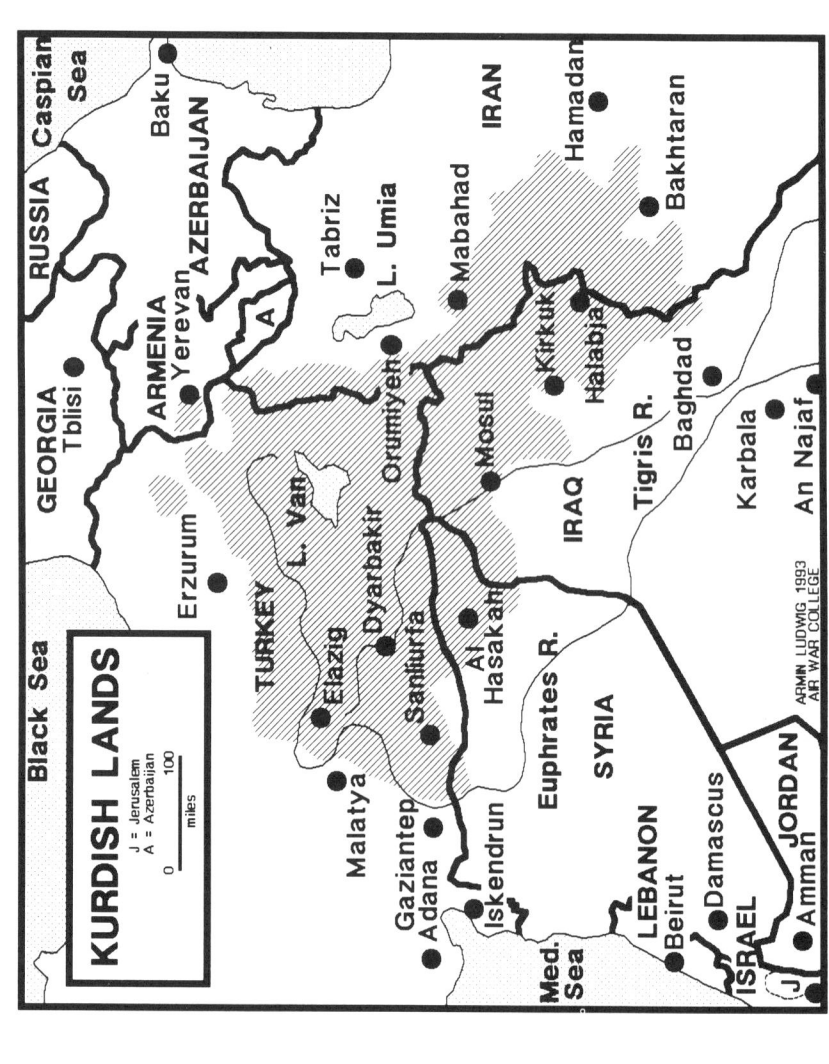

The Persian Gulf After the Cold War

Introduction: Background and Overview

M. E. Ahrari and James H. Noyes

The first two years of the 1990s have already brought about changes of revolutionary proportion in the international arena. As if the equally momentous mutations of the previous decade were not enough — the liberation of the erstwhile Soviet satellites and their adoption of democratic governments, the collapse of the detested Berlin Wall that symbolized the subjugation of eastern Europe, the unification of Germany, to name only a few — the 1990s also witnessed the banning of the Communist Party in the USSR, the eventual collapse of the Soviet Union itself as we have known it since the Communist revolution of 1917, and its replacement by the 11-member Commonwealth of Independent States (CIS) in 1991.[1] The viability of this commonwealth remains uncertain, given the remaining unresolved intractable issues, such as the control of the nuclear weapons, the issue of military command and control, and the basis of distribution of economic assistance from the West within the CIS.

Despite these remarkable changes in Europe, no one can state with certainty that the strategic affairs of the Persian Gulf will undergo much change. Even though both the United States and the USSR cooperated on measures that eventually led to the Gulf War of 1991, it is unclear that similar future cooperation between Washington and Moscow would ensue just because the Communist USSR was replaced by the CIS. Also uncertain is whether the various states of the former Soviet Union will act in concert on foreign policy issues or split to opposing blocks that seriously complicate Western security interests. This uncertainty overshadows prospects for dealing with future Kuwait-type crises in the volatile Gulf region. Experiments with intraregional integration, such as the Gulf Cooperation Council

(GCC), although more than rudimentary, are far from mature. The arms race continues unabated; intraregional competition for domination remains intense.

This book is aimed at examining strategic issues in the Persian Gulf in the post–Cold War era. The end of the Cold War itself was vividly dramatized by the "new political thinking" of Mikhail Gorbachev. This dry phrase only palely defines the cataclysmic changes in the domestic and foreign policies of the Soviet Union under Gorbachev. He realized that despite superpower status in the military sphere the USSR largely remained an underdeveloped country in the economic sector. For that country to make significant economic progress, therefore, its productive sectors needed to undergo a radical process of *perestroika* (that is, restructuring). Such a process, concluded Gorbachev, requires enormous amounts of capital investment. He understood that his country could not massively rebuild its economy while sustaining an extremely high rate of military investment to compete with the United States. However, the USSR could not afford disinvestment in the military sector prior to preparing a political environment conducive to such a measure. This realization was the basis of extending the new political thinking to the realm of foreign policy.

In foreign policy, Gorbachev rejected the age-old notion that an arms race can be won, making a virtue of the necessity imposed by the growing superiority of U.S. conventional military technology and management. He recognized that striving for military superiority can bring no political dividends in a failing economy. This thinking underscores the new cooperation between the superpowers as they confront global problems.

With respect to Third World countries, Gorbachev brought about drastic economic and military retrenchments. As he originally planned, the Soviet Union was not to become completely inward looking. Soviet gains were to be examined in terms of their strategic value. For instance, under new political thinking, the USSR withdrew from Afghanistan but continued its military support of the client regime. Similarly, without abandoning its military and economic ties with Vietnam, the Soviet Union persuaded that country to withdraw from Cambodia. This measure not only resulted in considerable goodwill from the People's Republic of China (PRC) and the United States but also saved the Soviet Union precious capital formerly expended as military aid to Vietnam.

Between 1985 — the year Gorbachev came to power — and 1989 — when the Berlin Wall came down — even an ardent warrior like President Ronald Reagan became convinced that the Cold War was over. Under his successor, President George Bush, the United States and the USSR continued to improve their relationship. Of transcendent importance in the new post–Cold War era is the emphasis on negotiations as opposed to confrontation, arms reduction rather than an extravagant arms race, and economic cooperation rather than military competition.[2] Therefore, during the post–Cold War era (that is, between 1989 and the collapse of the Soviet Union), both superpowers had agreed to de-escalate military competition and to enhance their endeavors to promote cooperation on all issues affecting their mutual interests. Finally, both superpowers had come to see that the Cold War drain on resources amounted more to exploitation by the various client states than vice versa.

AN OVERVIEW OF U.S. STRATEGIC PERSPECTIVES

Traditionally, because the United States and the USSR competed for strategic advantage (if not dominance) in different regions of the world, they envisioned this competition as a zero-sum game in which gains made by one roughly equalled losses absorbed by the other, and vice versa. The Anglo-American alliance of World War II definitely helped the United States establish its strong position in the Persian Gulf. The post–World War II U.S. predilection for forming anti-Communist alliance systems did not work in the Middle East except temporarily with the creation of the Baghdad Pact, whose members were Iran, Iraq, Pakistan, Britain, and Turkey. This alliance collapsed in 1958 when bloody revolution brought the rule of the Hashemite monarchy in Iraq to an abrupt end. The Leftist regime of Karim Qassem not only ended Iraq's membership in the Baghdad Pact — thereby causing a change in its name to the Central Treaty Organization (CENTO) — but also became one of the staunchest critics of U.S. endeavors in the Middle East.

The near-obsession with anticommunism in simplistic form deprived U.S. foreign policy of many opportunities, because although the blocking of Soviet expansion and influence was unexceptionable as a policy, the policy crudely applied could backfire. This was especially so during the John Foster Dulles era, when Third World countries were judged as friends or (potential) adversaries of the United States on the basis of their willingness, or lack thereof, to become part of Western alliance systems that were being established in different regions of the world. The nonaligned position, which was gaining popularity among the newly independent nations, became a target of considerable scorn by Dulles.[3] Such an attitude had its strategic advantages, but it also cost the United States heavily in goodwill during the early- to mid-1950s and resulted in acute anti-U.S. feelings in the late 1950s and the early 1960s. The policy created numerous strategic openings for the USSR. Perhaps the most glaring example of this phenomenon occurred in relations between the United States and Egypt, although President Eisenhower did earn some transitory goodwill with his stand during the Suez crisis.

Despite its rigidity, U.S. policy undermined chances of Soviet dominance in the Middle East during the 1950s. As a by-product, the United States contributed to defeating Nasser's brand of anti-Western pan-Arabism.[4] Because U.S. decision makers were so preoccupied with containing the Soviet Union, they often overlooked the underlying political intricacies of the Middle East. This deprived U.S. policy of the ability to make tactical adjustments on behalf of longer-range strategic U.S. interests. Dissenting Arab leaders were too quickly labeled "Communists" or "Communist sympathizers." The result was a kind of McCarthyism in foreign affairs. When Arab leaders went to the Soviet Union for arms or economic assistance, they did so for political or economic reasons, not necessarily because they favored communism. In fact, both Nasser and Qassem strongly repressed Communist parties in their own countries while they eagerly sought Soviet economic and military assistance. Similarly, successive Syrian regimes tolerated only tame and obedient Communist activities.

The political contest between Middle East Nasserites and monarchists in the 1950s was perceived by the United States as yet another manifestation of the struggle between Communist and anti-Communist forces. Thus, a pervasive anti-Sovietism and anticommunism guided U.S. foreign policy in the Middle East and the Persian Gulf, as in other parts of the world, throughout the 1950s and into the late 1960s. However, this policy could not find many anchors during those years except for the creation of CENTO, which, as previously noted, remained an ineffective alliance. The defeat of Egypt in the 1967 Arab-Israeli War eliminated Nasser as a viable anti-U.S. force. He died in 1970.

The U.S. war in Vietnam generated in the late 1960s and early 1970s enormous domestic divisiveness and acrimony. President Richard Nixon, mindful of the implications of this conflict for the United States' ability to intervene militarily in future contingencies, stated in 1969 that, thereafter, his country would rely on indigenous actors to promote stability in different regions of the world. This statement, referred to as the Nixon Doctrine, emerged as an important aspect of U.S. foreign policy in the Middle East and especially in the Persian Gulf in the 1970s.

The spectacular victory of Israel over Egypt in 1967 seemed to supply the United States with a helpful strategic partner in the Middle East. Of course, Israel never formally accepted this role; however, given the special relationship between the United States and Israel, no formal declaration seemed to be necessary.[5] Meanwhile, as an important aspect of its post–World War II strategic retrenchment, Great Britain in 1968 declared its intention to withdraw from the Persian Gulf by 1971. Shah Mohammed Reza Pahlavi of Iran began his posturing to fill the strategic "vacuum" to be created by the British withdrawal.

The congruity between the U.S. search for regional powers to protect Western interests and the shah's ambitions to emerge as a regional policeman became the basis for a new level of cooperation between the United States and Iran. Of course, another basis of cooperation stemmed from the fact that the shah owed his return to power in 1953 to the United States. Therefore, the shah became a medium for promoting and sustaining U.S. strategic interests in the Persian Gulf. This symbiotic relationship generally worked well until his fall. During the 1970s, the United States also relied (albeit to a lesser degree) on Saudi Arabia as a partner in promoting Gulf stability. U.S. policy vis-à-vis Iran and Saudi Arabia came to be called the "twin pillars" policy.

The Iranian revolution of 1978–79 replaced the stronger "pillar" with the stridently anti-U.S. regime of Ayatollah Rouhollah Khomeini. Under Khomeini, the Islamic Republic of Iran did not abandon the age-old ambition of that country's leaders to dominate the Persian Gulf area. The difference now was that Iran wanted the creation of its own sphere of influence wherein the Gulf nations were to be judged by their commitment to Islam and their neutrality vis-à-vis the superpowers. Any serious deviation from these conditions was to serve as sufficient ground for removal of the existing rulers by exportation of the Iranian revolution to their countries.

In December 1979, the Soviet Union invaded and occupied Afghanistan, predictably causing a powerfully negative U.S. reaction. Cumulatively, events in Iran and Afghanistan were seen from Washington not only as serious erosion of the erstwhile dominant U.S strategic position but also (typically, from the viewpoint of a zero-sum game) as enhancement for potential Soviet domination. Popular scenarios in the West envisioned a Soviet Union extending its empire through Pakistan and Iran and moving toward control of the international oil lanes in the Persian Gulf. Events in Iran and Afghanistan prompted a statement of U.S. determination to defend the political status quo of the Gulf, but with a new policy twist. That new twist emerged in the form of a substantial abandonment of the Nixon Doctrine and a manifest U.S. resolve in 1980, through the Carter Doctrine, to defend the pro-Western Gulf states, by military intervention if necessary. President Ronald Reagan further strengthened this commitment, especially toward Saudi Arabia. The military aspects of the radically altered U.S. commitment emerged in the creation of the Rapid Deployment Joint Task Force, which subsequently evolved into the United States Central Command (USCENTCOM) in 1983.

Even though these U.S. actions were taken in an atmosphere of crisis, when the Islamic Republic of Iran was perceived as threatening the stability of the Gulf monarchies and when the large Soviet military presence in Afghanistan constituted a much more proximate threat to international oil lanes, it was clear that the actual operational capability of USCENTCOM was limited to containing potential low-intensity conflicts. Any direct Soviet military threats to this area of vital U.S. interests would have to be deterred at the nuclear strategic level or, should deterrence fail, offset by recourse to horizontal escalation. It was also thought that deterrence would be strengthened by rapid insertion of a "trip-wire" force in certain contingencies.

The United States was provided with an opportunity to prove its commitment to the security of the Persian Gulf in 1987, when Kuwait invited both superpowers to protect its vessels from menacing Iranian attacks These attacks were part of an escalatory round in the Iran-Iraq War, which originally started in September 1980, when Iraq invaded Iran in response to Khomeini's strenuous efforts to destabilize the Ba'thist regime of Saddam Hussein in Baghdad. Iran's subsequent attempts to intimidate the Kuwaiti regime into eliminating its logistical and financial support for Iraq amply confirmed Washington's assessment of the threat from Tehran.

The Khomeini regime had humiliated the United States through the hostage crisis, then it continued to menace to the stability of the peninsular monarchies. Nonetheless, a complete defeat for Iran would not serve U.S. strategic objectives. A defeated Iran, at best, would become more vulnerable to Soviet ambitions of establishing a pliant Tehran regime; at worst, Iran might be driven into the Soviet camp. Moreover, there was no love lost between the United States and Iraq, although it was also recognized that a decisive defeat of Iraq would strengthen Tehran's hand in the Gulf. In sum, the defeat of either belligerent would not be an optimal outcome; in fact, there was no optimal choice in this war. An early political solution to the war would have enhanced the chances of stability, but as the war dragged on without a military victor and as Iran adamantly refused to meet Iraqi offers for peace negotiations despite its military setbacks, the prospects for mutually agreed settlement receded.

Given the hostile attitude of Khomeini's Iran toward the United States, Washington felt that the costs of a tilt toward Iraq would be minimal. The aim was to prevent an expansionist Iran from defeating Iraq. This was the basis for the U.S. decision to confront the Iranian navy; to supply satellite intelligence to Iraq on the deployment of Iranian troops; to encourage France to sell arms to Iraq; and to initiate Operation Staunch, which was aimed at closing all avenues of arms sales to Iran. These U.S. endeavors definitely played an important role in turning the tide of the Iran-Iraq War in favor of the latter or, at least, in preventing an Iranian victory. The Iranian acceptance of a cease-fire in August 1988 was a great relief to the moderate peninsular states, especially Kuwait, which had actively sought the superpower presence in the Gulf, and a vindication for U.S. policy. However, because it was Iran that called off hostilities after battlefield defeats, Iraq claimed victory, and as events were to demonstrate, Baghdad's regional ambitions grew accordingly.

AN OVERVIEW OF SOVIET STRATEGIC PERSPECTIVES

The Soviet Union, like the United States, operated in the Middle East and the Persian Gulf largely from a zero-sum Cold War perspective. However, its activities were limited in the 1950s. Joseph Stalin was too busy subjugating the Eastern European countries and working on the brutal domestic modalities of "socialism in one country." Nikita Khrushchev, Stalin's eventual successor, became involved in the Middle East when he agreed to provide economic assistance to Egypt in the building of the Aswan Dam. This was facilitated when the United States, in retaliation for the Egyptian decision to purchase weapons from Czechoslovakia and to extend diplomatic recognition to Peking, withdrew its commitment to help finance the dam.

The USSR also supplied military assistance to Egypt when Nasser fought a war in Yemen in 1962, assisting Republican forces against Royalist forces, which in turn were backed by Saudi Arabia. This war finally ended in the aftermath of the crushing defeat of the Egyptian forces by Israel in the Arab-Israeli conflict of 1967. The Soviet Union also supplied military assistance to Karim Qassem of Iraq, who came to power in 1958 after a coup against the Hashemite regime.

Throughout the 1950s and the 1960s, Soviet involvement in the Middle East remained largely that of supplying weapons to the pan-Arab or socialist/nationalist regimes, which were perceived as anti-Western by the United States. The humiliating defeat of Egypt in 1967 made that country more dependent on Soviet arms because Western, especially U.S., arms were not available.

The Soviet Union and the United States achieved rough strategic parity in the early 1970s. This equality was reflected in the growing complexity of the Soviet strategic objectives in the Middle East and the Persian Gulf. Because Soviet arms were playing a crucial role in the Arab-Israeli conflict, the USSR wanted to play an equally significant role in its potential resolution. Egypt, the largest Arab nation and one of the main protagonists of the Palestinian cause, was also undergoing major changes. The pragmatic quest of Nasser's successor, Anwar Sadat, for the resolution of the Arab-Israeli conflict finally bore fruit in the aftermath of the Arab-Israeli War of 1973. Even though Israel was not defeated as a result of this conflict, a respectable performance by Egyptian forces restored Arab pride, which had been badly wounded by the debacle against the Jewish state in 1967.

After the war, Sadat moved decisively to build bridges between Cairo and Washington. The financial backing by Saudi Arabia of Sadat's overtures toward the United States, together with the "shuttle diplomacy" of Henry Kissinger, succeeded in the virtual elimination of the USSR as a major participant in the Arab-Israeli peace process. The remaining option seized by the Soviet Union was alignment with hard-line (or rejectionist) states such as Libya, Syria, and Iraq.

In addition to establishing friendly ties with the United States, Sadat also made a bold overture toward Israel in 1977 by visiting Jerusalem and by opening a dialogue toward a potential resolution of the Palestinian question. Sadat's dramatic and highly publicized endeavors culminated in two developments: establishment of diplomatic ties between Egypt and Israel, and a related peace treaty that resulted in Israeli withdrawal from Sinai, the Egyptian territory occupied by Israel since the 1967 conflict. These results, following from the Camp David Agreement, were condemned by most Arab regimes as a "sellout." In the Arab world, this agreement became a euphemism for separate peace and a U.S. "plot" to divide the Arab countries, especially because the Israelis never delivered on agreed provisions for Palestinian autonomy.

The Soviet Union, however, reaped little strategic profit from the bad reception of the Camp David Agreement in the Middle East. Isolated from the U.S.-brokered Arab-Israeli peace process, it continued its support of the Palestine Liberation Organization and its alignment with the hard-line or rejectionist Arab states.

The Persian Gulf states achieved global prominence in the early 1970s because of their enormous deposits of petroleum. The industrial world had allowed itself to become inordinately dependent on oil imports, and the international oil markets were heavily favoring the Gulf states because of the quality of their oil and the technical ease with which it could be raised. The Organization of Petroleum Exporting Countries, although in existence since 1960, only in the early 1970s emerged as a vehicle for the exercise of oil power through a series of negotiations with the Western oil industry.

The cumulative results of these negotiations emerged in the form of intermittent escalations in the price of oil. Then, as hostilities broke out between the Arab (that is, Egyptian and Syrian) and Israeli forces in October 1973, the Organization of Arab Petroleum Exporting Countries, under the leadership of Saudi Arabia, imposed an oil embargo on the United States and the Netherlands. This organization offered to lift the embargo once the United States pressured Israel to withdraw from territories occupied since 1967. Although the oil embargo never attained its original objectives, it did underscore the significance of Saudi Arabia as a new leader of the Middle East and the Persian Gulf as a point of vital interest as well as a source of vulnerability for the industrialized oil-consuming nations. The volatile politics of that area underscored the need for vigilance and creative diplomacy on the part of the United States to contain instability. The Iranian revolution, another energy crunch, and the Soviet takeover of Afghanistan highlighted the high strategic value of the Persian Gulf area for the West and moved President Carter to enunciate the Carter Doctrine.

Mikhail Gorbachev's accession to power in the Soviet Union in 1985 initiated an era the likes of which is quite unprecedented in the history of superpower relations. As noted before, under his new political thinking, the Soviet Union was to give military competition with the United States a lower priority, and economic cooperation, instead, moved to the forefront. Gorbachev also decided to back away from a substantial portion of Soviet military and economic commitments to various Third World countries. The eastern European satellites were to be given freedom to choose governmental arrangements of their preference. Eventually, the USSR was also to allow the reunification of Germany. The Soviet withdrawal from Afghanistan restored many elements of goodwill for that superpower in the Middle East, especially the Persian Gulf.

Even though military competition took a low priority in superpower relations in the late 1980s, the interests of the CIS or other former Soviet states in the Middle East, and specifically in the Persian Gulf, do not promise to be low by any standard in the coming years. Moscow continues to attach great importance to the possibility of playing a significant role in the eventual resolution of the Palestinian question, as exemplified by the third round of Arab-Israeli negotiations in Moscow. Similarly, Moscow remains keenly interested in enhancing its diplomatic leverage in the Persian Gulf, especially now that it is no longer saddled by communism, an ideology that was abhorrent to the Muslim states of that area. Also worth noting are a number of agreements concluded between Iran and the former USSR that are apparently still honored by the CIS. As long as Western weapons technology remains largely unavailable to the Islamic Republic, the CIS is likely to emerge as a primary source for its arms in the foreseeable future. The Persian Gulf states also are likely to utilize the CIS avenue in the future when Western weapons are not available to them.

In the 1990s, when the European Economic Community (EC) emerges as an integrated entity and especially when economic competition intensifies among the United States, Japan, and the EC, both Japan and the EC may aggressively seek extensive trade agreements with the hard-line Arab states. As a great power, the CIS is also likely to build on its trade ties with a number of Arab states — especially Libya, Syria, Yemen, and Iraq — that might find it hard to do business with the United States for political reasons.

THE EUROPEAN COMMUNITY AND THE PERSIAN GULF

The western European countries did not adopt a sustained independent position on the Middle East until the 1970s. The Arab-Israeli War of 1973 was an occasion when these countries, overly conscious of the then-emerging petropower, did not want to antagonize the Arab states on the Arab-Israeli conflict. In the aftermath of the imposition of the Arab oil embargo of October 1973–March 1974, the western European countries not only went to great lengths in distancing themselves from the United States but also developed policies that were welcomed by the Arabs.

Even though the petropower all but disappeared in the 1980s, the precedence of political independence on the part of western Europe regarding the Arab-Israeli conflict remained alive and well. In the post–Cold War years, especially when the EC is edging toward reality, western Europe is emerging as an entity likely to alternate its position from cooperation to competition with the United States on different issues in the 1990s and beyond.

The most obvious issues of competition in the coming years are likely to be technology-related trade, agricultural, and arms sales. On all these issues, political clout invariably increases and decreases in accordance with the rise and fall of market shares of a trading state (or trading block in this instance). The western European countries have already established a record of strong competitive tendencies toward the United States on trade issues affecting Europe. There is no reason why similar tendencies would not surface between the United States and the EC regarding trade and arms sales in the Persian Gulf region in the future.[6]

The emergence of the EC promises to increase the chances of the resurgence of a new bipolarity in the international system (if one considers the enhanced role of Japan, the international political system would even appear a tri-polar one), except that this bipolarity, unlike the bipolarity of the Cold War years, would be devoid of ideology-related antagonisms between the United States and the former USSR. How antagonistic the new bipolarity of the post–Cold War years is likely to be would depend upon the intensity of the trade and arms sales-related competition during the 1990s and the next decades.

**CONTEMPORARY DYNAMICS OF SECURITY
RELATIONS IN THE PERSIAN GULF**

Mutations in the international arena that culminated in the demise of the Soviet Union did not seem to have a salutary effect on the issue of political stability in the Persian Gulf, where the strategic interests of Iran, Saudi Arabia, and Iraq are still dangerously at odds. The Iran-Iraq War was, however, evidence that a serious conflict could be contained and eventually shortened by the superpowers working in parallel if not in full cooperation.

A profound threat to Gulf stability that ensued soon after the cessation of the Iran-Iraq War was the Iraqi invasion of Kuwait in August 1990. Saddam Hussein had earlier served notice that Iraq had emerged from the war with Iran as a power to be reckoned with. He supplied arms to the Lebanese Christian forces that had been resisting Syrian military forces. This was one way of paying back Hafez Assad of Syria for his support of Iran in the recent war. Saddam also threatened to retaliate with chemical weapons against Israel if it attacked Iraq in a renewed attempt to preempt Baghdad's nuclear capability. Then came the unexpected blitzkrieg into Kuwait.

The Gulf War of 1991 — Operation Desert Storm — decisively eliminated Iraq as a source of potential military threat to its neighbors for at least one decade. The U.S.–Soviet cooperation prior to this "first post–Cold War crisis" played a crucial role in enabling the United States and its allies to attain their twin military objectives of extricating Saddam Hussein from Kuwait and shattering his military machine. The emergence of the CIS, along with a strong EC, is likely to change the nature of competition in the sense that it would be devoid of ideological underpinnings of the Cold War years. However, if the historical competition among great powers has taught us anything, we can foresee likely competition among the United States, the EC, and the strongest survivors from the former states of the USSR, be it the CIS, Russia alone, or some other combination. Part I of this book addresses the dynamics of this competition.

During and after the British military withdrawal from the Gulf in the late 1960s and early 1970s, the shah's Iran emerged as the leading regional power with the acquiescence of and, indeed, the encouragement of the United States. In the late 1970s, evidence emerged of what could be called an incipient "three-power entente" in the Gulf. In the wake of the Algiers Accord of 1975, which ostensibly settled longstanding problems between Iran and Iraq, a consensus seemed to be forming among Tehran, Baghdad, and Riyadh that together they would guarantee Gulf security and, further, that superpower presence and competition should be excluded, insofar as possible, from the area.

Following the overthrow of the shah, Iran and Iraq moved from tacit security cooperation to bitter enmity. While they were preoccupied with each other in a brutal eight-year war, the third Gulf "power," Saudi Arabia, spearheaded the formation of the GCC[7] in 1981, partially as a consequence of the six members' perceived vulnerability to dangers inherent in the Iranian revolution, the Iran-Iraq War, and the Soviet invasion of Afghanistan.

Historically, regional balances of power have been established or reestablished by resort to war when diplomacy failed to check the ambitions of actors bent on hegemony or on upsetting the balance to benefit themselves. Iran was viewed as the primary threat to the Gulf balance in the 1980s; Iraq, with is vast army, became the incipient threat after its victory over Iran.

When it invaded Kuwait on August 2, 1990, Iraq was the dominant Gulf power, a fact that was apparent in the blitzkrieg of that Gulf sheikhdom and in the lack of deterrence credibility of the extant collective security arrangements of Saudi Arabia and the rest of the GCC. However, in the aftermath of the decisive defeat of Iraq by a UN-sanctioned and U.S.-led military offensive, two of the three erstwhile Gulf powers became prostrate, and Saudi Arabia, with its GCC allies, constituted by default the strongest "pole" in the erstwhile tri-polar Gulf. This reality still does not guarantee the stability of the Persian Gulf, for a number of reasons. First, there are the potential negative repercussions of what the nationalist and Islamic elements in that area regard as the defeat of an "Arab" by a "Muslim" nation, that is, Iraq by a Western-dominated coalition of forces. Second, demands for the creation of democratic governments that were heard in Kuwait and Saudi Arabia and among the exiled Iraqi opposition groups were clearly discerned by the ruling monarchies as inherently destabilizing. Third, the conspicuous consumption in the rebuilding of the security apparatus by the Persian Gulf states is perceived as misappropriation of "Arab" assets by the forces of reform and democracy. Under these circumstances, the Saudi predominance will be threatened. Iran, a state of much greater military potential than the collective GCC, has been busy rehabilitating its military capabilities. Iraq is not likely to emulate Iran in the foreseeable future; however, the legacy of Saddam — especially his vision of dominating the Gulf — might be used by his successor as a rationale of the distinct emergence of Iraq as a major power.

In the 1990s, Iran and Saudi Arabia will continue to be the major indigenous players in the Gulf. Even as a considerably diminished actor, Iraq and its domestic developments, especially its treatment of the Kurdish problem, will be closely watched by its neighbors, the United States, and the USSR. Part II of this volume will focus individually on Iran, Saudi Arabia, and Iraq.

PERSISTENT REGIONAL STRATEGIC ISSUES

Even after the liberation of Kuwait after the Gulf War of 1991 (which was a conflict of major proportion considering the devastation of the Iraqi civilian and military infrastructures and the enormous loss of human life suffered by the armed forces of that country), a number of regional issues promise to persist throughout the 1990s and beyond. Part III of this book will explore the respective outlooks for the politics of oil, the role of Islam, weapons proliferation, and collective security.

According to many estimates, Persian Gulf oil will in the 1990s regain much of the economic and strategic salience attached to it in the 1970s. The facts are portentous: over two-thirds of the world's proven (and most easily exploitable) oil resources are located in the Gulf states; the United States is importing 50 percent of the oil it consumes; oil is fungible, and as recent events demonstrate, oil pricing is again very sensitive to events in the Gulf; and sustained low oil prices have driven up world consumption and have acted as a disincentive to development of alternative energy sources. Regarding the prospective role of Islam in the Gulf, the outlook is mixed. On the one hand, the once-shining example of the revolutionary Islamic Republic of Iran has clearly lost some of its luster. On the other hand, Saddam Hussein's invocation of Islamic jihad in the Kuwait crisis testifies to his belief in the continued potency of Islam as an anti-Western touchstone. Islamic resurgence, both of the Shi'ite and Sunnite varieties, continues to exhibit strong appeal in the Gulf and, indeed, throughout the Middle East.

The most conspicuous weapons proliferation issue in the Gulf region is the increasing acquisition of unconventional weapons of mass destruction together with means to deliver them, including ballistic missiles. The Gulf War of 1991 was the second conflict of the Persian Gulf (the first being the Iran-Iraq War) in which ballistic missiles were used quite extensively. What was unprecedented in this war was the use of missiles to expand the scope of conflict. Saddam attempted to do this by shooting Scud missiles at the Israeli cities, thereby dragging the Jewish state into the war. He hoped that such a development would bring about the weakening, if not the dissolution, of the international coalition that was so assiduously put together by Washington; much to his dismay, this did not materialize.

The most disconcerting aspect of missile proliferation in the Persian Gulf and the Middle East is that geographic distances between population centers have become meaningless, given the fact that a number of states have been busy building their inventories by acquiring more and more sophisticated missiles. Syria has reported to have purchased Scud-B missiles from North Korea and has also been acquiring missiles from the PRC.

In addition to missile proliferation, the nuclear issue also looms largely on the horizons of the Persian Gulf and the Middle East. The UN inspection of Iraq after the Gulf War has provided conclusive evidence that Iraq was considerably closer to acquiring a nuclear bomb than was originally estimated.[8] The Israeli nuclear capability, although still beyond confirmed specifics, is no longer a topic of mere speculation.[9] Conventional arms buildups also continue apace. Iran, Syria, and Algeria are reportedly busy acquiring nuclear technology. The uninterrupted supply of nuclear technology is likely to enable Iran to emerge as a nuclear power within ten years or less. The PRC, North Korea, India, and Pakistan are reported to be willing sources of providing this technology and know-how to these countries.

Prospects for collective security in the Gulf suffered a clear setback with Iraq's invasion of Kuwait. GCC mutual defense arrangements proved to be woefully inadequate. Future deterrence and defense credibility may require not only more robust and concerted actions among the GCC states themselves but also increased outside support from regional and extraregional allies, and in the end, the internal stability of the GCC states — how they deal with the challenges of political change — will be crucial to their external security posture.

In his chapter, "Policies of the United States and the Commonwealth of Independent States," James H. Noyes examines the intricacies and challenges faced in the Persian Gulf by Washington and Moscow. Regarding the future course of involvement of the CIS (or its dominant actor, Russia), he states that "there are more guesses than answers." Despite this uncertainty, the author sees the possibility of a situation when ultranationalistic elements in Russia could take an upper hand and establish a dangerous liaison "with those strong Middle Eastern movements basing much of their appeal on anti-Westernism." Concerning the future U.S. role in the Persian Gulf, Noyes is of the view that "the visibility and the extent of U.S. military presence will remain a tender and provocative political issue within the GCC context and as a dangerous component of Iranian and probably Iraqi propaganda."

"The Persian Gulf: A European Challenge to U.S. Hegemony?" a chapter by Leon T. Hadar, focuses on the dynamics of the growing competition between western Europe and the United States in the Persian gulf. As the European unity becomes a reality, according to Hadar, "the notion of Washington serving as a Gulf policeman, with Europe paying to support this leading role, is expected to be questioned by both Americans and Europeans." He states that the "Mediterranean bloc" of Europe, that is, France, Italy, and Spain, is sensitive to the security and economic problems of the Middle East and remains quite active in proposing solutions to these problems.

Another source of growing friction between the United States and western Europe involving the Persian Gulf (and the entire Middle East) is what the Europeans perceive as the U.S. predilection for military solution of various problems of that region, states Hadar. This is particularly true in the aftermath of the U.S. success stemming from the Gulf War of 1991. The Europeans perceived this war, notes Hadar, as an occasion to cut them, and especially Germany, "down to size," and also as "an evidence of a U.S. grand design to weaken Europe's ability to project power in the post–Cold War era."

In his chapter "Iran in the Post–Cold War Persian Gulf Order," M. E. Ahrari examines the dynamics of hyperactivism of Iranian foreign policy in the 1990s. Even though this activism is a direct response to the experience of Islamic Iran, almost all objectives of its foreign policy resemble those pursued under the late shah. Ahrari is critical of the U.S. and Saudi predilections to exclude and isolate Iran. He states that only by adopting an all-inclusive policy of collective security can the United States and her Arab allies create a permanent structure of peace and stability in the Persian Gulf.

Ahmad Hashim's chapter, "Iraq and the Post–Cold War Order," examines the dynamics of domestic and external challenges to Iraq. "Contrary to the conventional wisdom regarding Iraqi threat to regional security," he argues, "its weakened status in the 1990s poses a serious threat to the very survival of Iraq as a state." Some interesting aspects of this chapter include reasons for the failure of domestic uprisings against Saddam following the Gulf War of 1991 and the contemporary dynamics of Iran-Iraq and Iraq-Turkish relations and their implications for the security of that area. His analysis concludes with a series of questions related to the internal dynamics of Iraq in the 1990s. There is virtually no disagreement that Saddam must go. However, no one seems to have a clue as to what type of leader or political arrangement should succeed him and brutal rule.

Joseph Twinam's chapter, "The Saudi Role in the New Middle East Order," deals with the nuances of some of the crucial issues faced by Saudi foreign policy in the 1990s. The Saudi monarchy has never been known to create innovative approaches or solutions to conflicting issues of the Middle East. For instance, regarding oil, they preferred a moderate price increase in the 1970s, a decade when oil shocks rocked the global economy In the 1980s, they were preoccupied with finding avenues to firm up prices of oil. In the 1990s, their price moderation has remained intact, but in the aftermath of the Gulf War of 1991, when the U.S.-led coalition defended Saudi Arabia, that kingdom cannot help but feel obligated to keep an even firmer grip on the pricing issue so that the potential creation of price shocks remains minimal. Needless to say, Washington also prefers a policy of this nature. The "dusty ambiguity" of Saudi foreign policy to which Twinam refers remained somewhat less dusty in their decision to make their presence felt at the Arab-Israeli negotiations following the Gulf War of 1991.

The issue of oil in the Persian Gulf is dealt with by David Winterford and Robert E. Looney in "Gulf Oil: Geo-Economic and Geo-Strategic Realities in the Post–Cold War and Post–Gulf War Era." These authors' analysis of Saddam's invasion of Kuwait is quite interesting. According to them, this invasion was based on Saddam's calculation of what was beneficial to Iraq in the immediate future. Oil was needed by Iraq not only as an essential source of revenue but also to boost the failing legitimacy of the Ba'thist regime. Moreover, the Kuwaiti oil production policy at that time was at variance with Baghdad's preference for production cutbacks in order to boost prices in the global markets. The Iraqi irritation over the Rumallah oil field dispute with Kuwait only expedited its military action against that sheikhdom.

The issue of the arms race in the Persian Gulf is examined in M. E. Ahrari's chapter "Arms Race in the Persian Gulf: The Post–Cold War Dynamics." All five dimensions of the arms race — conventional weapons, missile proliferation, and nuclear, chemical, and biological weapons — are of utmost concern to the world at large. After all, the Persian Gulf was an area where two major wars were fought in the past 12 years. One of these two wars, the Iran-Iraq War, lasted approximately eight years.

Even after the elimination of Iraq as a major military power, the Persian Gulf continues to be a region where the arms race has not yet subsided. The Iranian and Saudi megaexpenditures on weapons acquisition continues to serve as an uneasy reminder to the world that the next conflict in the area is likely to be even deadlier.

Kenneth Katzman's chapter, "The Gulf Cooperation Council: Prospects for Collective Security," analyzes the intricate politics of the peninsular states and of the Persian Gulf region as a whole. An important aspect of this chapter is the simmering conflicts among a number of member states. In the post–Cold War and post–Gulf War years, the growing rivalry between Iran and Saudi Arabia and the escalating activism of Iran in the Persian Gulf emerge as two issues that would destabilize the security of that region.

This book concludes with a joint assessment by its editors of the outlook for the Persian Gulf region, taking into account the contributors' analyses, respectively, of the perspectives of great powers and regional powers and of regional strategic issues.

NOTES

1. "11 Soviet States Form Commonwealth Without Clearly Defining Its Powers," New York *Times*, December 22, 1991.

2. For an excellent overview of the meaning of the new political thinking see Roger Kanet, "Reassessing Soviet Doctrine: New Priorities and Perspectives," in *The Limits of Soviet Power in the Developing World*, eds. Edward Kolodziej and Roger Kanet (Baltimore, MD: The Johns Hopkins University Press, 1989), pp. 397–425.

3. For Dulles' views on nonalignment, especially as it involved Egypt in the 1950s, see John G. Stoessinger, "Evangelism as Foreign Policy: John Foster Dulles

and the Suez Crisis," in *Crusaders and Pragmatists: Movers of Modern American Foreign Policy*, (2d edition) (New York: W. W. Norton, 1985), pp. 107–32.

4. For a detailed discussion of this point see Malcolm Kerr, *The Arab Cold War* (New York: Oxford University Press, 1971).

5. Israel has, of course, proven to be both a strategic asset and a strategic liability to the United States in the Middle East.

6. For a good overview of trade- and security-related problems between the United States and the EC, see Joseph Lepgold, "The United States and Europe: Redefining the Relationship," *Current History*, November 1991, pp. 353–57.

7. Other members of the GCC in addition to Saudi Arabia are Kuwait, Bahrain, Qatar, the United Arab Emirates, and Oman.

8. David Albright and Mark Hibbs, "Iraq's Bomb: Blueprints and Artifacts," *The Bulletin of the Atomic Scientists*, January/February 1992, pp. 30–40.

9. For a good discussion of this issue see Seymour Hersh, *The Samson Option* (New York: Random House, 1991).

I

The Outside Powers and the Persian Gulf

1

Policies of the United States and the Commonwealth of Independent States: A Post–Cold War Perspective

James H. Noyes

The Gulf, often included within the wider region of Southwest Asia, was central to the Cold War. Just as post–World War II Soviet occupation of northern Iran was a midwife to the conflict, the long Soviet occupation and eventual military abandonment of Afghanistan sounded one of its death rattles. In both instances, forceful U.S. intervention deflected Soviet ambitions.

With the Cold War's passing, the Gulf seems destined to remain a focus of international tension. Well before the collapse of the USSR as a superpower, the region demonstrated full capacity to generate international crises independent of either U.S. or USSR action or influence. Mere cessation of superpower rivalry, then, is unlikely to stabilize the region. Too many military imbalances, deep antagonisms, and unsettled issues remain. Further, just as most assumptions regarding the direction of the surviving post-USSR entities dissolve into nearly pure speculation, doubts arise about the stamina of U.S. interest, because the Cold War provided the framework from which the generally bipartisan policy toward the Gulf was constructed since World War II. This framework's removal more clearly reveals the regional complexities that actually will drive the Gulf's future. Although vital U.S. national interests foreseeably will be engaged in the Gulf, it is no longer apparent that Washington's policy attention span will be sufficient to the task of sensitively sustained involvement. For U.S. policy, the challenge centers on patient reading of regional politics, particularly regarding the various quests for security and problems of political development. Throughout, military and energy issues will dominate the regional agenda one way or another.

Whatever policies emerge from the fragments of the old USSR, in turn, are unlikely to be unified and certainly not predictable. The Commonwealth of Independent States (CIS) has been aptly called "the world's largest fig leaf."[1] To write of it as the cohesive successor to the USSR would be grossly misleading; in fact, it is unwise to assume the continuance of the Russian Federation itself as a harmoniously unified state. Only as the political drama unfolds can the principal national characters be named and their policies identified. This uncertainty creates a jumbled potential for external feeding of rival Gulf forces should Russia and other ex-Soviet entities develop conflicting policies on the Gulf as a source of investment or aid, as an arms sales market, as an energy ally or competitor, or as either an important support for or dangerous inciter of radical Islamic forces.

THE GULF: AFTER THE COLD AND OTHER WARS

Regardless, the Gulf states, momentarily excepting Iraq, increasingly are bound to think of themselves as centers of power and influence, a generally apt impression. From the past emphasis on defensive actions to buy off enemies, the Gulf Cooperation Council (GCC) states now identify their own agenda freer of concerns about the demands of pan-Arabism and placating the Palestine Liberation Organization (PLO). Iran's ambitions dominate this agenda, but both sides of the Gulf emerge after the Cold War in more independent postures relative to the industrial world.[2] In part, of course, this is because the opening of the vast Central Asian republics has altered the geopolitical map. Iran will almost inevitably be drawn toward filling the void created by Iraq's military and political force. With the United States facing greater financial constraints and Europe increasingly preoccupied with integration, the problems of eastern Europe, and the disintegration of the USSR, it is the GCC states', Iran's, and, eventually, Iraq's importance as aid donors that will grow despite immense current drawdowns.

On top of Iran-Iraq War costs, the authoritative annual Arab Economic Report in early September 1992 estimated $160 billion and $190 billion losses to Kuwait and Iraq, respectively, from destroyed infrastructure alone. In addition, the GCC paid at least $92 billion to Western and Arab coalition members, not including the $51 billion in logistical support for U.S. and allied forces.[3] Nonetheless, GCC aid has formidable momentum. Saudi Arabia alone by 1988 was providing 2.8 percent of its gross national product for foreign aid, as opposed to 0.36 percent for the industrial nations. Between 1973 and 1989, combined Saudi loans and grants totaled $59.47 billion, making the kingdom the second largest donor after the United States.[4] Despite the heavy drain of helping support Iraq during its struggle with Iran (often estimated at over $30 billion) and the far greater cost of financing Desert Storm, the Gulf's financial clout remains, whether through international agencies, overt bilateral arrangements, or covert subventions. The GCC's capacity to exert influence within the former USSR was shown after disbursement of their $4 billion (including $1.5 billion from the Saudis) to the former Soviet republics was frozen following the disintegration of the USSR's central government. Riyadh reportedly has agreed to disburse its remaining $750 million commitment, but directly to the Islamic Central Asian republics rather than to Moscow.[5] The GCC states are not without influence in industrial capitals, of course. Beyond the obvious question of oil pricing, the Saudis in particular play a major investment role in financing U.S. debt.

The impediment to prospects for enhanced regional stability and influence arises primarily from the region's acute military imbalance. Eight years of war solidified the belief among both Iran and Iraq's leaderships that national security is achievable only through regional military dominance. During the mid-1980s and early 1990s, the West has intervened with military force twice to prevent just such a hostile dominance. The first intervention was to thwart Iran's intimidation of Kuwait during the reflagging operation; this and indirect Western military assistance to Iraq brought Iran's ultimate defeat. Second, of course, Desert Storm, again keyed to Kuwait, denied regional hegemony to Iraq.

Both Tehran and Baghdad, then, have been thwarted by Western intervention. In both cases, GCC military weakness and the need for Western support have been vividly demonstrated. Until dramatic governmental change occurs in both Baghdad and Tehran, a potential need for Western (essentially U.S.) intervention will remain. This Western role obviously grates against the region's growing nationalism and desire for independence on the popular level. Moreover, it is provocative to Moscow's longstanding sensitivities and ambitions. Whether this Western task can be done with the cooperation rather than opposition of the major surviving entities of the USSR will help measure whether the new era has simply fractured one overriding Soviet threat into a lesser but still dangerous multiple.

MEASURING SUPERPOWER INFLUENCE DURING THE COLD WAR

Projection of the Gulf's future in the post–Cold War era should be preceded by estimates of superpower influence on the major conflicts during the region's recent past. Were these conflicts generated from largely indigenous regional factors, or were they significantly provoked and stimulated by Moscow and/or Washington? The latter case might bode greater tranquility for the Gulf's future. In the former, less presence and influence by major external powers could portend a higher conflict level, even leading to Balkan-style communal fracturing. Although stimulative of conflict in some ways, a Cold War derivative in the Gulf was the imposition of reasonably fixed barriers to regional bullies.

The Afghan War was but one of four in the region during the 1980s. Essentially a direct Soviet product whose failure was caused by the West's material intervention, the Soviet misadventure was unique. It demonstrated the brittle and thin penetration of long years of Soviet cadre indoctrination. It reaped for the Russians deep waves of enmity throughout the Gulf and universally in the Islamic world. Similarly, but without the presence of Soviet forces or even direction, the civil war in the People's Democratic Republic of South Yemen (PDRY) in 1986 marked the demise of the Arab world's only Marxist state. The futility of decades of East Bloc effort there became evident as the ruling Yemen Socialist Party self-destructed together with its utopian doctrine that had sustained the country's long slide into deepening poverty. Like Afghanistan, Soviet actions in the PDRY had done much to galvanize the countries of the Arabian Peninsula against Soviet encroachment and subversion. Both Soviet involvements contributed to the rationale for U.S. and other Western military sales and training activities regionally, but both were contributing rather than primary factors in creating the Western presence. Thus, the Afghan example with its Soviet invasion, support for a made-in-Moscow Afghan regime, and lengthy military occupation is atypical of superpower regional behavior. Its reverberations continue to haunt Moscow as Afghan guerrilla factions and the presence of Afghan refugees stir the civil war in neighboring Tajikistan.

The other two wars were clearly a different matter and are the principal focus of concern for this chapter. The eight-year Iran-Iraq conflict was precipitated by the 1980s' most epic Gulf event, Iran's revolution. Although the revolution initially was seen as primarily a disaster for U.S. policy, the events it eventually propelled also damaged Soviet prestige in the Middle East. First, the USSR's efforts to reap large diplomatic benefits in Iran while retaining its position in Iraq failed. President Rafsanjani's visit to Moscow in June 1989 marked the high point of this expectation, as *Pravda* noted that "one of the most favorable situations — unprecedented in the history of ... Iranian Soviet relations — has arisen now."[6] Iran's lowest points throughout the war coincided with frantically publicized courtships of Moscow. However, this card, while still being dealt, was fast becoming a Cold War relic. Off-again, on-again Soviet support for Iraq fortified existing Middle East impressions of Soviet unreliability as a military supplier. Western military technology, doctrine, and support in the end were credited with Iraq's ability to withstand the Iranian siege.

These events also created the made-to-order episodes in superpower relations that enabled Gorbachev's demonstration of the compelling advantages of parallelism with Western policy despite outraged opposition from hard-liners at home. The West's capacity to mobilize naval forces during reflagging operations for Kuwait in 1984–88, as well as the UN's resolve, showed the Gulf's continued ranking as a vital interest to the industrial world at a level sufficient to justify military action and that without a dependable and logistically suitable ally in the Gulf, Moscow's military opposition would be hollow. Moreover, to what end would Moscow provoke greater instability on its own flank?

Like the West, Moscow saw grave disadvantages to a decisive victory by either Iran or Iraq and recognized the risks as well as the lack of rewards in blocking the industrial world's efforts to assure the orderly flow of oil while trying to become part of that world economy. Once again, larger Soviet interests were being jeopardized by a state, Iraq, whose utility as an arms purchaser and quasi ally, by comparison, dwindled to insignificance. Here, in dramatic form, and elsewhere in Africa and Asia, the USSR's transition to an establishment power was unfolding. That transition, as evidenced in the USSR's successor entities, remains far from complete in the political realm, as Russian nationalists and old party stalwarts continue to resist.

It was the region's fourth conflict that dramatized the Cold War's demise when the Desert Storm coalition performed without opposition from Moscow. Larger Soviet interests were so seriously jeopardized by Saddam's bizarre behavior that, again, his remaining old guard Moscow supporters became conspicuously isolated. Earlier, U.S. resolve to protect Kuwait from Iran coincided with the Soviet offer of tanker escort. Thus, what first appeared as a typical Cold War action-reaction actually signaled the opening of a new era.

This was clear evidence, to all but Saddam Hussein, that the industrial world was prepared to mobilize and act militarily to prevent a hostile power, Iran, from achieving major control of Gulf oil resources by intimidation. Further, it was clear that the USSR no longer found it desirable or even feasible to confront the West in a regional conflict in which a Moscow "success" would likely damage the health of the world economy upon which Moscow based its hope of salvation. Ultimately, the main force of these events from the Moscow reformists' perspective lay in their simple suggestion of the mutual benefit inherent in cooperation between major powers on dangerous regional problems.

Finally, comparison of the pre–Cold War and post–Cold War Gulf compels reflection on the change that local wars have worked on Gulf societies. Two defeated nations still seem able to poison the Gulf irrespective of Moscow's or Washington's past, present, or future designs. Casualties in the hundreds of thousands have left their mark. In precisely what way is uncertain. This uncertainty, associated with profound social and political upheaval, suggests the need for massive doses of humility for analysts recommending new formulas to reorder Gulf societies both internally and in relation to each other.

THE LARGER MIDDLE EAST EQUATION: IMPACT OF THE USSR'S COLLAPSE

The strategic implications of the Soviet evolution have been much discussed, but the related ideological impact of Moscow's disavowal of communism and its imperial role in a regional Middle East context have been less appreciated. The significance of the transition lies not in the collapse of communism per se; rather, it is the collapse of Soviet state power that has so altered the ideological landscape. To look ahead in the Gulf requires an appreciation of this evolution.

For the obscurantist core of radical Islamists, the USSR's collapse weakened their battle against the ravages of social and economic freedom associated with democracy and capitalism, but demise of the Left's citadels also removed a dwindling challenger. Eastern bloc atheism, however much an anathema, had never been as threatening and as intrusive as Western cultural and economic influence. Marxism's elite-oriented appeal had run its course. In Iran, for instance, although the Communist Tudeh Party had strength at one time, its acceptability arose chiefly as a tactical ally against the shah. Its power, moreover, derived from cadres that were eliminated. Similarly, Iraq's Communist Party was largely decimated by slaughter and exile. In contrast, Western influence flooded through both societies in amorphous waves of education, films, books, music, clothing, and the presence of tens of thousands of Western residents.

The Eastern bloc, then, represented not a system to be emulated but a useful non-Western model of central economic and political control coupled with imposed social codes. As a major world force opposed to the West, it presented an alternative social and economic system promising to outdistance the more-threatening Western world. The Eastern bloc was the "enemy of my enemy" and, therefore, an ally.

For many Middle East regimes, the Eastern bloc's tight economic and political controls represented attractive devices, when traditionally garbed for local use, to keep Western influence at bay and help legitimize military or theocratic dictatorship. The ideological utility of the Eastern bloc lay in its relentless propaganda assault on the West, its promise of eventual triumph over capitalism, privatization, enmeshment in the industrial world's economic system, and the spread of "cultural imperialism." Despite Soviet atheistic materialism, the model simultaneously served the religious Right wing, the secular far Left, and those basically nonideological rulers seeking justification for junta government. The Eastern bloc had backed the nonaligned movement as well as the post–World War II utopian "revolutions" of Nasserism, Ba'thism, and pan-Arabism that were the emotional props of an entire era.

Not only the secular far Left, of course, had leaned on Soviet and Eastern bloc clandestine support for secure bases, equipment, and training as well as communications networks now so well-publicized. Also, for what may be loosely categorized as the centrist regimes (and even moderate regimes in some cases), there was the even better known strategic support in weapons and training backed, rhetorically at least, in a broad strategic sense by Eastern bloc military and security forces. Particularly shattering for the Marxist ideologues dominating the intellectual climate of most Middle East regimes since World War II was the image of the former Soviet states scrambling to join the industrial West's economic organizations. In fact, since at least 1973, the states of the Middle East were becoming steadily integrated into the Western economy, despite the continuity of the prevailing intellectual ethos.

Although the new generation of pragmatic and educated leaders, whether in Egypt, Syria, Iraq, or even Iran, had long recognized that the post-colonial quest for autarky was a dead end, the sham cult was kept alive as a statist device. Economic control enabled political control, restricted foreign contacts, and provided the ability to politicize foreign trade. Post-Nasser Egypt, of course, had been the Arab world's most heavily excoriated leadership for its attempts to shift from East to West, particularly for its troubled efforts to cooperate with the International Monetary Fund's (IMF) dictums. After years of defending against such "humiliation," President Husni Mubarak of Egypt exuded particular satisfaction during his 1991 Labor Day speech. In recounting how Egypt had "passed the stage when the government ran economic activity," he detailed the upheavals of Soviet economic reform in which, for example, bread prices were raised 280 percent, flour 260 percent, public transportation 300 percent, all unrelated to the IMF but reflecting the same philosophy.[7] Although Mubarak once dubbed the IMF the "International Misery Fund," Egypt had felt compelled to endure the institution as the avenue to Western resources.[8]

As he went on to describe price increases and currency collapses throughout much of the Third World and the Eastern bloc, Mubarak mentioned IMF agreements with China, various Arab states, and countries throughout the world. His point was principally to educate Egyptians away from a lingering Marxist orthodoxy and to show how much worse than Egypt's were the transitions of many countries that had long eschewed reducing state subsidies, let alone dealing with the IMF. Shortly, of course, the situation had come full circle, as the IMF agreed to accept Russia, the Ukraine, and most of the other former Soviet republics as members in April 1992.[9] The completeness of Eastern bloc transformation was painfully dramatized even further by the rush of former rejectionist allies in the battle against Israel to open diplomatic and trading relationships with the Jewish state and facilitate Jewish immigration.

Although Mubarak's internal ideological battles are far from won and Egypt's turmoils are physically remote from the Gulf, Egypt, nonetheless, remains the most politically and culturally influential Arab state. Egypt, furthermore, is the natural balance for the GCC states against either of their more powerful Gulf neighbors, Iran and Iraq. Egypt's assistance to Iraq in the long war with Iran was just as illustrative of this role as was Egypt's lead among Arab states in supporting the Desert Storm coalition against Iraq's invasion of Kuwait. Although lacking the military mobility, modernization, and financial power to exert regional hegemony, Egypt has an underlying strength unequaled in the Arab Middle East.

Because Egypt is a primary focus of the ideological influences on the Gulf states from the wider Middle East, the fate of its struggle against poverty and the attendant rise of radical Islamists will determine the viability of the support link to the GCC. Like the other major Arab states, Egypt is trying to restructure a failed economic system with the consequent social pain while allowing greater political expression. The result, as evidenced even more dramatically in Algeria and Tunisia, is increasing confrontation between radical Islamists and the governments in power. In oversimplified terms, it is as though two worlds have drawn battle lines — the entrenched, largely Western-educated parties bent on modernization and integration with the world economy and the impoverished multitudes still more tantalized than uplifted by modernization. This increasing confrontation weakens the GCC's capacity to withstand Iranian pressure and accommodate internal pressures for more political expression. In turn, external powers, whether Western or Eastern, face mounting complexities in working with the Gulf states.

However imaginary, much of the Middle East dialogue during the Cold War centered on how events were being shaped by the superpowers. Now, without the USSR, the United States has become a more valuable political target to radical Arab Islamists whose routes to power are blocked by governments struggling for closer links to the Western economic system. This development is a beneficiary of Iran's new power status in the Gulf. The combined effect has the potential to magnify adverse pressures on the GCC states.

MOSCOW, MINSK, DUSHANBE, AND SO ON: POST-USSR INFLUENCE IN THE GULF

All of this dislocation and uprooting of an era's hard points of reference in the wider Arab world has affected the Gulf, just as Iran's revolution and the Gulf's wars radiated waves of influence outward to that world. The question of how the future course of events in the Gulf may be influenced by the successor states of the former USSR becomes an exercise approaching outright speculation. A major power, however, Potemkin, in many ways, has simply disappeared from the map, but the actual effect of this may not be so dramatic. This is so, first, because the USSR lacked real influence in the Gulf relative to the vital interests or relationships held by the West and, second, because the USSR's principal source of influence, military equipment and training, may well remain at least as available as before; in fact, through a variety of possibly competing or cross-purposed former Soviet entities, it will likely be available without the controls or restraints previously exercised by Moscow.

There are caveats, however. Some authorities define the disintegration of the former Soviet forces as dangerously chaotic, with various state and private entities rushing to sell off weaponry (including major naval assets like ships and submarines) for motives ranging from personal profit to the urgent need to build housing for former officers.[10] The entire former Soviet industrial military base is vulnerable to organizational disruption. CIS reliability as a supplier could collapse if cooperation among the republics' dispersed but highly integrated weapons manufacturers breaks down. India's Soviet-dependent defense establishment, for example, has complained about a seriously disrupted flow of CIS military spare parts so severe as to require new purchases of entire systems solely to cannibalize their parts.[11] Even at best, past Soviet military logistics for foreign clients was a serious source of criticism and friction. Unchecked, the now-worsening trend could discredit Moscow as a reliable military supplier.

This added unpredictability in the Gulf's military equation is magnified by the growth worldwide of other arms manufacturers that spurted during the eight years of the Iran-Iraq War. China's more aggressive and escalation-blind sales policy also became characteristic of North Korean and Latin American sellers. Iran's eagerness for Chinese military hardware may incline Tehran to become a conduit for Western defense technology back into China. Reports indicate Peking's acquisition of aerial refueling derived at least in part from Iran.[12] This development, plus the Western priority attached to arms sales, reduced the major powers' at least theoretical ability to moderate military development. The ease with which sellers by-passed their governments' restrictions (real or supposed) on the full spectrum of hardware and high technology was a hallmark of the period. The most embarrassing display of policy conflict in this realm during Desert Storm occurred as French warships and aircraft confronted Iraqi forces equipped with advanced French-manufactured electronic and other equipment not yet in French naval inventory.[13]

The continued flow of weapons, technology, and perhaps arms manufacturing capability from the former USSR military complex in one way or another, nonetheless, is reasonably predictable. Moscow's financial needs are clearly the short-term priority, whether from actual sales or in the form of investment loans from the Gulf states. Three senior delegations from Russia visited the GCC states in the spring of 1992, and Foreign Minister Kozyrev, who headed one, was forthright in defining the effort to develop new arms markets in "stable, moderate regimes" as opposed to previous buyers like "Libya, Iraq, and Iran, etc. ... an extremely unfortunate choice."[14] Iran's inclusion is noteworthy, identifying a dilemma discussed below. One product of the visits appears to have been an agreement by Oman to invest $500 million in Russian oil and gas development.[15] Although Russian past, and apparently current, military cooperation with Iran remains a concern in the Gulf (and in Saudi Arabia's case, probably a deterrent to military cooperation with Russia), there is little question that Moscow will become increasingly active in Gulf military sales.

Such activity in the near term, however, is unlikely to have significant policy implications for the West short of its unlikely extension into the nuclear arena. First, Desert Storm greatly enhanced the appeal and mystique of U.S./European military high technology and battle management. Second, given the apparent fragmentation and radical downsizing of former Soviet forces, it will likely be years before current reform and modernization plans can create a new post-Soviet cohesive military of sufficient stature to exert influence in the Gulf comparable to the USSR's. Third, short of the eventual emergence of a unified power comparable in mobility, logistic capacity, and cohesiveness to the USSR in its heyday, the mere availability of weapons systems without the implied backing of actual superpower support in crisis, both political and logistical, will sharply reduce influence.

More than likely, a principal preoccupation of the Russian military, as Vice President Alexander Rutskoi noted in May 1992, will be "the prevention of local conflicts and wars."[16] In a sense, a reconstituted Russian military may have to be preoccupied first with reordering Russia itself and then with protecting Russian enclaves throughout the former USSR empire. Should the military leadership then become infected with the extreme nationalist virus of groups like Sobor (described below), they might look to expansion in

Southwest Asia. At such a point, however, the nationalist cum militarist would need strenuous leaps through many hoops of fire in any search for past Russian success in the region. Too much debacle's debris lies fresh in the modern history of Afghanistan, Iraq, the PDRY, and beyond to the Horn of Africa and Egypt to form the rationale for another go. In the last stages of the USSR, it was the military themselves who began to challenge the use of military means to support the cause of socialism abroad; the role of Afghanistan in closing communism's chapter is well-documented. Fresh reminders are evident. As a Russian correspondent noted during a Gulf visit in May 1992, hotel guests in Kuwait were buying souvenir Soviet shell cases, and in Oman's Armed Forces Museum, Shpagin submachine guns and Kalashnikovs were displayed as trophies captured during the PDRY-supported Dhofar rebellion as "graphic evidence of our past mistakes."[17]

The outcome of current disputes over allocation of military assets among the republics is still in doubt, with division of naval forces between the Ukraine and Russia still unresolved. From the Middle East standpoint, the central question is whether a powerful Russia will eventually emerge as the sole significant military factor replacing the old USSR or whether several weaker and possibly competing entities might evolve. Apart from Russia, the Ukraine, as the second-largest country in Europe, has major military potential, with some 20 percent of the prime manpower of the armed forces and a traditional foothold in the upper echelons of the military-industrial elite.[18] With military production assets like the former USSR's main attack helicopter plant, several primary aerospace plants, and a principal tank design center, the Ukraine could eventually support an independent arms sales program. Should Ukrainian relations with Russia deteriorate seriously, a mini–Cold War is imaginable in which Kiev could not only tie down Russian forces but also stimulate anti-Russian actions elsewhere within the former USSR as well as abroad in places like the Gulf. The scenarios in such a context are endless, and in most of them, as well as in situations of a cooperative relationship between Kiev and Moscow, oil will be central. The Russian economy, hopefully, will require the foreign exchange to be derived from revitalized and greatly increased oil production, but will Kazakhstan, for instance, in the event of substantial production, be willing to accept rubles from Moscow as opposed to hard currency from direct sales abroad?

This complex question of how relationships will evolve between Moscow and the Muslim republics is obviously of material importance to the Gulf states. Attention has focused, rightly, on Turkish, Iranian, and Saudi competition for influence as these republics open to interaction with Middle East politics and commerce. How the republics' relationships with Moscow and with each other evolve is also central. The Moscow transition from aid and investment source to competing fellow supplicant to the West is a difficult and, for the most part, bitter concept to the Third World. The GCC states after the Cold War and Desert Storm seemed to have moved even farther from the orbit of the Third World into that of the industrial nations. The Soviet successor states, however, have edged closer to Third World status, thus, creating an even more unique financial and strategic status for the GCC.

Combining with, and to an extent partly determining, these relationships will be the emergence of a defining new world policy by Moscow. For now, there are more guesses than answers. "The key question is whether they [the Soviet Army General Staff] are ready to ... move step by step toward real military cooperation with Western Europe, the US, NATO, Japan and Korea," according to Sergei Blagovolin, president of the Institute of National Security and Strategic Studies, who added, "Up till now there is no real answer."[19]

Although such speculation may look idle in relation to current realities of Russian military weakness and further deterioration, the long view is essential. Moscow's young minister of defense, General Pavel Grachev, insists on the necessity for Russia to remain a nuclear power following the removal of all nuclear weapons from the other former Soviet republics.[20] He clearly sees the military as central to the reformation of Russian power and that, as Vice President Rutskoi has written, "While restoring the Russian Army we are restoring Great Russia."[21] These and similar expressions of the current leadership are not surprising as Moscow grapples with the giant morale problems of reabsorbing millions of military personnel into civilian life. Elements of assertiveness and even aggressiveness are expectable during the messy and competitive scramble to reassemble relationships and assets among the 15 former republics.

However, with prospects for the success of Yeltsin and his group far from certain, the powerful continuity of the old Russian ideas must be kept in mind. Not all are as far out as those of Vladimir Volfovich Zhirinovsky, head of the Liberal Democratic Party, who won 6 million votes in the June 1991 presidential election, placing him third. Zhirinovsky, who reportedly has strong ties to the Communist Party and the KGB and whose block unites various new parties, sees the West behind Soviet Union disintegration. His goal is to reinstitute the union, with the "ideal variant ... to return to the borders that existed 130 years ago in 1865, when Alaska was part of our state, and our state stretched over three continents."[22] The trend toward coalescence among antidemocratic groups, however, is valid cause for concern.

Referred to as the "national-patriotic movement" or "the red-brown axis," their most prominent leader is former KGB General Alexander Sterligov, who heads the Russian National Assembly,

Sobor, founded in June 1992. Combining ex-hard-line Communists, anti-Communist nationalists, and nationalist writers, Sobor extols the restoration of Great Russia. Further, it demands rejection of Western models while reinstituting state economic controls, all too reminiscent of Nazi propaganda during the 1930s in its campaign against "anti-national cosmopolitan forces." In making such a comparison, former Deputy Premier Sergei Shakrai, a prominent liberal, specifically warned of the threat of dictatorship from the nationalists, saying that "the danger in Russia" comes from the injured psychology and national feelings of millions of people [who] with the breakup of the Soviet Union feel cheated."[23] As the economic dislocations and deprivations accompanying the transition to privatization mount, their sting multiplies the force of this psychological injury.

Although future Russian capability to exert a credibly distinct and potent Middle East policy may be in doubt, there is little question about the widespread intentions of many even within the prodemocratic spectrum to move away from close cooperation with the West on Middle East policy. Sergei Tarasenko, an aide to former Soviet Foreign Minister Eduard Shevardnadze, calls this close cooperation, "just a confusion of the transitional period [which] cannot go on forever," a view amplified by Russian Deputy Foreign Minister Vladimir Petrovsky who defines the Middle East as "always a special case for us because of our geographical location, our historical ties, and our strategic interests amplified by our economic interests."[24]

Invariably, the historical momentum of Russian greatness animates these views beyond economic or strategic specifics. Oleg Derkovsky, deputy head of the Russian Foreign Ministry's Middle East Department, says, "Russia was, is, and will be a great power regardless of the problems.... Sooner or later, with economic reform we will be able to play the role of a great power again."[25] In the few cases in which foreign policy specifics of Moscow's post-Soviet Middle East policy have surfaced among academics or officials, prominent subjects have included oil, the security of the Muslim former Soviet republics, trade and joint ventures, and the potential for influence arising from major defense relationships such as that with Syria. Shorn of the old ideological crusade component, none of these are cited necessarily as sources of conflict with the West, with the occasional exception of oil. To Ratchik Avakov of the Institute of World Economy and International Relations, "Oil will increasingly be a cause of divergence with the West, because supplies, even in the Gulf, are finite [and] is the West going to give Russia access to them?"[26] The question postulates a Western "control" over Gulf oil that is dubious despite Desert Storm. Western ability to block hostile military seizure of Gulf resources should not be confused with a hypothetical Western ability to manage the global delivery of Gulf production. Moreover, Iran already has substantial direct gas pipeline delivery capability into the former Soviet Union, and with Turkish cooperation, Iraq's large pipeline to the Mediterranean — a consequence of the Iraq–Iran War — could bypass the Gulf proper.

A pertinent question is whether planned Western assistance in developing the vast former Soviet oil resources will be allowed to proceed expeditiously and whether Russia itself will be able to control the eventual production from major new fields like Kazakhstan's. The growing tension between Kazakhstan's half-Russian and half-Kazakh population points to a nationalist impetus for independence from, rather than cooperation with, Moscow. A similar potential for resource-related conflict was illustrated by a February 1992 Ukrainian report of an Iranian deal with the Ukraine to build a $7 billion pipeline for direct delivery of Iranian oil.[27] In the context of sharply diminished delivery of Russian oil to the Ukraine, the story may well represent a pressure tactic but is, nonetheless, suggestive. Given the magnitude of estimated former Soviet reserves (293.2 billion barrels estimated, second only to Saudi Arabia's 364.4 billion) any looming oil shortfalls in Russia would appear to derive either from a disrupted transfer of Western production technology and investment capital or from intrarepublic dispute, as opposed to resource depletion.[28] Near-term Russian oil prospects are bleak. Output dropped 13 percent during the first half of 1992, and in July 1992 government specialists in Moscow predicted that by 1995 the level might fall to half the level of 1991, from 460 million to about 228 million tons.[29] With oil comprising some 67 percent of hard currency exports, alarm over the trend is inescapable.

During this transitional period marked by dislocation and disruption, however, world oil supply shortage does not appear on the horizon as much as the divisive effects of excess production within the Organization of Petroleum Exporting Countries (OPEC). Iraq's eventually resumed production will exacerbate these effects. However, given the enormous financial debts owed Moscow by Baghdad and other Arab states, the undoubted continued acquisition of Russian arms, and the desire of both Saudi Arabia and Iran to influence developments in the Muslim republics, Gulf oil seems likely to remain available to at least some of the former Soviet republics. Further, in the long range, should Russian political and economic capabilities evolve so feebly as to create a dependency on Gulf oil, a credible Western motive for further damaging so crippled an economy is difficult to hypothesize.

Russia will continue the same quest for Gulf investment and arms export earnings as the Soviet Union. The new twist arises in the politically activist Islamic realm, with Saudi Arabia and Iran both exerting influence — and perhaps eventually being influenced by — the Muslim republics. Because the Gulf's basic markets and, increasingly, investments are in the industrial world and because the most holy seats of both Shi'ite and Sunni Islam lie in the Gulf states, the greater influence stream appears likely to flow east. Moscow's future capability to affect these relationships is unknown, but the unchecked development of hostile relationships between indigenous ethnic Russian and native populations in Central Asia could upset Moscow's apple cart in the Gulf.

Presumably, however, Russian use of arms sales will remain as the significant continuity of the Soviet era. The problem for the West may be not so much concerting policies with a Moscow government but coping with rogue deals made independently by units of fragmented and demoralized former Soviet forces or by republics hostile to Moscow. As evident during Desert Storm and in previous Middle East conflicts involving Soviet military clients, questions about the numbers and roles of Soviet technicians or advisers have been murky. The USSR's disintegration will vastly complicate the accountability aspect of the issue during future crises. The sale to Iran of several modern Russian Kilo class diesel submarines, the first of which arrived in the Gulf during late 1992, exemplifies the potential. As the sophisticated systems will absorb slowly into the Iranian navy, Russian training personnel expectably will be aboard for years. During a crisis involving Western navies, how will Moscow balance its commitments to cooperation with the West, new ties to the GCC states, and reliability as an arms seller? To forestall these dilemmas, Moscow might limit the commitment of its personnel to a brief initial period. Tehran could then draw on the ample pool of former Russian technicians and military as substitutes, leaving the West without recourse on a government level and Moscow plausibly without direct responsibility.

On a broader level, the West must recognize another continuity, one that predates as well as spans the Soviet era. Russian suspicion of the West and nostalgia for great power status as expressed in the nationalist movements described above could interact in powerful magnetism with those strong Middle Eastern movements basing much of their appeal on anti-Westernism. Although oriented today in radical Islam, these movements crave a foreign ally to balance Western power. Russian prospects for ideological influence, however, are threatened by the former union's communal turmoil in which Russian forces confront Muslims. Moscow's complex peace-keeping role throughout the former USSR already pits Russian soldiers against Muslim aspirations in Tajikistan, with a similar potential evident both within the Russian Federation itself and in other Central Asian republics.

Russian sensitivity to its Muslim secessionist pulls was reflected in what *Izvestia* called "one of the surprises" of Foreign Minister Kozyrev's May 1992 Gulf visit, namely, the lack of support expressed there for the desire of Chechnya, Tartarstan, and other Muslim (federation) republics to secede from Russia.[30] However, although the Gulf states may be unified in their fear of secessionist movements, Moscow's Gulf relations will remain complicated by Iran's and Saudi Arabia's conflicting overall policies toward Islamic issues in Central Asia. Grasping the Iran policy nettle, in fact, will be equally difficult for Moscow and for Washington. In its quest for lucrative and stable Gulf relationships, Moscow will be more handicapped than helped by the priority it has attached to its post-shah Iran relationship. Russian Foreign Minister Andrey Kozyrev reportedly told journalists while returning to Moscow from his Gulf visit in May 1992 that "military cooperation with Iran remains the only stumbling block in Russia's relations with the Gulf countries," a fear apparently not removed by his repeated reassurances in heavily Shi'ite Bahrain and elsewhere in the Gulf.[31] Kozyrev repeatedly denied that Moscow would sell Iran its latest weapons, but with MiG-29s (roughly comparable to U.S. F-18 Hornets) and SU-24s and SU-22 fighter bombers already in Iran's inventory, the exclusion of "latest" weapons represents the same cold comfort projected to the Arab side of the Gulf by Moscow's sale of diesel submarines later in 1992. Moscow undoubtedly argues that such sales, training, and extended support commitments provide scope for leverage and a moderating influence on the Tehran regime, but in retrospect, the outcome of Moscow's military tie with Iraq sours the point.

Nonetheless, Russian diplomats with Kozyrev spoke of United Arab Emirates (UAE) interest in security guarantees by Moscow, because of "the proximity of Iran, armed to the teeth and disputing a number of islands with the UAE."[32] Kozyrev reportedly said Russia is "ready to act as a guarantor of the UAE's sovereignty and territorial integrity," with a bilateral treaty on security soon to be prepared.[33] Kuwait, already engaged with British and U.S. security agreements, might also seek Russian guarantees based on past inclinations and on the assumption that Moscow may retain influence in Baghdad helpful in repatriating Kuwaiti detainees.

Certainly all of the Gulf states, including Iraq, view with apprehension Iran's exported radical Islamic zeal. That Russia shares this fear is clear. Russian journalist Vyacheslav Yelogin wrote at the time of Kozyrev's trip about "Iran ... giving an anti-Russian thrust to its relations with the former Soviet Muslim republics," and ominous statements were made by nationalists in those republics about "the rebirth of Greater Turkestan, the partitioning of Afghanistan ... and the formation of various confederations involving Iran, Afghanistan, and Pakistan," events with the potential to cause "Russia's geopolitical position to change drastically."[34]

U.S. POLICY CHALLENGES: CONFLICTING SEARCHES FOR STABILITY

The Cold War's demise brought particular benefits to the United States in the remote Gulf, which, as a locus of our vital interest, lay at the Soviet doorstep. During the decades when Moscow aided Iraq's and the PDRY's subversive efforts in the region, worked to subvert Iran through the Tudeh Party, and supported the small clandestine revolutionary parties operating in most of the Gulf states, the West constantly faced the contingency of a supporting Soviet military thrust into the region. Although that specter is gone and although Moscow's covert actions have been replaced by major diplomatic and commercial efforts to gain the confidence of the pro-Western Gulf states, the region remains at risk from itself.

As already noted, the two recent Gulf crises united most of the industrialized world to diplomatic and military action, but Iran's pressure to intimidate Kuwait toward the close of the Iran-Iraq War and Iraq's invasion of Kuwait were generated locally. Moscow could be blamed for Iraq's basic military development with the same kind of broad-brush application as the U.S. and European role in supporting Iran's defense expansion under the shah. However, although Moscow tried to save Iraq from defeat during is struggle with Iran, in uncomfortable concert with the West, there was no more hint of Soviet approval for Baghdad's two ill-fated invasions of neighbors than there was of U.S. encouragement of the Ayatollah Khomeini's reign of domestic and foreign terror. A vastly truncated and deeply self-absorbed Russia is now likely, at least during the 1990s, to seek stability in the Gulf with an urgency parallel to the West's. This abruptly alters the regional military and political equation.

What, then, now confronts U.S. policy makers in the Gulf? The end of the Iran-Iraq War and the Desert Storm conflict brought to some U.S. observers superficial visions of newly found balance in the region. Near and seemingly real, like those of Tantalus, they were quickly revealed as out of reach. Following Iran's acceptance of the UN-sponsored cease-fire, Iraq appeared to have overcome its basic strategic disadvantages. As the center of a new Arab mainstream, Iraq had mended relationships with Egypt, whose wartime manpower resources did much to free Baghdad's civilians for military duty. As prime mover in the newly formed Arab Cooperation Council, which included Egypt, Yemen, and Jordan, Iraq's long-frustrated quest for a wider Arab world role seemed within sight. Turkish and Saudi cooperation in building pipelines had reduced Iraq's vulnerability to maritime strangulation by Iran. Jordan's support for Iraq had supplied strategic depth and logistic avenues. The GCC states, in varying degrees, had provided enormous financial support to Baghdad and showed every sign of their continued interest in seeing a strong Iraq emerge as a balance to Iranian ambitions. With all this leverage, despite its staggering debts, Iraq had opened itself to a multitude of new commercial associations with the West and was articulating recognition of its need to move toward both economic and political pluralism. Whether this articulation was calculated deception or a genuine intention suddenly abandoned out of financial desperation and/or megalomaniacal ambition will long be debated, but, for whatever reason, debacle replaced the promising new course for Iraq. In the stunted world view of Saddam and his group, the concept of stability arising from mutually enforcing political and commercial regional relationships was rejected; instead, pursuit of regional dominance became the option.

A brief Tantalus vision similarly emerged from Desert Storm. Saddam seemed doomed by the weight of his stupefying errors and the draconian penalties his continued rule imposed on Iraq's people. A new Arab security arrangement linking Egypt and Syria in support of the GCC states — expressed in the Damascus Declaration of March 6, 1991, calling for increased political, security, and economic cooperation among the six GCC states plus Syria and Egypt — offered to square the circle of balancing both Iranian and Iraqi power. The Western states of the victorious coalition, particularly the United States, looked down from a catbird seat with a seeming ability to call the shots on everything from oil prices to security arrangements in the Gulf. However, the concept of an Arab security force in the Gulf consisting of other than GCC military soon dissolved before old fears and rivalries. Iraq's leadership survived sufficiently to impose a new set of security problems and uncertainties in the Gulf.

To a limited extent, the demonization school of Gulf policy analysis now so much in vogue has a valid role in explaining these evolutions. The demon side of both Saddam Hussein and the Ayatollah Khomeini brought havoc in uniquely perverse ways. Personality factors were key. The Ayatollah's personal hatred for Saddam was obviously one reason for his marking Saddam's Ba'thist regime for destruction as the revolution began. Saddam's personal hatred for the Sabahs in Kuwait undoubtedly figured in his aggression strategy.

Although the demons were there as brutal distortions of religious zeal and secular ambitions, it is the objective geopolitical circumstances that have staying power. Iraq dominates today's debate. A successor regime in Baghdad that reunites the country will confront $65 billion in foreign debt.[35] In addition, there are the pending claims arising from the invasion of Iran and Kuwait. Even with these aside, however, Iraq will remain prisoner to a difficult geopolitical set. Although the absence of natural boundaries is not unusual in the region, Iraq combines this problem with the fact that two neighbors, Turkey and Iran, are larger in population, land mass, and defensive capability. Both have recent historic claims to parts of Iraq. Modern ideological barriers pile upon historic ones — Turkey's NATO membership and European Community (EC) aspirations and Iran's messianic radical Islamism for which secular Ba'thism is rank apostasy.

Iraq's aggravated relations with Syria rest on the personal Assad-Saddam vendetta and Ba'thist ideological schism factors in part but extend deeper into historical origins. Also, in the Gulf, the animosities among Iran, Iraq, and the GCC states over oil pricing and production quotas, boundaries, and unsettled wartime issues are too obvious for elaboration.

War has dramatized Iraq's geographic disadvantages — an almost landlocked state whose 750-mile border with Iran demands more than the available defensive manpower against an enemy with a four-to-one manpower advantage. This deficit is sharply exacerbated by Iraq's lack of strategic depth over its long, relatively narrow confines in which the population is densely concentrated. Although Iraq is rich in water resources by Middle East standards, both Syria and Turkey retain the potential for interference with the flow of the two great river systems. Within the past few years, Turkey temporarily restricted the Euphrates' flow, affecting both Iraq and Syria; Syria has completed a large dam on the Euphrates that reduces the flow available in Iraq for agriculture.

However, it is the way in which Iraq's own communal divisions relate to its neighbors that threatens Iraq, as the aftermath of Desert Storm vividly demonstrates. The point was well made by the then-pseudonymous author of *Republic of Fear*, who attributes the improved performance of Iraqi forces as Iran began to triumph not to the strengthening of Iraqi nationalism, but to fear marked by "the growth of confessionalism, family loyalties, ethnic hatred, and religious sectarianism in Iraqi society — which Baathism simultaneously inculcated and kept at bay."[36]

Baghdad's repression of both Kurds and Shi'ite groups is a ghastly further demonstration of the ruling group's response to a vulnerability linked to foreign military threat. The Kurds helped Iranian forces during the darkest days of the Iran war. In the early 1970s, the Kurdish rebellion received substantial assistance from Iran and Israel, and although Iraqi Shi'ite conscripts formed the infantry bulk during the war with Iran, Baghdad's insecurity was reflected in mass deportations of those accused of Iranian origins or sympathies. In April 1980, Iraq's leading Shi'ite cleric, Ayatollah Muhammad al-Sadr, was executed along with large numbers of the Al-Dawa extremist Shi'ite party for terrorist acts against the Baghdad regime These events were central to the outbreak of war in

September 1980. For Saddam Hussein, Iraq's Kurdish and Shi'ite rebellions are paranoid delusions become real.

The point is not to weigh the loyalties or separatist ambitions of Iraq's Kurdish or Shi'ite communities but to underscore the security problem faced by Baghdad in its regional setting. The post–Desert Storm debate has focused short term on the anticipated benefits of Saddam's eventual removal. The stubborn continuity of problems that will outlive Saddam's rule, however, form the real issue for U.S. policy, because although we may hope for the emergence of a democratic, compassionate, and statesmanlike Baghdad government, these ingredients are wishful figments despite clever Washington propaganda exploits by Iraqi opposition groups. UN enforcement of protective zones for both the Kurds and the Shi'ites (in the limited "no fly" context) and the many other international pressures bearing on Baghdad are undoubtedly encouraging pluralist tendencies within Iraq. Whether the developing agendas are more separatist than democratic for all of Iraq is questionable, however. The externally based and sharply divided expatriate "leadership" for the most part remains severed from grass roots. The vision of new government among most of the opposition leaders stops well short of a unified and democratic Iraq; in fact, the elimination of immediate community rivals and independence from Baghdad assume priority.

Iran, with all its internal problems, has profited strategically from Iraq's debacle. The gain, however, created even more of a Gulf security role for the United States and increased the GCC states' fear of Iran. This new U.S. role complicates the potential healing process between Tehran and Washington. Tehran's split objectives are worth close analysis. Excessive attention has been given to the religious motivation behind Iran's export of radical Islam at the expense of neglecting the realpolitik aspect. For the shah, Iran's expansion from its Shi'ite and Persian particularism to a more powerful regional role was to come about through revival of the ancient Persian empire. This was to be achieved through extraordinary military and financial power sufficient to humble Gulf neighbors.

The Ayatollah Khomeini's revolution delegitimized this secular imperial rationale along with its creator. Retained, and considerably magnified by war, was the thrust to bolster Iran's security through power beyond its borders. Only now, an aggressive, radical, antimonarchical Islamic rationale was employed to break from Persian and Shi'ite isolation that confined Iran to a peripheral and defensive role in Middle East affairs. Therefore, the religious crusade must also be viewed as a fundamental foreign policy device to forward the interests of the Iranian state. The crusade's anti-Western and anti-Israeli emphasis strives to weaken relationships between the United States and moderate Arab states, particularly Egypt and Saudi Arabia, that block Tehran's ambitions in the Gulf, whether on security or on related oil pricing issues. Support for Shi'ite parties in Lebanon opposing the Syrian-backed Amal movement hedges against any Syrian Iraqi signs of reconciliation. Similar are Iranian activities in the Sudan to weaken Egypt, in Central Asia to counter Saudi and Turkish influence, and in Afghanistan to undercut Saudi and Western ambitions for a friendly regime. Speculation has mounted that disintegration of the USSR has opened avenues for the "sweep" of Tehran-inspired radical Islamic influence into the Muslim former republics. In fact, the nearby instability and ferment may work to increase Iranian fears of unfriendly encirclement and communal separatism. The rising force of Azeri nationalism in the old Soviet Azerbaijan must worry Tehran, which, like Baghdad, is vulnerable to numerous secessionist threats. The editors of *Middle East Insight* speculate that this worry is a factor in reducing any Iranian inclination to support the dismemberment of Iraq as well as a moderated attitude toward Saudi Arabia, which is determinedly building on its Islamic relationships in the former republics.[37]

There are, of course, many sides and many voices to Iranian policy. For every moderate and accommodating statement, there is eventually a countering threat or action. Cases in point are Tehran's concurrent efforts to restore correct relations with the GCC states, the expulsion of Arab residents from the small Gulf islands of Abu Musa and the two Tunbs in violation of agreements with the UAE, with whom rule is shared, and reneging on an agreement to return to Kuwait six passenger (Airbus) planes originally seized by Iraq and later flown to Iran to escape Desert Storm bombing.[38] However, Tehran has made hesitant efforts to liberalize its foreign investment laws and experiment with free market activities. Ample optimistic views of Iranian intentions are available,[39] but Tehran's unresolved core political and economic problems suggest a continued need for U.S. caution.

The skeptical view of Iranian policy aims to correct an imbalance of perceptions, not to fuel anti-Iranian fervor or to suggest the usefulness of a U.S. policy to ritually scapegoat or isolate Iran. Iran could eventually emerge as an important balance to a resurgent Iraq again consumed with hegemonic ambitions. Rather, the purpose is to illuminate the unfortunate coalescence of radical Islamic evangelism and old Iranian fears about Arab intentions. These are partly the by-products of revolution and the humiliation of defeat by an Arab world–supported Iraq (minus Syria) allied with the West — an ultimate Iranian nightmare. It is this impetus that magnifies Gulf security problems to a level that seems dominated by fear, the need for revenge, and the inevitability of renewed war. In states like Egypt, whose stability is important for the GCC countries, mounting poverty and a growing level of religiously linked violence offer Tehran tempting targets.

From this it is evident that the GCC states, clearly of priority significance to U.S. policy, now suffer from a regional security imbalance that has even further deteriorated. Although both Iran and, particularly, Iraq have been severely weakened militarily by war, both now have extensive experience in organizing for warfare and in arms production. Iran is obviously committed to major defense modernization, justified by its equipment and training shortfalls during the conflict with Iraq. No leadership in Iran appears likely again to sanction the sending of hundreds of thousands of its untrained civilians, including children, into combat as a substitute for sophisticated weapons systems and professionally trained forces. As Iraq's prospects languish, Iran's potential for Gulf military hegemony grows.

Iraq, however, still remains strong relative to the GCC and, regardless of its future leadership, will doubtless continue to circumvent most international limitations on the acquisition of military systems. The GCC states can foreseeably aspire only to credibly deter, but not balance, either Iran or Iraq in military strength. Yemen cannot be ignored in the equation, particularly given Yemen's support for Saddam's invasion of Kuwait and the bitter Sana-Riyadh dispute over the kingdom's Asir province. Longstanding Saudi fears about the potential strength of a combined North and South Yemen made this support all the more threatening and triggered the bitter expulsion of an estimated 1 million Yemeni workers from the kingdom.[40]

For each Gulf player, then, the urgent quest is for military sophistication — Iraq, to compensate for the strategic weaknesses cited above and to regain regional prestige; Iran, to preclude repetition of its experience with Iraq and to fortify its "bastion of Islam" claim; the GCC, to build against repetition of the kind of threats posed against Kuwait and the UAE (and, by extension, the entire GCC, of course) by Iran during the Iran-Iraq War and eventually by Saddam Hussein's invasion of Kuwait.

The principal continuing requirement of U.S. Gulf policy is to prevent and, if necessary, defeat further attempts by Iran or Iraq to gain control of the GCC oil fields. The Gulf's inherent military imbalance will continue to dictate this requirement until entirely different political relationships develop among the Gulf states. The visibility and extent of U.S. military presence will remain a tender and provocative political issue within the GCC context and as a dangerous component of Iranian and probably Iraqi propaganda. Iran, perhaps with Iraq, is likely to continue periodic aggressive provocations against the GCC, precisely to increase U.S. visibility as a delegitimizing device, portraying the GCC rulers as archaic protectorates.

Arms control measures theoretically might reduce tension and risk. The early post–Desert Storm attention focused on such a hope, however, has faded. Following the recommendations presented to Congress by Secretary of State James Baker on February 6, 1991, President George Bush called for a regional freeze on acquiring, producing, or testing surface-to-surface missiles and a ban on production of plutonium.[41] Meetings of the "Big Five" — the United States, the United Kingdom (UK), France, the USSR (succeeded by Russia), and China — in July and October 1991 and in May 1992 have produced little but statements of pious intention.[42]

There are several formidable barriers. Agreements to eliminate or reduce sophisticated systems would almost inevitably have the effect of enhancing Iran's manpower and geographic natural advantages. Iraq vis-à-vis the GCC would similarly benefit. Also, given the financial stress prevailing throughout most of the world and the particular unpredictability of China, chances for enforceable agreements appear dim. China has announced a decision to provide Iran with its first nuclear power plant despite U.S. opposition. The United States had better success with dissuading Argentina from a sale to Iran of enriched uranium not designed for peaceful nuclear purposes.[43] However, it is the nuclear problem that raises the third barrier to realistic expectations for arms control in the Gulf.

Ever more clearly after Iran's revolution and war with Iraq followed by Desert Storm, the Gulf's military and political problems are inseparable from the core Middle East political tangle of Palestinian and Israeli-Arab state relations. Although the United States can work to block nuclear proliferation in the region (as in the Argentinean case), Washington cannot act credibly on behalf of serious agreements, for instance, over medium- and long-range missiles, until Israel's nuclear, chemical, and biological programs are clearly on the table. Israel's overwhelming military superiority as a regional superpower is simply accepted in Washington as a given, without weighing of the political effects on the rest of the region. Israel successfully portrays the Middle East military balance as something delicate, skillfully utilizing U.S. arms sales in the Gulf as leverage to acquire new levels of sophisticated equipment and cooperation from the United States. These, incidentally, have rub-off benefits for the Israeli arms industry, for example, the September 1992 U.S. agreement to sell Saudi Arabia 72 F-15 fighter aircraft produced a new "major military cooperation package" for Israel.[44]

Thus, arms limitations efforts for GCC security inevitably become linked to prospects for accommodation between Israel and its neighbors. Perspective on the problem can be improved by imagining the terror within the Western alliance had the USSR possessed a nuclear weapons monopoly and vastly superior conventional military advantage over the West during the past 40 years. Yet, this is the comparable prevailing status for the Arab states in relation to Israel. The primary issue now is not who is at fault or who is the aggressor, potentially or in the past, but how to generate trust and confidence. Part of this challenge lies in gradually putting all the military cards on the table.

Even if Israel suddenly agreed to dispose of its nuclear arsenal (most unlikely), the bomb has become the reigning status symbol of power in too many other areas of dispute (for example, Iran and Iraq), and the regional quest for nuclear weapons would not likely cease; however, this event would help and greatly strengthen Western, and, hopefully, Russian, nuclear nonproliferation efforts. Alternatively, one could follow James Schlesinger's injunction that "under the Nuclear Non-Proliferation Treaty, the United States has large responsibilities — in brief, to provide protection for the non-nuclear-weapons states."[45] But whither? Could the United States respond, for instance, to Kazakhstan's request for security guarantees against nuclear attack by Russia or China while also pursuing arms limitations agreements and cooperative relationships with these major powers?[46] Would the U.S. umbrella fit over an Iraq threatened by a nuclear Iran, or vice versa? Would even the most puckish suggest a U.S. guarantee of Syrian, Jordanian, or Egyptian security against Israeli nuclear weapons? Washington cannot be a credible guarantor against Israel's nuclear option. However, a continuing priority U.S. interest in peace negotiations may eventually lead to the point of arms limitations where Israel's nuclear weapons could become highly valuable bargaining chips as regional security arrangements are discussed. This distant prospect will diminish in attractiveness if nuclear club aspirants like Iraq, Iran, and Libya succeed beforehand in their development or acquisition programs.

Aside from the tangles surrounding these security issues, U.S. Gulf policy will be most acutely challenged on the closely related question of Iraq's political evolution, a part of the larger regional democratization question. Given the continued applied strength and grit of the UN coalition, Saddam Hussein eventually will fall. In doubt are the continuity of this pressure and the character of the regime replacing him. This new regime, while trying to move Iraq back into the world stream, will first have to reestablish the Iraqi state. The efforts of the United States or regional states to micromanage the latter process unfortunately point toward the further disintegration of Iraq's polity. The countries of the Gulf need not look as far as the Balkans; across to Ethiopia and Somalia, to Afghanistan, and to Lebanon, nauseating Grand Guignol disintegration performances abound. Syria, Iran, and Saudi Arabia support expatriate Iraqi opposition factions that, for the most part, have no influence in Iraq. However, dreams of influencing Baghdad's future political evolution are one thing; the risks of partitioning Iraq are another, and rejected, option. There is sufficient energy to communal antagonisms almost without exception throughout the former Soviet state, South and Southwest Asia, and the Middle East that encouragement seems cruelly ill timed.

Yet, although there is finally wide recognition in the West that a disintegrated Iraq would leave Iran in charge of the arena, there has been a persistent stream of confusion in U.S. academia between communal and democratic aspiration in the wake of Desert Storm. To one analyst, for instance, "the inconsistency of Washington's cynical postwar abandonment of anti-Saddam Hussein forces in Iraq is why so much of the pro-democratic potential of the Persian Gulf war was negated."[47] Short of a protracted U.S. occupation of Iraq that would gradually try to encourage the essential underpinnings of a democratic polity, one could only search among the pitiful wreckage of Iraqi society for the instruments of democratic movement. Communalist fervor would, however, occur in abundance, be it Kurdish, Shi'ite, Sunni, Marsh Arab, or Christian. And where to stop? Should economic collapse or renewed war in Iran open the same issues for U.S. policy there? Would we be wise to assume the mandate to accommodate separatist aspirations of the Baluchis, the Azerbaijanis, the Kurds, and other communities?

William Pfaff writes that "The past lies in strata of human experience, never totally forgotten even when deeply buried in societies consciousness, but too often, in the east of Europe, still raw at the surface."[48] He goes on to quote the defense minister of newly independent Croatia in August 1991, who, speaking of the struggle with Serbia, said, "We have been waiting for this moment for centuries."[49] The Gulf region reflects the force of these strata dramatically with the rest of the Middle East. There will be strong inclinations in the absence of the unifying Cold War simplifications for U.S. policy to find substitutes. Issues of democratization and radical Islam can all too easily be molded to dangerous oversimplification when the requirement is for cautious pragmatism.

In an odd way, there is a parallel between the military and the political requirements of U.S. Gulf policy. Militarily, we still need to be largely "over the horizon" as the Gulf states wisely insist for the sake of regime stability. Our forces must be credible in deterrent capability yet not so visible a presence as to become targets of xenophobic fervor. This stricture creates military disadvantages and frustration. Politically, although more closely allied to the GCC than ever before, we also remain "over the horizon" in our ability as a government to influence democratization in an era when popular demands are more pressing, locally and worldwide. We are there, our interests are acute, but we cannot be too visible. This in turn creates frustration and political vulnerabilities for any U.S. administration unprepared to explain in some detail to the U.S. public the evolutions taking place in Gulf societies.

The potential for confusion in the U.S. role became most evident as Desert Storm ended. Some critics contended that our assemblage of military might had created the moment for Washington somehow to lever the region's problems into solution. In fact, this fantasy still persists. However, nothing would have been more foolishly counterproductive than to have embarked on a political engineering program based on in-place military forces. U.S. political prestige in the region and, in fact, beyond was sustained precisely because we withdrew the bulk of our forces promptly.

In a U.S. political atmosphere hungry for fresh symbols, it may be dreary to remain stuck with what can only be called a traditional balance of power and realpolitik approach to the Gulf. Without the formation of compatible governments in the region, however, there is little alternative. The United States will probably have new opportunities to rebuild its relationship with Iran and eventually, we may hope, with a responsible new government in Baghdad. Until then, diplomacy with the ultimate backup of military force will work to assist the region, but without the ability to settle its many disputes.

U.S. Gulf policy will be criticized for emphasis on military force rather than on diplomatic problem solving — handily attractive grist for the mills of politics. The reality, however, derives from an almost total absence of Washington's political leverage in either Baghdad or Tehran, where the Gulf's principal physical power resides. Should the UN's sanctions eventually work on Baghdad to bring hope of respectable leadership, new avenues toward resolving fundamental regional problems could open.

NOTES

1. Paul Goble, "Forget the Soviet Union," *Foreign Policy* 86 (1992): 56.
2. The GCC states include Saudi Arabia, Kuwait, Bahrain, Qatar, the United Arab Emirates, and Oman.
3. New York *Times*, September 8, 1992, citing "The Arab Economic Report," annual study by the Arab Monetary Fund, the Arab League, the Organization of Arab Petroleum Exporting Countries, and other leading institutions.
4. *Saudi Arabia*, Royal Embassy of Saudi Arabia, November 1990.
5. *Wall Street Journal*, January 15, 1992.
6. *Pravda*, June 22, 1989, p. 29.
7. FBIS-NES-91-088, May 7, 1991, p. 6.
8. New York *Times*, April 26, 1992.
9. New York *Times*, April 28, 1992.
10. *Wall Street Journal*, April 13, 1992.
11. Washington *Post*, October 6, 1992.
12. New York *Times*, August 23, 1992.
13. *Aviation Week and Space Technology*, August 27, 1990, p. 23.
14. *Izvestiya*, May 6, 1992, p. 25.
15. Ibid.

16. Daniel Sneider, "Turning Russia's Army Into a Lean Machine," *Christian Science Monitor*, June 9, 1992.
17. *Krasnaya Zvezda*, May 6, 1992, p. 26.
18. Steven Zaloga, "Soviet Military Development," *Armed Forces Journal International*, October 1991, p. 19.
19. *Christian Science Monitor*, June 9, 1992.
20. Ibid.
21. Ibid.
22. *Wall Street Journal*, March 18, 1992.
23. *Christian Science Monitor*, July 14, 1992.
24. *Christian Science Monitor*, February 5, 1992.
25. Ibid.
26. Ibid.
27. *Radio Liberty Daily Report*, February 5, 1992, p. 2.
28. *Oil and Gas Journal*, September 23, 1991.
29. John Lloyd, *Financial Times*, August 5, 1992, p. 10.
30. *Izvestiya*, May 6, 1992.
31. Ibid.
32. *Rossiyskaya Gazeta*, May 8, 1992.
33. *Izvestiya*, May 6, 1992.
34. "Map of the Islamic Factor," *Rossiyskaya Gazeta*, May 6, 1992.
35. *Middle East Economic Digest*, September 7, 1990, p. 6.
36. Samir al Khalil, *The Republic of Fear: The Politics of Modern Iraq* (Berkeley: University of California Press, 1989), p. 276.
37. "Middle East Foresight," *Middle East Insight* 8 (1992): 3.
38. New York *Times*, April 16 and September 13, 1992.
39. James A. Bill, "The Resurrection of Iran in the Persian Gulf," *Middle East Insight* 8 (1992): 29–35.
40. James H. Noyes, *The Clouded Lens: Persian Gulf Security and U.S. Policy* (Stanford, CA: Hoover Institution Press, 1982), p. 38 (regarding Saudi concern over possible merger of the two Yemens).
41. *Middle East Policy Survey*, February 1, 1991. Secretary Baker's recommendations represented the report of an interagency commission chaired by Deputy National Security Advisor Robert Gates.
42. New York *Times*, May 31, 1992.
43. New York *Times*, September 11, 1992.
44. New York *Times*, September 15, 1992.
45. James Schlesinger, "New Instabilities, New Priorities," *Foreign Policy* (Winter 1992–92): 20. Dr. Schlesinger served as Director of Central Intelligence, Secretary of Defense, and, finally, Secretary of Energy during the Nixon and Ford administrations.
46. *Christian Science Monitor*, April 27, 1992.
47. Larry Diamond, "Promoting Democracy, *Foreign Policy* (Summer 1992): 43.
48. William Pfaff, "The Absence of Empire," *New Yorker*, August 10, 1992, p. 59.
49. Ibid.

2

The Persian Gulf: A European Challenge to U.S. Hegemony?

Leon T. Hadar

The fall of the Soviet Union and the collapse of the post–World War II bipolar system coupled with the U.S. military victory in the Gulf War and its leading diplomatic role in the Arab-Israeli peace process have created growing expectations about the emergence of a new international system dominated by the United States. The Middle East and the Persian Gulf, the central focus of the superpower rivalry during the Cold War, now seem to be falling under an exclusive U.S. hegemony.

EUROPE: THE JUNIOR PARTNER?

Reflecting this new conventional wisdom about the emergence of a "unipolar international system" and a "one-superpower world," the Defense Department in a 1991 policy paper stated that the U.S. mission in the post–Cold War era would be "convincing potential competitors that they need not aspire to a greater role or pursue a more aggressive posture to protect their legitimate interests." The Pentagon paper made the case for a world dominated by one superpower — the United States — whose position can be perpetuated by constructive behavior and sufficient military might to deter any nation or group of nations, including the United States' Cold War allies in Europe, from disputing U.S. primacy. To secure its leading role, the United States "must sufficiently account for the interests of the advanced industrialized nations to discourage them from challenging our leadership or seeking to overturn the established political and economic order." In the Middle East and the Persian Gulf, Washington should "remain the predominant outside power in the region and preserve U.S. and Western access to the region's oil." The United States is going to continue to pay the costs of maintaining order in the area. It will "seek to deter further aggression in the region, foster regional stability, protect U.S. nationals and property and safeguard our access to international air and seaways."

The national security establishment expects that in the revitalized North Atlantic Treaty Organization (NATO), Europe will continue playing the role of junior partner of the United States. U.S. military forces will remain in Europe, albeit in reduced numbers, discouraging moves toward a European-only security arrangement that could undermine NATO and the leading U.S. role in it. Europe is expected to support, in the future, reruns of Desert Shield/Desert Storm and U.S.-led efforts to maintain order in the Gulf as well as a post–Cold War/Gulf War U.S. hegemony scheme in the region, based on a security system that includes bilateral military agreements with a selected number of Arab states and excludes two major regional powers, namely, Iran and Iraq. Stated the Pentagon paper, "As demonstrated by Iraq's invasion of Kuwait, it remains fundamentally important to prevent an hegemon or alignment of powers from dominating the region.... This pertains especially to the Arabian peninsula," where the United States "must continue to play a strong role through enhanced deterrence and improved cooperative security is emphasized."[1]

However, as the post–Cold War era is beginning to take shape and as the memories of the Gulf War are fading away, the notion of Washington serving as a world and a Gulf policeman, with Europe paying to support this leading U.S. role, is expected to be questioned by both Americans and Europeans. As the tensions between the former Cold War allies intensify, the Persian Gulf could emerge as a major arena for the new competition between the U.S. and European trading blocs. Because of its strategic location and its natural resources (being the world's greatest producer and reserve of oil), the stakes in that region for the two major players in the new global economy, the United States and the European Community (EC), are very high. Because oil is the fuel that powers industrial society, control of the oil reserves in the Gulf will give any nation enormous power over the international economy by manipulating the supply of oil. Also, the profits that result from oil production can make a producer a major (and, sometimes, controlling) power in the international economic system.

The Cold War, as well as the Gulf War (during which the United States assumed the role of securing Western access to oil resources in the Gulf), created an illusion of close U.S.–European cooperation in the region. Behind it, however, lay the long-standing competition for preeminence in the region between Washington and the leading European powers, Great Britain and France. This fierce rivalry could reemerge now that the Cold War glue that tied the U.S. and European interests in the region is melting away and as the struggle for economic power between the United States and the EC is beginning to dominate the new international agenda. Instability in the Middle East can be expected to become a major feature of the international system and could determine the level of peace and prosperity of the new world order. The geopolitics of oil will make the twenty-first century resemble the nineteenth in certain ways. The world will continue to be marred by constantly shifting regional alliances, the power of nationalism, and the need for great powers to be able to project military power in order to control vital economic interests.

The Gulf could become, therefore, a major arena for such competition in a multipolar system in which the United States will be one among several economic and military powers. With its economic base shrinking, Washington might find it more and more difficult to mobilize support from the U.S. public and the former Cold War allies for paying the growing diplomatic and military costs involved in maintaining the U.S. position in the Gulf. These costs include the containment of regional challenges like Iran and Iraq and opposition forces in the autocratic regimes in the region as well as those of continuing to facilitate the Arab-Israeli peace process. Washington's problems could be exacerbated especially if tensions in the Middle East — and skillful exploitation of them by U.S. oil companies and the Arab Gulf states — keep the price of oil higher in the next five years than it was in the latter half of the 1980s and could worsen the conditions of the U.S. economy. Not less significant, much of the potential "peace dividend" from the end of the Cold War could be lost as the U.S. defense establishment exploits fears about Islamic Fundamentalism and threats to U.S. interest in the Gulf to keep the military budget intact — one of the rationales behind the Pentagon paper.

Even without moving toward full political and economic unification, Europe and, especially, its Mediterranean bloc (particularly France, sensitive to instability in the Middle East because of, among other things, the possibility of growing immigration from there) could be expected to begin challenging the U.S. position in the region. Neither a federal "Fortress Europe" with a strengthened German-Franco military cooperative structure nor a "Europe of states" dominated by growing right-wing nationalist, protectionist, and anti-immigration governments will continue to back U.S. unilateral control of Europe's Middle East backyard and its oil resources as a way of forcing them to accept U.S. hegemony. Europe, whose ability to offset rising oil prices would be met by effective energy policies and higher economic growth, could compete with the United States in the Gulf and the Middle East by providing alternative military solutions and, especially, by devising new diplomatic and economic agendas, in the form of long-term European–Middle Eastern economic or trade arrangements or through ad hoc bilateral agreements on immigration and economic policies between European and Middle Eastern governments based on balance of power considerations and national economic interests.

In the short run, in the transition period from the Gulf War era to a new international system, the United States and Europe will devise ways of moderating their competition in the Gulf and the Levant, combining military resources in order to maintain their shared interests there. Washington, supported by the United Kingdom, the Netherlands, Turkey, Israel, and its allies in the Gulf and by the financial resources of Germany, Japan, and the Arab oil states, will be able to maintain its preeminent role in that region while leaving the Maghreb to Europe's Mediterranean countries. The U.S. position in the Gulf will be backed by a system of multinational military forces and intervention resources with multiple commands for different operations in the Gulf, with the possible intersection there between current military structures such as NATO and the Western European Union (WEU) and regional military forces. Europe will not want to break with Washington in that period of transition.

In the long run, however, at the end of that transition period, as the new political, economic, and military centers of the new international system begin to solidify and as Europe (particularly Germany and France) translate their economic strength into military power, Washington will face growing challenges to its Pax Americana project in the Gulf.

THE GULF AND THE OLD STRATEGIC BALANCE

After World War II, military and economic weakness caused Britain and France to pass the Middle Eastern torch to the United States. Washington hoped that its oil companies would capture the British-dominated Gulf oil market and that its anti-imperialist image would help it replace the two former colonial powers as a major player in the region. The Truman Doctrine, which sought to counter Soviet moves in the eastern Mediterranean that had threatened Western access to oil, symbolized the U.S. assertion of power in the region. The 1956 Suez campaign and its diplomatic aftermath, in which the United States used its political and economic power to pressure London and Paris to withdraw from Egypt, highlighted the U.S. objective of undercutting Europe's status in the area. The British withdrawal from the Gulf and the granting of independence to Algeria by France marked the end of the domination of the region by the European powers, while the Eisenhower Doctrine projected the U.S.-preeminent position there.

The close cooperation and, at the same time, fierce rivalry that marked the U.S.–European relationship in the Middle East until the Gulf War reflected their different perspectives on the linkage between the Gulf and the Arab-Israeli conflict. "Whereas the U.S. sees the problem of access to the Gulf in strategic terms, West Europeans see it primarily in political terms," explained a former State Department official in an attempt to explain the fracturing of the Western alliance during the 1970s over Middle Eastern politics. The Europeans, "seeking to respond to the political and trade concerns of the nations of the Gulf region," and motivated by their own economic interest in increasing trade, including arms sales to the states of the area, wanted to forge an unbreakable political linkage between the Palestinian-Israeli conflict and the security of the Persian Gulf. The Europeans argued that the U.S. refusal to accept a linkage reflected the power of the Israeli lobby, while Americans interpreted Europe's commitment to that linkage as a surrender to Arab oil blackmail.[2]

In the late 1960s and early 1970s, the transformation of the U.S. global and economic position and the emergence of the U.S. alliance with Israel encouraged the Europeans, who were moving toward closer economic and political integration, to begin competing again with Washington for influence in the region. These tensions reached a painful climax with the 1973 Middle East War and the ensuing Arab oil embargo. The Europeans pressured Washington to make concessions to the Arabs, then exploited the U.S. refusal to do so by concluding separate deals with the Middle Eastern states. The U.S.-sponsored Egyptian-Israeli peace process again seemed to enhance the U.S. position in the region, but the Europeans took advantage of the fact that the Camp David accords failed to solve the Palestinian problem and in 1980 put forward the Venice Declaration, demanding that the Palestine Liberation Organization be included in a Middle East peace conference. This initiative was aimed at tarnishing the U.S. diplomatic victory and at winning support from the Arab Gulf states opposed to the Camp David accords. Israeli and U.S. opposition helped sink it.[3]

After the election of Ronald Reagan, Europe found itself paralyzed in the face of increasingly unilateral U.S. posture in the Middle East, which was based on close strategic cooperation with Israel, on one hand, and Saudi Arabia and Egypt, on the other hand, as a way of countering the powers of the Soviet Union and of Khomeini's Iran. Feeling the consequences of the post-1973 oil shocks, unable to develop cohesive foreign and defense policies, and under the impact of the growing superpower tension, Europe accepted U.S. hegemony in the region. However, U.S. policies in the Middle East deepened the desire among the Europeans to maintain distance from the U.S. security posture and to emphasize diplomatic measures to resolve conflicts before considering military options. Occasionally, the Europeans did clearly distance themselves from Washington — after the 1985 attack on Libya, for example. Meanwhile, they were suffering directly, in the form of terrorism, from the consequences of U.S. policies and its alliance with Israel, which led to the 1982 invasion of Lebanon and to the suppression of the Palestinians.

Already in the mid- and late-1980s the Europeans were beginning to define a security role for themselves in the Gulf. What NATO calls the "out-of-area" questions had undergone subtle changes in that period. The Suez crisis of 1956 was the most dramatic case of European intervention in the region and proved extremely divisive for the alliance. In addition to the differences between Europe and the United States over Middle Eastern issues, there were major disagreements on how and under what circumstances national defense resources would be utilized for non-NATO contingencies in the Middle East with its intermingling of the East-West divide, the Arab-Israeli conflict. The Europeans, especially France and Italy, were becoming more assertive on out-of-area questions. In Lebanon from 1982 to 1984, during the Red Sea minesweeping operation in 1984, and in the Gulf during the Iran-Iraq War in 1987–88, there were projections of European military power, but even those actions were only in coordination with the United States.

THE GULF WAR STRATEGIC INTERMEZZO

By the early 1990s, the end of the Cold War, the growing economic problems facing the United States, the rise of Europe as a new global power, and, in particular, the moves by the EC toward a single market in 1992 suggested that U.S. interests in the Middle East would decline and that Europe could return to playing a leading role in the area. After all, strict geopolitical reasons would have dictated that with the decline of the superpower rivalry and with no other global power threatening to establish hegemony, regional powers could be counterbalanced either by other regional powers or by players adjacent to the region, for example, Europe, whose interests in the area were more direct and immediate than those of the United States. With the combination of the end of the Cold War and rising economic problems, Americans were expected to question the wisdom of maintaining their presence in the Gulf. An international system was emerging in which economic power was beginning to replace military power as the modicum of international competition and in which Europe would assume a role equal to that of the United States. Why should Americans continue to pay the costs of defending access to the oil resources in the Gulf from the Europeans who were trying to beat them in the trade competition?

The reunification of Germany, the growing German-Franco military cooperation, and the reactivation of the WEU as an instrument of independent European security coordination suggested that Europe would be able to act independently in the Middle East. The potential prominence of the WEU could have meant a new instrument for the Europeans to contemplate out-of-area responses in the Middle East. The Europeans could then decide "whether to combine or integrate national rapid deployment forces and define what contingencies will require such responses."[4] At the same time, the Europeans were expected to translate their growing political unity and their economic power into diplomatic and military might and try to drive forth their own Middle Eastern agenda, with its emphasis on diplomatic and economic rather than military power and, especially, the need to link a Palestinian-Israeli solution with the security of the Gulf.

The Gulf War seemed to reverse those post–Cold War trends. The crisis in the Gulf found the international system in transition. The United States as a declining hegemonic power was not ready to transfer some of its Middle East responsibilities to the rising Europe, which was not yet ready to accept it. Washington resisted giving up its leadership prerogatives. Europe, the up-and-coming player, was in no hurry to take them.

From the U.S. perspective, the Europeans played the role of free riders during the Gulf War, counting on the hegemon, the United States, to provide them with cost-free defense of the region's oil. Americans, antagonized by European behavior — German peace demonstrations, French ill-timed diplomatic initiatives — believed that the Europeans should have kept quiet and footed the bill presented by Washington. There was resentment in the U.S. capital at the initial reluctance of the EC (with the exception of Great Britain) to commit significant numbers of troops or provide large-scale support for the U.S. effort in the Gulf. Senator David Boren expressed the then-prevailing U.S. view when he asked, "Is it going to be American taxpayers who are going to foot the bill so that when it's all over we end up with their economies enhanced?"[5] The European approach reflected the free-rider problem: Europe wanted the benefits of a stable world order, including the containment of Iraq and the security of the oil resources in the Gulf, without bearing the costs.[6]

However, viewed from Paris and Bonn, the Gulf War was an opportunity for the United States to send a "I am back" message to the world and put the Europeans, who had begun to challenge U.S. hegemony, in their place. Bush's aim, according to *Le Monde*, was to "drive a wedge between the Arab and European worlds, further slow down the creation of a grand European economic alliance, and set up a New World Order dominated by Washington."[7] The Europeans were far less enthusiastic about the prospect of military action against Saddam. Not only was there little sympathy in Europe for the exiled leaders of Kuwait, but also there was concern that a prolonged and bloody war with Iraq would produce chaos in the Middle East and harm that region's close economic and political relations with Europe. Responding to those sentiments, French President Francois Mitterrand tried, on the eve of the war, to lead an independent European effort based on a linkage between Iraqi withdrawal from Kuwait and Israeli withdrawal from the West Bank. Sounding a familiar Gaullist battle cry, he asserted France's independence from the United States: "I do not feel I am in a position of a second class soldier who must obey his commanding general."[8]

France, Italy, and Spain were particularly apprehensive because of their large Muslim populations and strong ties with North Africa. A war with Iraq, warned the Spanish Foreign Minister Francisco Fernandes Ordonez, could lead to "a collision course between Islam and the West."[9] There was concern that a war would fuel anti-European attitudes among Muslims in Europe and that support produced for Saddam Hussein in North Africa, manifested in several large pro-Iraqi demonstrations, would threaten the relatively moderate regimes there and create new waves of migrants to France, with potentially explosive political effects.

Germany drew strong criticism from the United States for not contributing more directly to the war effort. Germany's response reflected a consensus among Germans that their country should play a peaceful international role with strict limits on the use of military force. That consensus is embodied in the German Basic Law, which restricts the use of German forces to NATO territory. Many Germans also expressed concern that the war with Iraq would divert international attention and resources from the political and economic reconstruction of eastern Europe.[10]

For one major European power, Margaret Thatcher's British government, determined to prevent U.S. "decoupling" from Europe and concerned over the growing power of the Germans, the war provided an opportunity to revive the special relationship between Washington and London. Not surprisingly, Bush's decision to send troops to the Gulf was made following a meeting with Thatcher, in which she persuaded the president to take an unyielding stand against Saddam. Britain's interest in going to war also stemmed from its historical ties with Kuwait, as well as from the fact that Kuwaiti money helps prop up the pound in the world's financial system.[11]

Many Europeans have perceived the U.S. attempt to reassert its hegemony in the Gulf as part of an effort to turn back the post–Cold War trends and to reestablish U.S. leadership in the Western alliance. The Europeans saw Bush as a sheriff in search of his "high noon" role in the Arabian desert, whose aim was to achieve "Europe's submission" to Washington and to prevent it from becoming "the new challenger to American domination."[12] Because the war bolstered the British position in Europe and secured the interests of Israel and the Arab oil states, there was talk about the convergence of a "Washington–London–Tel Aviv axis" that would dominate the Middle East with the passive acquiescence of the EC.[13]

The success of the war in cutting Europe down to size was seen in Europe as evidence of a U.S. grand design to weaken Europe's ability to project power in the post–Cold War era and to develop independent policies toward the Middle East and the Gulf. The Gulf War was "America's War," stated then–Defense Minister, Jean-Pierre Chevenement, arguing that by sending troops to the Gulf, "France attempted to help the U.S. restore a world domination that its economic situation no longer assured."[14] In his view, the war was an effort by Bush to remedy U.S. economic problems and avert a recession through wartime stimulation of the economy and the establishment of permanent U.S. control over the Gulf oil resources. The fact that Washington set out to destroy Iraq, France's main and most powerful ally in the gulf and a counterweight to the more pro-U.S. Saudi Arabia, was seen as part of an effort to erode Paris' interest in the region. Similarly, on the French Right, former Prime Minister Jacques Chirac suggested that the U.S. president had foreseen that Europe would be a great economic power 20 years hence, and because it lacks independent sources of oil, Bush set out to make control of oil the United States' equalizer.

The prevailing view among the European leaders was that Washington was trying to force them to implement U.S. policies in the Gulf and endure their negative effects, in the form of terrorism and oil shortages, without allowing the Europeans to participate in the decision making. "Behind the public facade in London as well as in Bonn and Paris there is impatience and not a little exasperation with the U.S. Administration," concerning the drive to war in the Gulf, reported the *Guardian* of London in December 1990; in the world of an EC official quoted in the same newspaper, the situation was a "classic case of taxation without representation."[15] If Washington wanted them to cease being free riders, argued the Europeans, it should allow them to sit in the driver's seat of Middle East and gulf policy making. After all, if Europe had wielded significant influence over Middle Eastern policies during the 1980s, it might have been able to prevent disasters like the 1982 Lebanon War or to push more effectively for an Israeli-Palestinian peace. That, in turn, would have strengthened the moderate Arab bloc and would have made the region less hospitable to Saddam's aggression. The message to Washington was that the United States cannot have its cake — call the shots unilaterally in the Middle East — while eating it, too — expecting Europe to pay the costs.

THE GULF: A NEW PAX AMERICANA?

At the same time, in the United States, the military victory of the U.S.-led coalition in the Gulf suggested to some that we have entered a new period of Pax Americana, with an interventionist United States reigning supreme in a unipolar world, especially in the Middle East, in which Europe will play a secondary role.[16] From the U.S. perspective, the Gulf War heralded a new division of labor in the Western alliance, in which Europe would be expected to "deliver plenty of political support backed by hardware and a lot of money" while "leaving the driving to President Bush."[17] Europe should, therefore, abandon the "romantic" and "dangerous" notion of a united and independent Europe capable of sharing international security responsibilities in regions like the Middle East, argued former British Prime Minister Margaret Thatcher.[18]

However, some leading U.S. foreign policy thinkers — who coined the term "geo-economics" to supplant "geopolitics" — were arguing that as economic competition was superseding political-military rivalry as the dominant current in the international affairs of the post–Cold War era, it was neither a U.S. interest nor a responsibility to maintain the world order. Washington should begin diverting resources from its military budget to revitalize its civilian economy in preparation for the economic battles with Europe and Japan. According to this economic nationalist view, in the new world, Europe and Japan have emerged as the United States' prime antagonists. For the United States to bear the costs of maintaining global security constitutes a direct subsidy to its rivals. Securing the oil from the Gulf by helping to maintain the balance of power there is one example of subsidizing the European free riders. Because Europe and Japan are the prime consumers of Gulf energy resources, they should be the ones to make the sacrifices to keep the flow of oil from that region stable and the price low, argued the geo-economists.

However, Bush and his advisors, who belong to the Rockefeller wing of the Republican Party, have continued to support the notion of the United States' military superiority and its hegemonic role in the Gulf. Their geo-strategic model, in contrast the geo-economic one, called for a policy based on a U.S. role guarding the Western world's principal trade routes and sources of raw material against insurgency, sectarian violence, and regional adventurism and instability.[19] It seems that the Clinton administration has decided not to deviate from the foreign policy predilections of the Bush administration toward that region. If Washington continues to control the Gulf, its status as a political superpower would be supplemented by vast economic power. In addition to controlling the world's oceans, the United States would be in control of the world's oil supply, because North American production, combined with that of the Persian Gulf, would be about 35 percent of world production and 65 percent of world oil reserves. "Controlling the Persian Gulf would open a period of enormous imperial power unprecedented in history, dwarfing even the Anglo-French imperial system."[20]

Unlike the economic nationalists, who perceive Washington's domination of the Gulf as a burden, the geo-strategists, whose views dominated the 1991 Pentagon paper, contend that the United States should control the Gulf and prevent both regional and external powers from challenging its power there. For the geo-strategists, the Gulf and its oil resources can be used to extract both political and economic concessions from the Europeans. The success of the U.S.-led military operation in the region has left the United States effectively as the greatest oil producer. It is now in a position to set production quotas and prices and to control the movement of oil. With more than 20 percent of its oil originating in the countries within the Straits of Hormuz and with the Arab Gulf states being its fourth largest economic market, Europe would find that its greatest economic competitor was in direct control of its supply of oil and its major market. The United States could conceivably use its dominant status in the region to extract concessions from the Europeans on various trade issues. It could, therefore, use its military power in the Gulf to gain a hammerlock on the international economy and impose unfavorable trade relations on the other industrialized nations, especially Europe.

According to this view, the end of the Cold War and the outcome of the Gulf War have provided Washington with an opportunity to reestablish U.S. supremacy over Europe in the post–Cold War era, especially with regard to the prime out-of-area bone of contention — the Middle East. The Bush administration's vision of a new world order was that of a reformed NATO under U.S. leadership that continues to guarantee the security of the West while expanding to other regions. The oil-rich Persian Gulf became a focal point for applying that new approach. Its control enables Washington to establish its new power relationship with Europe. In order to formalize its dominant power vis-à-vis Europe and the Gulf, Washington has pursued in the aftermath of the war a new model of trans-Atlantic relationship, called the New Atlanticism. It envisions a renewed U.S.–European partnership in dealing with security threats to the Western alliance, including out-of-area challenges emanating from the Middle East. U.S. military forces would remain in reduced numbers in Europe and would continue to provide the continent with a nuclear umbrella. NATO would redefine its role to include out-of-area threats in regions such as the Middle East.

Under this security structure, NATO could have a stronger "European pillar." The WEU could serve as bridge between the United States and the EC, and the NATO commandership would alternate between the United States and Europe. Europe would enjoy a greater say in decision making while bearing a greater share of the defense burden, but it would continue to rely on U.S. security leadership, especially outside Europe. Since the Gulf War, Washington has been promoting this vision of a New Atlanticism. It has stressed the need to create a large multinational rapid-deployment force under NATO auspices that could respond immediately to crises outside Europe. NATO commanders agreed in April 1992 to expand the alliance's European-staffed rapid-defense force, perhaps to as many as 100,000 troops, to deal with such eventualities.[21]

That move reflected a lesson of the Gulf War, pointing to the need to redefine NATO's out-of-area role, over which the United States and Europe have clashed often since 1945. During the 1973 Middle East War, for example, the Bonn government strongly objected to the movement of U.S. tanks from bases in West Germany to Israel because this overstepped NATO's geographical mandate. In 1987, when the United States provided an escort to protect Kuwaiti tankers from Iranian gunboats, the European allies that participated in the mission carefully refrained from identifying it as a NATO operation.

The Gulf War, notwithstanding the short-term consensus that developed between the Europeans and the Americans, has accentuated the tensions between them over the out-of-area entanglements and, in particular, has raised the question of if and how the Gulf could be integrated into the strategic structure of the Western alliance. For example, a controversy arose when the NATO Air Mobile Force, including 18 German aircraft, was sent to Turkey. Bonn insisted that these forces were to be used only in defense of Turkish territory and not for attacks on Iraqi soil, rejecting Ankara's goal of expanding NATO's responsibility to the Gulf.

U.S. planners downplay the importance of such differences. The Gulf War, they argue, showed that no individual European state or combination of states is able to raise the military forces required to contain large armies, modern air forces, and weapons of mass destruction controlled by Saddam-like regimes in the Middle East. France and England might be able to tame an Arab dictator for a short period by either bombing raids or gunboat diplomacy. However, only massive land power and large naval forces on the scale commanded by Washington during the Gulf War are capable of containing the growing security threats to Europe from its southern flank. It is essential, therefore, that as part of the New Atlanticism scheme, the United States and Europe coordinate their military policies in the region. The sine qua non of Europe's security policy in the Gulf would continue to be the United States' large navy, marine, and airborne divisions, which the New Atlanticism would provide. In that context, the main danger of nuclear proliferation, by U.S. calculation, is that it might instigate other industrial countries like

Germany and Japan to develop such weapons as well, thus broadening the areas of challenge to the U.S. hegemony. A rise of a nuclear power in the Middle East would, after all, pose almost no threat to the United States. It could, however, induce both Middle Eastern powers and Europe to develop their own independent nuclear military strategy to counter the new threats from, say, a nuclear Iran to Iraq. That, in turn, would make it unnecessary for them to rely on the U.S. nuclear umbrella.

The proponents of the renewed Pax Americana, masquerading as a new U.S.–European partnership, contend that in the Gulf War, the United States has finally overcome the Vietnam syndrome and is once again ready to play the role of a global policeman, with Europe as its supporting units and Saudi Arabia, Egypt, Turkey, and Israel serving as its Middle Eastern cops on the beat. U.S. military power will continue to function as the ultimate arbiter of international conflicts, as the "balancer" in the Gulf, containing radical anti–status quo states there, while Europe will help finance U.S. intervention. The Middle Eastern states, like other Third World nations, generally will be induced through threats or friendly persuasion to conform to the interests and views of the only remaining superpower. The U.S. objective to "remain the predominant outside power" in the Middle East, will be achieved, according to the Pentagon paper, by reducing the five existing theater commands (Atlantic, Pacific, European, Southern, and Central) to three: Atlantic, Pacific, and Contingency. The anticipated military engagement is clearly in the south: the Atlantic and Contingency commands combined would have the capacity to replay Desert Storm.[22]

Europe and the United States are seen in the Pax Americana/New Atlanticism perspective as a single political and cultural unit, an entity *The Economist* called "Euro-America." Together, Europe and the United States face threats within (from an angry Russian bear and insurgent German militarism) as well as from radical forces in the Arab and Muslim countries, which *The Economist* lumps together under the term "Islamistan."[23] The cultural and military tensions between Euro-America and Islamistan (which, with its control over oil and large military forces, directly threatens the core interests of the West) are bound to rise. The emergence of new Saddams and, especially, the growing movement of Islamic Fundamentalism in the Muslim states between Morocco and Iran, whose youthful populations are susceptible to radical and anti-Western nationalism and religious ideology, are going to confront the West with a new global threat. It will replace the Soviet menace and will be symbolized by the color of Islam, the Green Peril.[24] The Muslim threat not only will pose a military challenge to the West in the form of possible military nuclear capability in the hands of states like Iraq and Iran but also will give rise to increased immigration and terrorism from the Middle East. The Gulf War demonstrated that only a unified U.S.–European security structure, supported by the efforts of the four pillars of Saudi Arabia, Egypt, Turkey, and Israel, will be able to contain future threats from Islamistan.

Notwithstanding Bush's Gulf War Wilsonian rhetoric, the primary goal of Euro-America in the Middle East, according to the Pax Americana paradigm, should be to maintain stability, not to engage in crusades for democracy or promote self-determination. The West should be content to see the rise of a more compliant dictator in Iraq instead of taking steps that might lead to Kurdish independence, which could threaten Saudi Arabia and Turkey. Similarly, Washington's efforts to promote an Arab-Israeli peace and achieve Israeli withdrawal from the occupied territories are not grounded in any idealistic notion of supporting self-determination for the Palestinians. Their realpolitik sources are tied directly to the main goal of the war — to maintain control over the Gulf's oil resources.

Indeed, a lack of a solution to the Arab-Israeli conflict raises the costs of U.S. hegemony by forcing Washington to juggle its commitments to Israel and to the pro-U.S. Arab states and prevents the integration of the Jewish state in its overall strategic game in the region. This juggling act was reflected in Washington's efforts to convince Jerusalem during the Gulf War not to retaliate against Iraq's Scud attacks or by opposition to arms sales to the Saudis from the pro-Israeli lobby on Capitol Hill. The continuing Arab-Israeli conflict also provides anti–status quo powers in the Gulf, such as Iran, to exploit U.S. support to Israel as a way of igniting anti-U.S. feelings in the region. At the same time, a stalemate in the efforts to solve the Palestinian problem could play into the hands of a potential European player. It could challenge U.S. hegemony in the region by trying to propose alternative agendas based on a more forceful approach toward Israel aimed at its withdrawal from the occupied territories, an approach that Washington cannot adopt because of domestic pressure from the pro-Israeli lobby.

EUROPE: ACCEPTING U.S. HEGEMONY?

In the aftermath of the Cold War and the Gulf War, it looked as if Washington's unipolar agenda and hegemony schemes in the Persian Gulf were being implemented. After all, the Bush administration succeeded in winning support from its European allies for maintaining the current structure of NATO and for suppressing any serious moves toward development of an independent European military structure. Europe, in the deep gloom that engulfed it in the war's immediate aftermath, seemed to be receptive to U.S. proposals for a New Atlanticism and for the United States' leading role in the Middle East. Several European observers suggested that Europe's new line on NATO should be "Yankee, don't go home." (The number of U.S. troops assigned to Europe in 1992 [220,000, down from 325,000 in August 1991] is expected to be cut in half, and perhaps even to 60,000 over the remainder of the 1990s.[25]

With the initial concern over the possible rise of hard-liners in Moscow, the disarray in eastern Europe, and the perception of possible new dangers emanating from the Middle East, including military nuclear weapons in the hands of Iraq and Iran, there was a certain eagerness to see Washington continuing to play a security leadership role. Some analysts even argued that France's decision to send troops to the Gulf stemmed from its interest in keeping U.S. troops in Europe to offset Germany's pacific tendencies and economic clout. "To argue for an American presence in Europe, there had to be a French presence in the Gulf," explained Dominique Moisi, deputy director of the French Institute for International Relations. His country's performance suggested that French President Francois Mitterrand wanted to prove to Washington that France is a reliable ally, especially "if we want to sit down at conference tables and have a say in world affairs," as Defense Minister Pierre Joxe put it.[26]

Europe seemed to accept Washington's leading role in the Gulf and its own limited role in the Arab-Israeli negotiations launched in Madrid. Europe ended up as a marginal player in the peace negotiations, relegated to the role of an "observer" in the Madrid Conference, "completing, complementing and adding nuances" to U.S. ideas on the region and expected by Washington to finance economic development projects in the Middle East following the signing of the peace agreement.[27] The fact that Russia, a bankrupted remnant of the Soviet Empire, continued to serve with the United States as a cosponsor of the peace negotiations while the EC played, with the Gulf states, the role of a silent observer was a clear sign that Washington refused to give the Europeans a place in the Middle East driver's seat, a position they believed was commensurate with their rising economic and political power. The New Atlanticism and its little brother, the new order in the Gulf, were gradually seen by the Europeans as a disguise for U.S. hegemony.

At the same time, with growing economic problems at home, Americans were beginning to resent continuing to shoulder the heavy burden of leadership and providing security to their allies across the Atlantic while Europe beat them in the global market and eroded their economic security. After all, despite the "America is walking tall again" post–Gulf War rhetoric, the real lesson could be that Washington could no longer go it alone: the United States is simply incapable of financing a Pax Americana in the Gulf or, for that matter, anywhere else. In Desert Storm, it took 75 percent of the

United States tactical aircraft and 40 percent of its tanks to defeat a country with the gross national product of Portugal. Washington could not have afforded such an effort without the $54 billion in aid pledged by its allies. The United States will probably never again receive such massive support for a foreign policy initiative, nor is it likely to continue maintaining forces that would permit action on the scale of Desert Storm. The Gulf War, as former Secretary of State Henry Kissinger pointed out, was "an almost accidental combination of circumstances unlikely to be repeated."[28]

While the Bush administration continued to advance its unipolar agenda, the U.S. public was beginning to recognize the gap between Washington's continued pretensions to world leadership and the diminishing resources available to advance this global role. The result was a 1992 presidential election campaign dominated by rising trends of isolationism and protectionism and by calls for cutting the defense budget and disengaging from the costly overseas commitments, including support by several candidates for reducing the number of troops in Europe. Even the administration was responding to that public pressure. During a visit to Europe, then–Vice President Dan Quayle stressed that the United States saw a linkage between the security and trade areas, threatening to reconsider U.S. commitments to maintain a military presence in Europe unless the EC makes major concessions in the General Agreement on Tariffs and Trade (GATT) talks.

As the United States was moving inward, Europe was showing some signs of diplomatic and military assertiveness, projecting, albeit in an incoherent way, an alternative scenario to that of the New Atlanticism, one based on the idea of developing an independent European bloc that would make its own decisions on foreign policy and defense and present them as *faits accomplis* to Washington. As Europe reasserts itself on the world scene and the United States begins to disengage, it is almost inevitable, as Kissinger suggested in testimony before the Senate Armed Services Committee in November 1990, that U.S. leadership in the Middle East and its hegemony in the Gulf is going to end. He said, "We are in a transitional period. I would think that over a period of 10 years, many of the security responsibilities that the United States is now shouldering in the Gulf ought to be carried by the Europeans who receive a larger share of the oil from the region."[29]

The United States, like other declining hegemonic powers, is resistant to giving up its leadership position, especially when it comes to the Gulf, whose resources can provide the United States with bargaining chips in its competition with Europe. After all, it was only after the humiliating 1956 Suez Crisis that Great Britain and France were willing to recognize the limitations on their power in the Middle East and to shift their leadership responsibilities to

Washington. The EC itself might not be ready yet with the necessary political-military mechanisms to play a larger role in the Middle East or, for that matter (as the case of the former Yugoslavia suggests), in Europe. Continuing intra-European rivalries could complicate the adoption of a unified security approach. Another question is whether the transfer of responsibilities from the United States to Europe, in general, in the Gulf, in particular, would occur in an amicable fashion or would lead to growing tensions between the two pillars of the Atlantic alliance.

Washington has become more critical of the idea of European unity. One of the outcomes of the war was that Washington began to confront what might be called the "European unity paradox." The United States has long supported the idea of a united Europe and has also taken for granted that a Europe that spoke with one voice would be a simpler and more straightforward entity with which to deal as part of a general Western approach to various global problems, such as the Gulf Crisis. A strong Europe was perceived in that context as a U.S. asset, but Washington failed to consider the possibility that a common European voice would not necessarily be a sympathetic one. "Certainly the evidence suggests that had Europe had a common foreign policy and common defense structure at the time of the Iraq seizure of Kuwait, Britain would have been restrained from giving the support it did," suggested one European analyst.[30] In particular, it is unlikely that a British leader would have urged the United States to go to war as Prime Minister Thatcher did. Thus, there has been a growing sense in Washington after Desert Storm that progress toward a unified Europe might actually harm U.S. interests and prevent a replay of the Gulf War.

EUROPE REASSERTS ITS POWER

For the Europeans, the Gulf War was in a way a wake-up call. It gradually became clear to many European officials that one of the major reasons for their inability to meet the U.S. challenge during the war was the lack of European institutions for developing independent political and security policies. That fact was especially apparent when it came to Europe's continuing reliance on a U.S.-led NATO in out-of-area conflicts, such as in the Middle East. The war was seen, therefore, as a reason to redouble efforts to more closely integrate the political and security policies of the European nations. "From patronizing the United States as the country of can't-shoot-straight bumbledom, European elites have once more turned into envying and admiring it as the competent organizer of a dazzlingly smooth high-tech victory." commented one observer.[31]

Concerns that Washington's victory would lead to a triumphal attitude and an attempt to reassert U.S. hegemony enhanced support for the idea of a new European political and security order. Turning Europe into a superpower whose military status would be comparable to that of the United States would have been seen as "costly folly before the thrilling video games of the Gulf War."[32] Although the press' attention has been on the lack of a coordinated European approach toward the events in the former Yugoslavia, there have been several moves toward serious exploration of a distinct security role for the EC, including in out-of-area contingencies. Similarly, France, Spain, and Italy have been moving in the direction of developing a more independent Middle East agenda with emphasis on diplomatic and economic cooperation that is clearly more distinctive than that of Washington. These signs of a more assertive Europe, including the Franco-German discussion of plans for developing greater coordination of EC foreign and security policies, have produced anxiety in Washington.[33] More than any other issues, the political differences over out-of-area issues, especially those involving the Middle East, could create divisions between Europe and the United States. Greater European defense self-sufficiency would mean, in the long run, the development of new tools that would enable the EC to contemplate out-of-area responses free of direction from Washington. In that case, Europe will not necessarily have to follow Washington's lead in Saddam-invades-Kuwait–like contingencies in the Gulf.

In a move that angered Washington, the French government, which believes that Europe should prepare for a U.S. withdrawal from Europe by establishing an independent defense capability, proposed the creation of a rapid-deployment force under the EC auspices. According to the plan, which was backed by EC chief Jacques Delors and perceived in Washington as an attempt to compete with its own proposals for a similar NATO force, multinational forces would be assigned to defend European interests within and outside western Europe. The French plan suggested that the forces would be under European control and take part in everything from peacekeeping and humanitarian assistance to direct military action against Middle Eastern bullies. Spain, Italy, Greece, Belgium, and Luxembourg expressed support for the proposal. The United States saw it as a way of accelerating the demise of NATO and creating a basis for independent European security policies and warned against the formation of a "European caucus."

The result of the trans-Atlantic debate was the activation of three security structures. The first was the announcement by France and Germany in May 1992 of the formation of a 35,000-member joint army corps, called "Eurocorps," with the aim of turning it into the nucleus of a future European army that would handle defense responsibilities outside Europe and NATO's sphere of operation. Second, there was the decision in December 1991 by the EC to turn the WEU into a new defense pillar, subservient to NATO in European military matters but free to act outside the NATO area.[34] Third, as a compromise with Washington, NATO set up a European Rapid Reaction Corps with a British commander to deal with out-of-area contingencies; the case for a British commander was underlined by "the decisiveness of their response to the Gulf Crisis," that is, their attachment to Washington's view of it.[35] However, although Britain has projected a more "Atlanticist" and pro-U.S. policy than both France and Germany, Thatcher's successor, John Major, has brought his country closer to Europe and established good personal rapport with the German Chancellor Helmut Kohl. Major has promised to move Britain in a more "European" direction and, to Washington's satisfaction, has emphasized London's support for a wider and more diffused European structure, in contrast to Paris' support for a smaller but more unified and federally oriented Europe.

Washington's hopes that the "British model" would prevent moves toward a more independent European policy might be premature, however. It is true that the relationship between the three new military structures to deal with out-of-area issues seems to be confused. Certainly, without amending the German constitution, Bonn and, by extension, the Eurocorps would not be able to defend European interests outside the NATO area (such as in the Middle East). The key to understanding future European policy is not necessarily by focusing on the existence or the lack of a unified European organizational structure. International structures, after all, reflect nothing more than a certain balance of power. What is important is to uncover the interests of the economically powerful states in the continent, which are going to determine its foreign policies, that is, Germany and France. As the interests of Washington and some of the European states diverge in the Middle East, Germany and France are bound to find ways to defend them.

Germany, the economic locomotive of the EC, whose own model of Europe is closer to that of France than to that of Britain, still has a long way to go if it hopes to translate its economic power into political-military influence. Nevertheless, in December 1991, Germany succeeded in using that influence to force the EC to recognize the former Yugoslavia republics of Slovenia and Croatia, even though several European governments and the United States were not eager to do so. A few days later, in another example of muscle flexing, Germany raised bank interest rates without consulting the European partners.[36] Finally, in March 1992, Germany led the EC in an important confrontation with Washington over Middle Eastern policies when it decided to halt deliveries of military goods to Turkey, a NATO member and one of Washington's major Middle Eastern pillars, after Ankara used German equipment in a drive against Kurdish separatists.

Turkey, which, at the end of the Cold War, has lost its value to the West and to NATO, in particular, as a strategic asset, has been trying to revive its importance to Washington by positioning itself as a bastion against Arab radicalism, Iranian expansionism, and Islamic Fundamentalism in the Middle East. Ankara's close cooperation with the United States during the Gulf War was "primarily designed to reaffirm Ankara's commitment to U.S.–Turkish bilateral relations and to highlight Turkey's importance to U.S. strategic interests and concerns in the Middle East."[37] Washington and Ankara share a common interest vis-à-vis NATO and Europe. Both are interested in extending NATO's out-of-area military role under U.S. leadership to the Middle East. In that way, Turkey could reestablish its significance to the organization, this time as the defender of Euro-America's interests in Islamistan and could perhaps even succeed in mobilizing support for its joining the EC. For Washington, anchoring NATO in the Middle East through Turkey fits with its overall strategy of cementing European–U.S. military cooperation in the Middle East under U.S. control.

However, NATO's European members, especially Germany, resisted the efforts by Washington and Ankara during the Gulf War to approve the possible use of NATO forces to attack Iraq as opposed to strictly defending Turkey from Iraqi attacks. The German military embargo against Turkey over the Kurdish issue, which enjoyed the backing of most of the EC members, was far from being a side show. It demonstrated the potential conflict between the U.S. project and the European approach.[38] Although the U.S. Middle East game plan is tied to a U.S.-dominant role in the region and relies on an alliance with strategic pillars like Turkey, the European approach is more responsive to demands for self-determination for the Kurds and the Palestinians, perceiving them as the root causes of the problems of instability in the region. Kurdish or Palestinian terrorism or Islamic Fundamentalism cannot be dealt with, according to the European view, by the exclusive use of military power; it is necessary to address the underlying problems that caused them. Washington's policies with their reliance on military powers like Turkey and attempts to draw military balance of power structures in the region have the potential of drawing the Europeans into new entanglements there that have little to do with their direct interests. Thus, Washington's efforts to establish Ankara as a counterweight to Tehran are seen by Germany and France as a dangerous policy that could lead to Europe's involvement in a potential Iranian-Turkish conflict.

The Europeans have, indeed, distanced themselves from Washington's efforts to build up, by press leaks and press statements, the notion of an Iranian-sponsored Islamic Fundamentalist threat. The U.S. policy is a way of sustaining U.S. public support for U.S. military commitments in the Gulf and of establishing a new "strategic consensus" among Washington's allies in the region, now that the Soviet threat has disappeared. Rejecting U.S. advice, all the EC members, including Britain, reestablished diplomatic relations with Tehran that were severed in the 1980s. When French Foreign Minister Roland Dumas prepared in 1991 for a visit to Iran to settle some of the financial problems between Tehran and Paris, French sources indicated that improving relations with the regime in Tehran and rejecting Washington's efforts to demonize the Iranian regime is part of "France's determined effort to maintain an independent policy in the region despite increasing American predominance."[39]

The EC rejected U.S. efforts to isolate Iran diplomatically and economically and argued instead that the West should try to improve political and trade ties with Tehran as a way of strengthening the moderate groups around President Ali Akbar Rafsanjani in his struggle against the more hard-line forces concentrated in the parliament (Majlis). In particular, the Europeans were upset over Washington's attempts to restrict their trade with Tehran, and only in the beginning of 1992 were they able to settle a long-standing conflict with the Bush administration after the latter withdrew its objections to the sale to Iran of the European-made Airbus passenger jet, which uses U.S.-made engines. In April 1991, the "troika," the rotating presidents of the EC, met with Rafsanjani in Tehran to discuss ways to improve trade relations between Iran and the community and take advantage of Rafsanjani's efforts to open his country to foreign investment. Moreover, although Washington and Saudi Arabia continue to reject Iranian demands that it play a major role in any future scheme in the Gulf, the EC seems more willing to accommodate Iran's interests in the region and, like Iran, emphasizes the need to supplement military arrangements in the region with economic cooperation and development.[40]

Indeed, the differences between the United States and the EC over the long-term approach toward Iran tend to reflect two different long-term visions of the Gulf and the Middle East. Washington's vision of its presence in the region tends to be in general military oriented and focuses almost exclusively on its oil interests in the region and on the defense of the Arab oil-producing states as well as on maintaining its commitment to Israel. U.S. policy is aimed, as former French Foreign Minister Michel Jobert put it, at turning the region into "the oil colony of America" and at imposing a solution on the Palestinians that would conform to Israeli interests.[41] However, from Europe, the Middle East is its backyard. Europe is, after all, a Mediterranean entity that, like other Middle Easterners, views the United States and Russia as foreign powers. "Why are you, the superpowers, here? We never asked you to come," asserted Jobert.[42] Although Washington has the luxury of distance to focus heavily on Israel's survival and on key Arab states, like Egypt and Saudi Arabia, in Europe there is a concern that unless the Middle East achieves growth and stability soon and moves toward adopting forms of democracy and self-determination, new radical regimes will come to power. Europe, especially France, Spain, and Italy, will then be overrun by new waves of Muslim immigrants.

TOWARD A EUROPEAN–MIDDLE EASTERN ZONE?

Indeed, the relationship between Europe and the Middle East is much more akin to that between the United States and Mexico; problems are, after all, more pressing on the border than thousands of miles away, and many of these problems, such as economic and political underdevelopment, cannot be solved by the use of military power. Moreover, these problems, especially the gap between the haves and have nots in the Middle East, make it necessary to adopt a more comprehensive regional approach in which the issue of the Gulf cannot be decoupled from that of the Maghreb. It is not surprising, therefore, that the southern European states — France, Italy, Spain, and Portugal — have been the most active in advancing an independent European approach to the Middle East. Their closer geographical proximity and demographic ties to the Middle East have tended to make them more sensitive to developments in that region.

Several years ago (after the signing of the Helsinki agreement in the mid-1970s), the southern states began to discuss the need to create a Conference on Security and Cooperation in the Mediterranean (CSCM), modeled after the Conference on Security and Cooperation (CSCE). The CSCM idea originated with the southern European states' concern about the potential for social and economic instability in North Africa and about the growing economic and demographic disparities between the northern and southern shores of the Mediterranean that might produce massive waves of immigration from countries like Algeria to France. The southern Europeans hoped that CSCM would contain instability and radicalism in the Maghreb by helping the North African countries to address their acute social and economic problems.[43]

With the end of the Cold War and the Gulf War, France and Italy have reintroduced the proposal and expanded its scope beyond North Africa to include other regions and issues that affect Mediterranean security, such as the Persian Gulf and the Arab-Israeli conflict. One of the interesting aspects of CSCM is its attempt to expand the very definition of security. As European Commission President Jacques Delors explained in a speech before the International Institute for Strategic Studies, security means not only maintaining militarily defensible borders but also providing a livable environment, economic prosperity, and stable and legitimate political institutions.[44] The

U.S.–Middle East paradigm views the Iraqi-Kuwaiti and Arab-Israeli conflicts through political-military lenses, focusing on such issues as the regional balance of power, but the CSCM perspective suggests that a real and lasting peace in the region will also have to deal with such problems as social and economic gaps between the have and have-not states, diminishing water resources, human rights, self-determination, and educational and environmental problems.

CSCM might follow the CSCE pattern of focusing on three distinct categories of issues: security, economic cooperation, and human rights. It would apply a comprehensive regional approach to traditional security problems such as disarmament by promoting the denuclearization of the region, the recognition of the inviolability of borders, and the implementation of military confidence-building and arms-limitation measures. CSCM's regional security system would not be imposed from the outside through foreign military forces, according to Italian Foreign Minister Gianni De Michelis, but would draw on local players and be backed by international guarantees.[45]

The CSCM proposal has been criticized for being in essence an "idealistic" project. After all, even the CSCE was established only to formalize the post–World War II balance of power system in Europe, and in any case, its power to influence developments in Europe, such as the civil war in Yugoslavia, has been limited; that is to say, without a political/military player to back it, the CSCM could turn out to be nothing more than a paper organization. Although such criticism is valid, it glosses over the possibility that the way that Germany is leading in reconstructing the eastern European nations and linking them to the EC, southern Europe, led by France, could play, in the long run, a similar role in dealing with Europe's Middle Eastern periphery.

Even if an ambitious program like the CSCM would not materialize, France's political and military power could be utilized to advance a similar comprehensive approach to the region that links the stability of the Gulf to a Palestinian-Israeli solution. Even the more diffused EC structure advanced by Britain could lead to an interesting division of labor between a Germany oriented toward middle Europe and a France with a face toward the Middle East. Germany, aware that a protectionist Europe that discriminates against eastern European products could find itself swamped by poor refugees from Poland and eastern Europe, has emerged as the main lobbyist for eastern European economic interests in the community. In the same way, France could become an important force in supporting expanding economic and trade ties between the EC and the Middle East, recognizing the fact that an unstable and poverty-stricken Middle East could produce a flow of Muslim immigrants to southern Europe.

However, without a cohesive Middle Eastern policy on the part of Europe, economic problems and, especially, protectionist tendencies on the part of the EC could inhibit its ability to establish its political and military interests in the region, especially in the Gulf, as part of the competition with the United States. For example, the EC and the Gulf states face a major problem regarding the growing petrochemical and refining industries of Saudi Arabia and the Gulf states, the potential competition between these and similar facilities in Europe, and the level of tariffs placed on these imports into the EC. The imposition in June 1983 of a 13.5 percent tariff on Arab Gulf petrochemicals imported into the EC caused friction in the relations between the two regional organizations, and it was not until 1988 that settlement was reached.[46]

More recently, there were growing efforts to move toward removing trade barriers between the EC and the Gulf Cooperation Council, leading to "the highest possible level of trade liberalization" between the two and, eventually, to the establishment of a free trade zone between these two groups. However, there is still strong opposition to such a dramatic move in the EC. Indeed, both the success of the EC Maastricht Summit and the collapse of the GATT talks have raised the specter of a "Fortress Europe" in the Gulf and in the Middle East. The status of the existing trade preferences is an issue of great concern within the region in general and in Saudi Arabia in particular. Of equal concern is "the fear that EC members will be increasingly distracted by the investment and trade prospects offered by Eastern Europe and the newly constituted Commonwealth," as well as by the enlargement of the Common Market itself, following the agreement between the EC and the European Free Trade Association members in November 1991.[47]

REALPOLITIK INSTEAD OF IDEALISM?

An increasingly protectionist EC and rising anti-immigration and anti-Muslim tendencies in Europe (especially in France) could make it more difficult to build new structures of relationship between the EC and the Middle Eastern region. Instead of the progressive CSCM vision with its emphasis on comprehensive diplomatic and economic solutions to the region's problems, the EC states could adopt a more realpolitik approach to the area, reaching ad hoc agreements with various regimes there, tying, for example European arms sales and special trade preferences to Middle Eastern support for stemming immigration and preferential oil pricing systems.

This balance of power approach is reminiscent of European behavior in the region during the nineteenth century. It would combine the occasional use of gunboat diplomacy with pressure for trade concessions. Europe will then lose its ability to compete with

Washington in the ideological realm and to ally itself with the forces pushing for change and modernization in the region. The European–U.S. competition will not be won over the hearts and minds of the Middle Eastern people but over the hearts and minds of its authoritarian leaders — military dictators, traditional monarchs, and Muslim Fundamentalists.

Lacking the constraints of an idealist public opinion, strong Congress, and a powerful Israeli lobby and with a long historical tradition of involvement in the cynical power and trade competition in the region, Europe could beat Washington in this game. European public opinion is not expected, after all, to set diplomatic constraints on the ability of its foreign policy managers to make diplomatic and military deals with a new Saddam or a new Khomeini or to take advantage of the anti-Israeli attitudes in the Arab and Muslim worlds. As a matter of fact, with no progress in the U.S.-sponsored Arab-Israeli peace talks, and if no change occurs in the Israeli policies toward the Palestinians, the Israeli–U.S. connection could be exploited by a more assertive Europe in order to advance its interests in the region.

The key to determining the results of this competition, at least in the short run, will be Saudi Arabia. Saudi policy makers are trying to retain U.S. military support while avoiding too close a relationship with Washington for fear of promoting a domestic and regional backlash. Certainly the idea of a U.S. imperial presence defending the country is disturbing to both Saudi policy makers and large segments of the society. Moreover, a set of developments such as political unrest in the kingdom, pressure from Iran on Riyadh to distance itself from Washington, a stalemate in the Arab-Israeli peace process, and continuing efforts by Israel's supporters on Capitol Hill to veto arms sales to the kingdom may lead the Saudis to reevaluate their ties with Washington.

It is not inconceivable that Saudi Arabia, which is now the largest trading partner of the EC, will begin, in that case, to reevaluate its ties with the United States and to strengthen its relationship with the less-threatening and more logical partner, the EC. It is also possible that Riyadh would also encourage a new round of oil hikes and arrange a preferential pricing for Europe as part of a deal that will include a European agreement to pressure Israel to withdraw from the West Bank, including the imposition of an economic boycott against the Jewish state. The combination of the new Saudi-European relationship and the declining value of the dollar might drive Mideast producers to shift to European-currency unit–based pricing, with other raw material producers in other parts of the world following suit. Such a development would be, of course, a major blow to U.S. international economic position.[48]

CONCLUSION: THE COMING U.S.-EUROPEAN STRUGGLE OVER THE GULF

Notwithstanding the post–Cold War "end of history" visions and the expectations for a new world order based on new modes of international cooperation and collective security, it seems that, if anything, the new international system will continue to be characterized by a lack of centralized management structures and by continuing chaos and anarchy. As a matter of fact, with the collapse of the bipolar system, it looks as though we are moving toward a new world disorder in which new power configurations reflecting political, military, and economic competitions among the three major trading blocs of North America, Europe, and Japan will intertwine with regional, national, ethnic, and religious rivalries. The Middle East, particularly the oil-rich Gulf, could become a focal point for this post–Cold War struggle.

Indeed, with the end of the Cold War, the geopolitical focus on the Gulf is dissolving and the economic focus becoming more significant. In the short run, the disappearance of the Soviet threat has strengthened U.S. military power to such an extent that the United States is in a position to impose its dictates on the region and to contain the challenges from regional powers like Iran and Iraq and to push to the sidelines potential external competitors, in particular, Europe.

Thus, the political regionalization of the Middle East has run directly against the countervailing tendency of the globalization of the economy. Without oil, the rising economic superpower could have treated the Gulf and the Middle East with the same benign neglect they are projecting in their attitudes toward sub-Saharan Africa. However, with oil, the dependency of the industrialized world focuses on the region.

Notwithstanding its current prominent position in the Gulf, Washington, in the long run, will find itself in a position other declining empires faced in the past. Like other empires, it won its position by developing the most efficient and industrious economy and by translating it into international military and political power. However, like other empires, it then maintained its power by political and military effort, not by economic efficiency. This military power was used to transfer wealth from dependencies and allies — the control of Gulf oil being one example — rather than the political effort being made to rebuild the domestic economy. At the same time, military expansion and overstretching continued to erode the economic base. The result is that the United States finds itself in the aftermath of the Cold War with a vast military power and a weakened economic center.

The end of the Cold War and the Gulf War provided Washington with an opportunity to use its military power and its control of the oil resources in the Gulf as a way of maintaining its domination of the international economic system and of dealing with the trade competition from the EC and Japan. It is doubtful that the executive branch and the Congress will be able in the near future to agree on measures to reform the U.S. economy. In that case, the temptation on the part of the U.S. political elite, Republicans and Democrats alike, would be to try to solve the U.S. economic crisis by the application of the geo-strategic model, that is, not by internal effort but by the use of military power, a path of least political resistance (it is easier, it seems, for a U.S. president to win congressional approval for sending troops to the Gulf than for cutting entitlement programs). The Gulf War reflected, in that regard, the shape of things to come.

The Gulf will almost necessarily become the center of rivalry between the United States and Europe (and Japan). Europe's vulnerability to the flow of oil from that area means that rising U.S. military power in the region would increase European economic insecurity. For example, Washington would be tempted at some point in the future to manipulate Europe's oil supply from the region as a way of pressuring Europe to cut its subsidies to its agricultural sector.

Although during this post–Cold War transition period, Europe, lacking the necessary political-military means, will refrain from seriously challenging the U.S. position in the Gulf, it is doubtful that, in the long run, Europe will accept such subordination to Washington. Instead, moves toward translating the economic power of Europe, especially that of France and Germany, into military power that could be extended to the Gulf and the Middle East independently of U.S. policy are inevitable. The growing tensions between Washington and Bonn and Paris over the May 1992 decision by Germany and France to form an independent European military corps pointed to U.S. fear over the possible development of a non-NATO military power not under U.S. leadership.[49]

Similarly, it is unlikely that the EC will continue to accept its marginal role in the Arab-Israeli peace process and the task Washington assigned to it as a source of financial support for development projects in the region. Paris has already complained about the refusal of the United States and Israel to integrate Europe into the Arab-Israeli negotiations. Unless Washington succeeds in moving the negotiations forward, France can be expected to lead an effort to mobilize European and international support for the establishment of a Palestinian state.

Indeed, France will probably lead the way in moving Europe toward more assertive policies in the Middle East, exploiting U.S. failure to maintain its four pillars policy in the region, and facilitating the Arab-Israeli peace process (coupled with the growing support in the United States for disengaging from the region). A division of labor in Europe between a German hegemonic role in eastern and central Europe and a French leadership role in the Middle East could then develop.

NOTES

1. Quoted in Patrick E. Tyler, "U.S. Strategy Plan Calls for Insuring No Rivals Develop," New York *Times*, March 7, 1992. For a discussion of the Pentagon paper, see Joe Stork, "New Enemies for a New World Order," *Middle East Report* 176 (May-June 1992): 28–34. Since March 1992, the Defense Department has been trying through new leaks and public statements to modify the unilateral "one superpower world" approach, reflected in the original draft of its policy paper, and to stress instead the multilateral elements in its post–Cold War strategy. Nevertheless, even this "multilateral" approach assumes a leading global role for the United States in general in the Persian Gulf in particular.

2. David Newsome, "America Engulfed," *Foreign Policy* 43 (Summer 1981): 26.

3. On European diplomatic efforts, see Raymond Cohen, "Twice Bitten? The European Community 1987 Middle East Initiative," *Middle East Review* 20 (Spring 1988): 33–44.

4. Ellen Laipson, "Europe's Role in the Middle East: Enduring Ties, Emerging Opportunities," *Middle East Journal* 44 (Winter 1990): 16.

5. Quoted in Walter S. Mossberg, Urban C. Lehrer, and Fredrick Kempe, "Some in U.S. Ask Why Germany, Japan Bear So Little of Gulf War," *Wall Street Journal*, January 11, 1992.

6. For an analysis of the debate on the burden sharing during the war, see Gary J. Pagliano, "Iraq/Kuwait Crisis: The International Response and Burden Sharing Issue," Congressional Research Service Issue Brief, Washington, March 25, 1991. See also Hobart Rowan, "The Free-Lunch Countries," Washington *Post*, November 3, 1990.

7. *Le Monde*, December 6, 1991.

8. Quoted in Alan Riding, "French Maneuvering; Taking the Lead for Europe," New York *Times*, January 6, 1991.

9. Quoted in "The Second Trajan's Empire," *The Economist*, September 29, 1990, p. 57.

10. For a discussion of the German position, see Ian Buruma, "The Pan Axis from Germany to Japan," *New York Review of Books*, April 25, 1991, pp. 25–28, 38–39.

11. For a discussion of the British position, see Nicholas Henderson, "The Special Relationship," *The Spectator*, January 19, 1991.

12. Daniel Singer, "Braving the New World Order," *Nation*, March 25, 1991, p. 368.

13. Quoted in Tominlav Sunic, "The Gulf War in Europe," *Chronicles*, May 1991, p. 49.

14. Quoted in Flora Lewis, "A Shabby French Sulk," New York *Times*, February 29, 1991.

15. Quoted in Hella Pick, "Europe 'Left Out of Gulf Decisions,'" *Guardian* (London), December 14, 1990.

16. For examples of this U.S. position, see Charles Krauthammer, "Bless Our Pax Americana," Washington *Post*, March 22, 1991; Joshua Muravchik, "At Last, Pax Americana," New York *Times*, January 24, 1991.

17. Josef Joffe, "In the Gulf, Allies Are Doing Their Part," New York *Times*, October 9, 1991.

18. Thatcher made the remarks before an audience at the American Enterprise Institute in Washington, D.C. The quote is from David Broder, "The Thatcher View: America Must Lead," Washington *Post*, March 13, 1991.

19. Michael T. Klare discussed the debate between the geo-economic and the geo-strategic schools of thought in "Policing the Gulf — And the World," *Nation*, October 15, 1990.

20. George Friedman and Meredith Lebard, *The Coming War with Japan* (New York: St. Martin's Press, 1991), p. 209.

21. Craig Whitney, "Europe Discovers the German Colossus Isn't Big after All," New York *Times*, April 21, 1991.

22. Joe Stork, "New Enemies for a New World Order: From the Arc of Crisis to Global Intifada," *Middle East Report*, 176 (May/June 1992): 32.

23. Brian Beedham, "A Survey of Defense and Democracies: A New Flag," *The Economist*, September 1, 1990.

24. For an analysis of U.S. efforts to replace the Cold War with Islam versus the West paradigm, see David Ignatius, "Islam in the West's Sights: The Wrong Crusade," Washington *Post*, March 8, 1992.

25. "Europe's New Line on NATO: 'Yankee Don't Go Home,'" *Business Week*, April 1, 1991, p 14.

26. Ibid.

27. Quoted in William Drozdiak, "Mitterrand and Bush to Nurture Rapport," Washington *Post*, March 8, 1991.

28. Quoted in Theo Sommer, "A World Beyond Order and Control," *Guardian Weekly*, April 28, 1991, p. 10.

29. *Crisis in the Persian Gulf Region: U.S. Policy Options and Implications*. Hearings before the Committee on Armed Services, U.S. Senate (Washington, D.C.: U.S. Government Printing Office, 1990), p. 278.

30. Gerald Frost, "America and Her Friends," *National Review*, May 27, 1991, p. 30.

31. Anthony De Jasey, "Lessons from the Gulf War," *National Review*, May 27, 1991, p. 28.

32. Ibid.

33. See Allan Cowell, "Bush Challenges Partners in NATO over Role of U.S.," New York *Times*, November 8, 1991.

34. William Drozdiak, "France, Germany Unveil Corps as Step Toward European Defense," Washington *Post*, May 23, 1992.

35. Quoted in *The Independent* (London), March 7, 1991, p. 8.

36. See John Tagliabue, "How to Be Europe's Big Power Without Awakening the Old Fear?" New York *Times*, January 2, 1992.

37. Sabri Sayari, "Turkey: The Changing European Security Environment and the Gulf Crisis," *Middle East Journal* 46 (Winter 1992): 14.

38. See Marc Fisher, "Bonn Condemns Turkey for Attack on Kurds," Washington *Post*, March 27, 1992.

39. Robert Swann, "Self Interest Wins Out," *Middle East International*, December 20, 1991, p. 13.

40. For a discussion of Iranian relations with the United States and Europe, see Mohammad Jafar Mahallati, "The New Persian Gulf Security Arrangement and the Relevant Factors," *Middle East Insight* 8 (July/August 1991): 22–24.

41. Quoted in Scott B. McDonald, "European–Middle Eastern Relations: What Looms on the Horizon," *Middle East Insight* 8 (July/August 1991): 41.

42. Ibid.

43. For a discussion of the CSCM, see Barry James, "De Michelis Urges 'Helsinki' Talks on War's Aftermath," *International Herald Tribune*, February 18, 1991.

44. Cited in Glenn Frankel, "European Rethinking National Security Policies," Washington *Post*, March 23, 1991.

45. Gianni de Michelis, "Global Viewpoint," San Francisco *Chronicle*, February 2, 1991.

46. Abdulaziz Bashir and Stephen Wright, "Saudi Arabia: Foreign Policy after the Gulf War," *Middle East Policy*, 1(1) (1992): 107–16.

47. *Guardian Weekly*, November 3, 1991.

48. Daniel Burstein draws such a scenario in *Euroquake: Europe's Explosive Economic Challenge Will Change the World* (New York: Simon & Schuster, 1991), pp. 342–43.

49. See William Drozdiak, "U.S.–French Tensions Called Peril to Alliance," Washington *Post*, May 27, 1992.

II

Dominant Indigenous Players

3

Iran in the Post–Cold War Persian Gulf Order

M. E. Ahrari

The Islamic Republic of Iran has emerged as a major Middle Eastern military actor in the 1990s. This reality is partially related to the dismantlement of the Iraqi military power as a result of the Gulf War of 1991. However, on a more substantial basis, the emergence of Iran as an important regional power is the fulfillment of its natural role in that region. This reality has been on the minds of all Iranian rulers, Shah Mohammad Reza Pahlavi as well as leaders of the Islamic revolution.

In the post–Cold War Persian Gulf, especially after the dismantlement of Iraq as an important military force, Iran has been viewed as a major challenge to the stability of that area by both Washington and Riyadh. Such a shared perception became the basis of the U.S. decision to continue large arms sales to the Saudis. Of course, one cannot ignore the economic payoffs stemming from this decision, either. Iran, on its part, views the alliance between the United States and Saudi Arabia as a major source of concern and as an equally significant justification to continue its own massive arms buildup. However, this is only one disconcerting aspect of the relationship among the United States, Iran, and Saudi Arabia.

Another source of irritation for Washington and Riyadh is the hyperactive foreign policy of Iran in North Africa and Muslim Central Asia. Whenever Iran makes a presence anywhere in the Middle East and its contiguous regions, an almost automatic U.S response is to view it as a threat to both stability and U.S. strategic interests in that area. The regional rivalry between Tehran and Riyadh also complements the U.S. interpretations of the ominous implications of the high-profile Iranian presence. The thesis here is that in the post–Cold War Persian Gulf, the United States has been forced to sustain a policy of "watchful neglect" regarding Iran. The "watchful" aspect of this policy forces Washington to keep track of the hyperactivistic foreign policy of Iran, because this hyperactivism is regarded as essentially anti-U.S. However, the "neglect" part of the U.S. attitude toward Iran is manifested in its sustained refusal to establish even business-like ties with Tehran. The burden of blame in this regard is not to be borne by Washington alone; Iran must be made partially responsible for this state of affairs. In this chapter, I will elaborate on the "how" and the "why" of this relationship among Iran, the United States, and Saudi Arabia and on its implications for the security and stability of the Persian Gulf in the 1990s and beyond.

FROM A "STABILIZER" TO A "SPOILER" OF POLITICAL STATUS QUO: CHANGING PERCEPTIONS OF IRANIAN ROLE

The significance of Iran in the Persian Gulf is recognized by all major actors in the post–World War II international order. The former Soviet Union coveted its northern territory in the early 1940s but was forced to back down under pressure from President Harry S Truman. Since then, good political relations with Iran were sought by both the United States and the USSR.

However, the fact that the Anglo–U.S. endeavors brought the shah back to power in 1953 enabled the United States — which inherited the dominant strategic role of Britain in the post–Cold War Middle East — to have special ties with Tehran. Although the shah never forgot the significance of the U.S. role in his return to power, he also had to establish himself as an independent leader. This sensitivity on the part of the shah might have created noticeable strains on the Iranian relationship with Washington if not for the Cold War–related designs of the Soviet Union vis-à-vis Iran.

The Cold War in the Middle East, as was also true in other regions of the world, established a zero-sum relationship between the United States and the USSR, whereby the strategic gains made by one superpower roughly equalled the strategic losses of the other. Iran also became quite important for the United States in the Cold War years because of its common borders with the former Soviet Union. Then, in 1970, the Nixon Doctrine became one of the bases for the creation of even stronger strategic ties between Washington and Tehran (the other basis being oil). Iran emerged as the gendarme of the Western (read "U.S.") interests in the Persian Gulf. Even though students of the Middle East almost habitually speak of the "twin pillar" policy of the United States in that area in the 1970s, the fact is that the only pillar of this policy that had the potential of emerging as a major regional power was Iran. About the only significance Saudi

Arabia had (and this significance, indeed, had merits of its own) stemmed from the fact that it had the largest known oil reserves in the world. However, viewed from the perspective of military significance, Iran was decidedly a more important actor. Perhaps one can, more realistically, describe the U.S. policy as a "one-and-a-half pillar," not a twin pillar, policy.

Regardless of how this policy should be characterized, it enabled Iran to emerge as a symbol of stability and a defender of political status quo in the Persian Gulf. The shah's ambitions in this regard could not have been fulfilled in a more efficient manner. He was given carte blanche by President Richard Nixon to purchase U.S. weapons of all levels of sophistication.

Saudi Arabia and Iraq, the other major actors in the Persian Gulf, remained envious of the Iranian role and its attendant prestige. Saudi Arabia had oil but had no other vital characteristics — such as a large population, the existence of military and economic infrastructures, or a high level of technical knowledge on the part of the people — to emerge as a dominant factor. Iraq, even though it signed a friendship treaty with the Soviet Union in 1972, could not fulfill its aspirations to become a major military state in that decade.

The shah also matched his ambitious arms purchase policy with an activist and anti-Soviet posture in the Persian Gulf. In November 1971, Iran occupied the islands of Abu Musa and the Greater and Lesser Tumbs, located at the base of the Persian Gulf, halfway between Iran and the United Arab Emirates (UAE). One of the reasons given by Iran for this action was to ensure the security of the Persian Gulf. When the pro-Communist Dhofar rebellion broke out in Oman in 1975, his military might played a visible role in crushing it.

It should be pointed out that this tradition of activism, which may also be labelled as a persistent hegemonic tendency in the 1970s on the part of Iran, was quite in harmony with the U.S. predilection for a pro-Western status quo. As long as this status quo prevailed, international oil lanes remained open and the Soviet Union remained on the sidelines of Persian Gulf affairs. Washington did not really care how this Iranian activism was perceived by other Arab states.

On oil affairs, Iran continued a hawkish policy of intermittent price escalations. In this regard, strains developed between Riyadh and Tehran. However, these tensions remained quite manageable, primarily because there were no other overriding, clashing, foreign policy perspectives between the conservative and status quo-oriented rulers in these two countries. Iraq was not really able to exercise much leadership in oil affairs in the 1970s, largely because its own oil industry remained undeveloped because of a long-standing dispute in the 1960s with the international oil companies that were operating within its borders.

Therefore, the most visible actors of the Organization of Petroleum Exporting Countries (OPEC) in the 1970s were Saudi Arabia and Iran. The price moderation of Saudi Arabia and Iranian hawkishness on this issue could always find common grounds in an international market that was strongly favoring the oil states in that decade. Although the newly found power of OPEC states resulted in intermittent price escalations and even an oil embargo (imposed by the Organization of Arab Petroleum Exporting Countries [OAPEC]), there always remained a number of significant issues on which the United States could cooperate with Tehran and Riyadh. The most significant one was the Arab-Israeli conflict, on which the strategic objectives of the United States, Egypt, and Saudi Arabia converged after the Arab-Israeli War of 1973. The Iranian revolution of 1978–79 brought about significant changes in the relationship among the United States, Iran, and Saudi Arabia, however.

The Islamic revolution was one of the most significant developments in the Middle East, for a number of reasons. First, it established the first Islamic government in the post-colonial Middle East. Even though both Pakistan and Saudi Arabia claim to be Islamic states, neither country's government was established as a result of a revolutionary change. Second, the creation of the Islamic Republic also initiated an era when the Iranian perspectives on the nature of political order in the Persian Gulf underwent radical changes. Iran was no longer to remain one of the players in the Cold War; in fact, the Islamic rhetoric of Ayatollah Rouhollah Khomeini, the Islamic revolution's spiritual leader, depicted both superpowers as "evil." Third, the language of politics also underwent major changes in Iran. After the revolution, Khomeini's Iran utilized a new litmus test for the legitimacy of ruling elites in the neighboring states: it was not necessarily their adherence to Islam but, instead, their ties with the United States that became the basis for judgment on their legitimacy by the Khomeini regime. "Illegitimate" (read "pro-U.S.") regimes were given intermittent warnings that their rule would be ended by exporting Islamic revolution to their polities.

The Islamic revolution converted Iran into an unconventional state, a potential destabilizer, and a spoiler of the political status quo. Modern nation-states did not know how to deal with Iran. The Gulf sheikhdoms were scared, and Iraq was befuddled and angry over the continued public exhortations of Khomeini to overthrow Saddam Hussein. The United States — the "Great Satan" — bore the fury of this revolution through the hostage crisis. Although the USSR initially welcomed the end of a pro-U.S. regime, it could not find a basis for close ties with Iran. Especially after the Soviet invasion of Afghanistan in 1979, Moscow had no chance of establishing friendly ties with an Iran that was highly voluble in condemning the superpower domination.

The Islamic revolution added a new — and perhaps a long-lasting — dimension to the rivalry between the United States and Iran. The most disconcerting aspect of this development is that it couches the double standards, hypocrises, and all other negative aspects of the relationship between the West (as the developed part of the world) and the Arab and Muslim world at large (as the underdeveloped part of the world) in the lexicon of religion. Thus, when the United States pursues policies that are detrimental to the Iranian strategic objectives, the present rulers of Iran could very well argue that Washington was behaving as an "anti-Islamic" state. The potency of this argument can be demonstrated by its adoption by Saddam Hussein, a lifelong secular Ba'thist leader, during the Gulf War of 1991. One only has to travel in the Middle East to realize how successful he was in phrasing his war with the U.S.-led coalition as a struggle between Iraq as a Muslim state and the devout supporter of "anti-Islamic" Zionism, the United States. When the Western allied aircraft attacked Iraq on January 13, 1993, Saddam once again utilized the Islamic jargon to condemn this act by vowing to "defeat the infidels" and by imploring his armed forces to fight the attackers "the way you fought God's enemies before."[1] The use of religious phraseology and symbols to condemn one's enemy has been a tactic of politicians through the course of history in the Middle East, but the Khomeini revolution, perhaps, brought this practice to a new height.

The Islamic government of Iran in the 1980s was clearly interested in establishing in the Persian Gulf its own region of influence, something of an Islamic subsystem. However, the trouble was that it went about creating such a system in a wrong way.

The threat of exportability of the Islamic revolution to the neighboring states was inherently self-defeating. The Arab sheikhdoms, most of them were quite weaker than Iran, could not have been intimidated into becoming part of an Islamic subsystem in which Iran was to be the dominant actor. The Arab states had a variety of choices, and they exercised them throughout the 1980s. Their first response to the Iranian revolution was the creation of the Gulf Cooperation Council (GCC) in 1980. One of the raison d'être of this organization was to provide collective security for the Peninsular states. Between 1980 and 1987, the GCC continued a nuanced policy of offering "carrots and sticks" to Iran. Regarding the Iran-Iraq War (which was also triggered in 1980), Saudi Arabia and Kuwait actively supported Iraq. Saddam was viewed as a lesser of the two evils. At the same time, the GCC maintained a policy that all conflicts of the Gulf should be resolved without recourse to the interference of outside powers. This policy was in harmony with the insistence of Khomeini's Iran on excluding both superpowers from the affairs of the Persian Gulf. The GCC members were also aware that as the worst case scenario, they could rely on the intervention of the United

States, especially because they had good relations with that superpower, Saudi Arabia and Kuwait having special ties with Washington and London, respectively.

However, the Iran-Iraq War had a logic (or lack thereof) of its own. When Saudi Arabia and Kuwait continued to be targets of the fury of Iran for their support of Iraq, Kuwait, in 1987, invited both superpowers to make their presence known in the Gulf. The longstanding zero-sum relationship between Washington and Moscow was triggered once again, even though the USSR was observing a number of revolutionary changes stemming from glasnost (openness)- and perestroika (restructuring of the Soviet economy)-related policies of Mikhail Gorbachev.

The United States had two other significant reasons for being in the Persian Gulf in 1987. The controversial "arms for hostage" policy of the Reagan administration caused a considerable credibility gap for that country. Here was an administration in Washington that sounded so supercilious about not doing business with states sponsoring terrorism. In the aftermath of the disclosures of this controversy, the Reagan administration wanted to retain the trust of its Peninsular friends. Also, this was an occasion Washington could utilize to teach the Islamic Republic a lesson for all the humiliations it had caused, stemming from the hostage crisis. More importantly, however, this was a moment when the United States could prove that it was really serious in sustaining the political status quo in the Gulf. All the U.S. strategic maneuvers that began with the enunciation of the Carter Doctrine and culminated in the creation of the elaborate United States Central Command would have meant nothing if its military muscles were not flexed against Iran in 1987. The potential "spoiler" of the status quo had to be put in its place.

The United States succeeded in this objective not only by destroying a substantial portion of the ragtag Iranian navy but also by enabling Iraq to gain an upper hand over Iran in the last phase of the Iran-Iraq War. The Islamic Republic's decision to accept the UN-sponsored cease-fire in July 1988 was the termination of an important phase of the ongoing confrontation between the United States and Iran.

THE "OTHER MEANS" OF CONFRONTATION: THE POST–COLD WAR MANEUVERS OF IRAN

One of the problems encountered by Iran in the 1990s was that the United States and Saudi Arabia continued to view its activities through each other's frame of reference. Although these frames of reference have common variables, they are not exactly a carbon copy of the other. Let me elaborate.

For the United States, Iran remains an unconventional state. The Islamic aspect of its foreign and domestic policies are an anathema to Washington. On the issue of incorporation of Islam in politics, both the United States and Iran suffer from similar types of suspicions and paranoia toward each other. The Iranian paranoia is apparent in its thinking that the U.S. goverment is intent on bringing an end to Islamic government in that country. At the same time, given the U.S. record of 1953, one cannot be too sure whether the Iranian government is really paranoid on this point. An important part of the U.S. frame of reference — that at times borders on paranoia — is that Iran's foreign policy activism in the Middle East and in Muslim Central Asia is regarded as inherently anti-U.S. in nature. Although Washington's perception is not totally without merits, one has to be concerned about overstating this reality. Another ingredient of the U.S. frame of reference is that if Iran establishes strong diplomatic presence in any country of the Middle East and Central Asia, that country would automatically become anti-U.S. in its political orientation. On this point, Washington responds more to its paranoia than to a genuine fear or concern. No country that establishes close ties with Iran has any reason to become automatically anti-U.S. Even the Shi'ite elements in Lebanon were not anti-U.S. when the U.S. forces first went into that country to keep peace. It was only after the Reagan administration decided to become a partisan in Lebanon by overtly supporting the Maronite domination that the United States was regarded as an enemy by those who opposed the Amin Gemayal government. By the same token, the Central Asian Muslim states do not regard the United States as either their enemy or an enemy of Islam. It is only by promoting the Turkish secular model, as the former Secretary of State James Baker did in the beginning of 1992, that the United States might be viewed by the Islamic parties of that region as anti-Islamic.

Saudi Arabia shares almost all aspects of the U.S. frame of reference, except on the issue of Islam. On this issue, Riyadh and Tehran appear to practice "competitive superciliosity." Saudi Islam, which is both Sunni and Wahabi, definitely regards itself as superior to the Shi'ite Islam of Iran. The Islamic republic, because it views the Saudi regime as almost obsequious to the United States, has on occasions berated that government as a practitioner of "made in America Islam." However, the repugnant nature of this depiction kept the Iranian government from harping on it too often or too visibly, even at the peak of their differences with Riyadh. In the 1990s, one hears this characterization of Saudi Arabia only from radical functionaries in Iran.

One has to be cautious, however, about overly emphasizing the differences regarding the Islamic variable, because the real competition between these two Muslim states is that of a strategic nature. Which actor would (or should) have an upper hand in the affairs of the Persian Gulf, especially those affairs that would determine the regional balance of power? Which state would (or should) emerge as a superior in the field of military power, technological know-how, and economic power? These are some of the questions that tend to stimulate competition between Tehran and Riyadh. Then, there is that Saudi paranoia that stems from the fact that it is an authoritarian society in which the ruling elite's chief source of legitimacy is the guardianship of the Islamic shrines and their ability to manage domestic dissent through cooptation, mild repression, and economic payoffs. The fact that the Islamic revolution succeeded in dismantling an imperial order will never be forgotten by the Saudis. It is not the ability of the current rulers of Iran to export their revolution that should worry the Saudis; rather, by overthrowing the shah, the leaders of the Islamic revolution continued to remind Riyadh that a happenstance along the same line *could* happen in Saudi Arabia. This is also a crucial point of convergence between the U.S. and Saudi strategic concerns in the Persian Gulf.

Despite the fact that Iran under President Ali Hashemi Rafsanjani has abandoned its rhetorical threats of exporting the revolution, Riyadh and Washington remained concerned about what Karl Von Clausewitz labelled as "other means" of confronting its adversaries. There are three important aspects of these "other means" of confrontation, as viewed by the United States and Saudi Arabia.

The Dynamics of the Continued Diplomatic Competition in a Redefined Middle East

The redefined Middle East includes the conventional regions of the Levant, the Arabian Peninsula, and North Africa. In addition, since the emergence of six independent Muslim republics of Central Asia — Azerbaijan, Khazakhstan, Khyrghistan, Tajikistan, Turkmenistan, and Uzbekistan — one has to incorporate them in the broadened map of the Middle East.[2]

Of course, the inclusion of Muslim Central Asian states in the new definition of the Middle East stems from the fact that they are Muslim and economically underdeveloped, but the most significant aspect of these countries is the fact that as they develop their national personality, Islamic perspective is likely to permeate almost all spheres of their polities. This also means that one or more of them might be forced to consider some form of Islamic government. This is an issue in which Iran and Saudi Arabia might be able to play an important role — Iran because of its proximity to these countries and Saudi Arabia because of its significance as a Sunni state and also as the birthplace of Islam. This is also an issue that created a flurry of diplomatic activities on the part of the United States in Central Asia in the beginning of 1992. At that time, as previously noted, Baker visited a number of countries of that area, largely to persuade them to consider adopting the Turkish secular model. The United States has been concerned that potential adoption of the Iranian-style Islamic government by any of these countries would be detrimental to U.S. strategic interests in the area.

Iran enjoys a certain number of advantages in Central Asia. It can provide economic assistance in kind and some financial assistance. However, its Islamic government may not be of much use to the Muslim countries of Central Asia, all of which are Sunni except Azerbaijan. Even Azerbaijan looks at Turkey as a source of emulation, largely because its population is to Turkic origin.

The highly proactive aspect of Iranian Islam is a variable that might be a source of inspiration for one or more of the Central Asian states. Tajikistan and Uzbekistan might turn out to be such states. Therefore, Iranian activism in Central Asia remains a source of consternation for Saudi Arabia, the United States, and even Turkey.

In the Persian Gulf area, Iran has initiated its "diplomatic offensive" since the death of Khomeini. The thrust of these activities is to persuade its Peninsular neighbors that it has no intentions of exporting the Islamic revolution. However, Iran has had limited success in translating its activities into tangible strategic payoffs.

The Persian-Arab rivalry has remained a reality whose fissiparous effects have always been felt in the Persian Gulf region. A chauvinistic manifestation of this rivalry on the part of the Arab states is the way the Persian Gulf is referred to as the "Arabian" Gulf or the Khuzestan province of Iran is frequently referred to as "Arabistan." On a more grand level, the Sunni-Shi'ite divisions are also felt strongly in the Persian Gulf.

The Persian-Arab differences also were underscored on security matters, especially in the 1980s. In the aftermath of the Islamic revolution, the GCC has emerged as an "Arab" organization. The Iranian concerns about its exclusivistic nature were pooh-poohed by its dominant member, Saudi Arabia. At the same time, that country remained the chief opponent of Iran's possible entry into the GCC.

After the cessation of the Gulf War in 1991, when the Peninsular states were considering future security arrangements, Iran was once again excluded. The security agreement — the "GCC plus two" or the Damascus agreement — remained focused on Arab participation in the security of the Persian Gulf. Egypt and Syria were to contribute their forces in the "plus two" part of this equation. However, as an ironic tribute to the considerable weakening of pan-Arabism, the Damascus agreement did not materialize. Saudi Arabia and Kuwait were fearful of the potential Egyptian or Syrian interference in their domestic affairs. Egypt was not happy because the smaller GCC states were also considering potential inclusion of Iran in a larger collective security arrangement.

Another reason for the exclusion of Iran might have been the fact that Washington continues to perceive the Islamic Republic as a potential threat to the security of the Persian Gulf. Such a U.S. perception also complements the Saudi aspiration (albeit an unrealistic one) to dominate the Persian Gulf region.

Emphasis on the Military Buildup

Post-Khomeini Iran has remained focused on emerging as a regional military power. The aspirations of the current Iranian rulers in this regard have been in harmony with those of the late shah. Iranian experience since the Islamic revolution also propels that country toward military preparedness.

The fury of the Iranian revolution consumed a substantial part of its military technology and its experienced and highly trained manpower. Saddam Hussein tried to exploit this reality by attacking Iran in September 1980. The ensuing eight-year long and bloody war ravaged its military and economic infrastructures. During the same time, because Western arms were not available to its forces, Iran was forced to diversify its supplies, largely from the Communist camp and from the former Warsaw Pact countries. Developing proficiency in the use of arms from the Eastern bloc while fighting a war is not exactly an efficient way of training one's armed forces.

During this war, Iran was a target of some of the worst missile attacks. Saddam had also used chemical weapons to destroy the morale of the Iranian armed forces. Its oil processing facilities absorbed the brunt of Iraqi attacks during that war, while Baghdad could deliver its own oil through pipelines that passed through Turkey and Saudi Arabia. Then, the U.S. presence in the Gulf, as previously noted, also led to further dismantlement of the already-ravaged naval power of Iran.

The cumulative effects of these experiences appeared to have created among the Iranian rulers a resolve that their country must rebuild its military muscle. When one looks at the Persian Gulf from the Iranian shores, there is Saudi Arabia, which has manifested a continued frenzy of arms buildup from the United States, Britain, France, and even the People's Republic of China (PRC). A number of smaller Gulf states have signed bilateral security arrangements with the United States, enabling the latter to have a long-term presence in that area. This development is one of the major sources of concern for Iran.

According to one study, between 1980 and 1988, Iraq, Saudi Arabia, Kuwait, Bahrain, and the UAE had either contracted or deployed some of the world's most advanced military aircraft, including AWACS, F-15, F-16, F-18, "Hawk" 200, Mirage F-1, Mirage 2000, Tornado, MIG-25, MIG-29 SU-24, and SU-25. By contrast, the Iranian aircraft imports for the same period include MIG-19, MIG-21, Chinese F-6s, and F-7s. Compared with its Arab neighbors' supplies, these aircraft were at least two generations out of date and even less capable than Iran's existing stockpiles of 1960 and 1970 F-5 Tigers, "Phantoms," and "Tomcats."[3]

Another source of grave concern for Iran is that Saddam has managed to survive the U.S. resolve of destroying his regime during and in the aftermath of the Gulf War of 1991. Although the continued rule of Saddam is regarded as a threat by Iran, the potential fragmentation of Iraq is also considered as an equally crucial source of consternation. Iran has been watching with dismay the potential division of Iraq through the Western-imposed "no-fly zones" (thirty-second and thirty-eighth parallels) beyond which Iraqi aircraft cannot fly. In addition, it has been witnessing the creation of an autonomous Kurdish region in northern Iraq. These developments have convinced the Iranian rulers that in the unpredictable Persian Gulf neighborhood, they had to be militarily strong in order to survive. There are two significant aspects of Iranian military buildup: reconstruction of its economy, and development of arms sufficiency through indigenous production and importation of missile and nuclear technologies.

Economic Reconstruction

Comparing the economic performance and priorities of the Rafsanjani government with those of the shah's, one is struck by the similarity of objectives and tactics to attain them. The shah's regime was severely criticized for its excessive reliance on industrialization at the expense of enhancing the agricultural sector and for wasting oil as a national asset on defense. Even his industrialization policy was berated for its lack of emphasis on creating heavy industries. The revolutionary leaders were expected to correct these imbalances. However, Iran's war with Iraq might have been one of the major reasons for the failure of the new rulers to implement a different economic policy.

Like the shah's government, Iran under Rafsanjani gave a top priority to rebuilding its oil industry, including petrochemical plants. Iran also removed control from investments and production, deregulated banks and foreign trade, opened a stock exchange, and considerably expanded private ownership.[4] However, the heavy Iranian reliance on oil revenues became a constant source of irritation with Saudi Arabia in the 1990s, a characteristic that also prevailed in the previous two decades, except that in the 1990s, the conflict between Iran and Saudi Arabia appears to be more intractable.

Saudi Arabia is also utilizing oil to finance its strategic ambitions in the Persian Gulf. Cooperation with Iran means that the Saudis have to agree to incorporate unrealistic price escalations in tandem with absorbing production cutbacks. These concessions are unacceptable to Riyadh, given the facts that the Saudi government had absorbed billions of dollars worth of expenditure stemming from the Gulf War of 1991 and it is faced with bankrolling an equally capital-intensive military buildup.

Development of Military Capabilities through Indigenous Production, Joint Ventures, and Importation

Another characteristic that is common to the imperial government in the 1970s and the Islamic government in the 1990s is the Iranian determination for massive rearmament and the strategies to attain it. In the 1970s, Iran armed itself to dominate the Persian Gulf region. In the 1990s, its rationale is that it is only responding to an unsettling strategic environment that could turn against it (as it did during the 1980s) without much notice. However, the outcome of this major military investment in the 1990s, especially as its Arab neighbors see it, would enable Iran to dominate the Persian Gulf and even Central Asia. What exactly is the nature of this rearmament?

The pioneering work for enabling Iran to emerge as a major military power was done by the late shah when, in 1970, he initiated his "import substitution industrialization" program. Its underlying purpose was to facilitate military self-sufficiency for Iran.[5] As an integral part of this program, the shah's government signed production assembly agreements with seven major defense producers from the United States and United Kingdom, which covered an unprecedented amount of transfer of technology, including nuclear technology, from the West to Iran. A number of joint ventures between major U.S. defense companies and Iran started producing military equipment of different sophistication.[6] Since 1989, these programs have been resuscitated by the Rafsanjani government, the major exception being that Iran now is relying heavily on military joint ventures with the former Soviet Union and its major successor, Russia. The reverse engineering taught by the Chinese is reportedly being utilized to make spare parts for F-4s and F-14s. Iran's ambitions also include manufacturing indigenous fighter aircraft.

Iran made a major breakthrough in 1989, when Rafsanjani, then speaker of the Iranian Majlis, signed a $15 billion trade deal with the Soviet Union during his trip to that country. Moscow agreed to sell Iran a total of $4 billion worth of equipment that included MIG-29 fighters, T-72 MBTs, air-to-air missiles, antiaircraft missile systems, and air-defense radar systems. Iran further diversified its repertoire of weaponry by signing agreements with the PRC, North Korea, Czechoslovakia, Romania, and Poland for the purchase of advanced

Warsaw Pact–type weapons systems. In addition, during the Gulf War of 1991, Iran gave shelter to dozens of Iraqi military aircraft that it later decided to keep as a partial payment of war reparations.

Iran's purchase of Russian built kilo-class attack submarines were prominently covered by the Western media. The United States unsuccessfully tried to persuade President Boris Yeltsin not to go through with this deal. The general thinking in the West was that through the purchase of these submarines, Iran somehow would emerge as a naval power. Another frequently mentioned objective of Iran that is related to this issue is its capability to control the Strait of Hormuz.

The fascination with the acquisition of missile technology was reportedly developed by the revolutionary leaders of Iran during their war with Iraq. According to one study, "The 'war of cities' and the 'tanker War' ... presented [them] with convincing evidence that possession of widespread missile inventories had both psychological advantages, even if they outweighed short-term military advantages."[7] Since then, Iran is reported to have developed a huge inventory of missiles from a variety of sources. It purchased from the PRC Oghab tactical artillery rockets, C-801 (comparable to the French Exocet), and R-17/Scud-B. In addition, the PRC sold the following technologies to Iran: technology for 130-kilometer range Iran 130, facilities to indigenously produce 1,000-kilometer SRBMs, the Tonder-68, 1,000–125-kilometer SRBMs, transfer of "M-class" missile technology to produce 600-kilometer range missiles, and infrastructures to produce HY-2 Silkworm antiship and "M-class" missiles. Iran contracted with North Korea to produce "Mod B" versions and signed a joint production agreement with Syria to produce Scud Mod-C by the use of North Korean technology. A number of SRBMs were also supplied to Iran by the former USSR.[8]

During the shah's rule, Iran had signed with the French government a uranium-enrichment agreement, but because the revolutionary leaders initially suspended the Iranian nuclear program, Iran refused to accept from 1980–90 about 1 million "separative work units" of enriched uranium from the French company Eurodif. Then, in 1991, the Iranian government began to put pressure on France for the supply of the enriched uranium. Even though Iran won a complicated agreement to receive uranium, France continues its refusal to supply Tehran the agreed-upon material.[9]

Nuclear power is reportedly considered by Iran as vital to its quest for a dominant role in the Persian Gulf. Whether or not that country is in possession of nuclear technology is a speculative subject. Even when it is assumed that it does possess the technology, the question still remains as to how far Iran is from producing nuclear weapons. The United States is leading the West in making it quite difficult, if not impossible, for Iran to have access to a variety of complex technologies for nuclear weapons. The PRC, North Korea, and even Pakistan and India are mentioned as significant collaborators of Iran on this matter.[10] Iran is also reported to have acquired Soviet-made nuclear-capable strike aircraft (MIG-23BNs) and learned nuclear delivery techniques and tactics from Cubans.

The North African Connection

During the post–Cold War decade of the 1990s, Iran has increased its diplomatic maneuvering in North Africa, a region where poverty is rampant and structural aspects of economic underdevelopment are quite intractable. For all countries of North Africa, the population between the ages of 18 and 30 has been growing steadily, and with this growth are also increasing the rates of underemployment and unemployment. Sudan is an economic basket case. Algeria, thanks to the highly corrupt and inefficient rule of the National Liberation Front, is not too far behind, despite the fact that it is an oil-producing country. Among the North African states, only Morocco and Libya hold a promise of economic growth and development. Of course, one has to remember that Libya is a sparsely populated country, and it has been ruled by one of the most unpredictable leaders of our time, Muammar Qaddafi.

Among the North African states, Islamic parties are becoming increasingly popular. In fact, in Algeria, the Islamic Salvation Front (FIS) made such a powerful presence in the popular elections held in December 1991 that the military junta nullified it.[11] A not frequently mentioned factor underlying the Algerian dictators' decision to outlaw the FIS — and thereby to undermine democracy — was that this party made its intentions well-known that once elected, it would reduce the inordinately high expenditures of the armed forces. The Islamic forces are also quite active in Tunisia. In Egypt, these forces have initiated a terror campaign, drastically affecting the thriving tourist industry of that cash-strapped country.

Iran has been accused of exploiting the Islamic forces with a view to overthrowing the existing regimes. Iranian strong presence in Sudan is depicted as the nerve center of such activities. Sudan is a state where Hassan al-Turabi, secretary general of the National Islamic Front, is regarded as the de facto leader because of his close ties with the government of General Zubair M. Saleh. Al-Turabi has publicly expressed his warmth toward Iran. President Rafsanjani's trip to that country in December 1991 is described as an occasion when Iran's "African connection," whose purported aim is to destabilize North African countries, was really reinforced. Even though Sudan is an Arab state, its support for Saddam during the Gulf War of 1991 became the reason for its diplomatic isolation and the severance of its attendant economic assistance from the oil sheikhdoms. Iran has tried to fill the gap by providing a limited amount of economic and military assistance.

Egypt has been in the forefront of states that are accusing Iran of aiding and encouraging the extremist activities of the *Jami'at Islamiya* (the Islamic party) by providing limited economic and military assistance. There is no doubt that the Islamic parties have become quite active in a number of North African states. However, it is only a matter of speculation as to how much Iran is behind their increased activism. Given the acute economic disparities that prevail in those countries, it can be prudently stated that extremism associated with the Islamic elements is the direct outcome of a growing sense of frustration and despair of the population at large regarding what they perceive as patently incompetent economic policies of their corrupt ruling elites. It is quite possible that Iran might be exploiting these forces.

From a strategic perspective, the Iranian presence in North Africa might be the intensification of a long-standing rivalry between Tehran and Cairo. Iran regards a potential participation of Egypt in the future Arab security arrangements in the Persian Gulf as a source of major concern. Therefore, it is possible that by escalating the level of its own activities in North Africa, Iran might be interested in extracting a quid pro quo type arrangement from Egypt — downsizing its own support for the Islamic forces in North Africa in return for a promise of a hands-off policy from Egypt in the Persian Gulf. Such an Egyptian concession is likely to pave the way for potential inclusion of Iran in future security arrangements in the Gulf.

There is another variable in the rivalry between Iran and Egypt. The revolutionary leaders of Iran never forgave Egypt for signing a separate peace with Israel. Even though they were disillusioned with the fact that the Palestine Liberation Organization publicly supported Iraq during its war with Iran, the present Iranian rulers maintained their solidarity with the Palestinian struggle. In this sense, an interesting but minor variable in the ongoing rivalry between Iran and Egypt might be the degree of commitment to the Palestinian cause. However, on this issue, a rapprochement between Iran and Egypt can be reached if the former were to offer a promise of nonintervention in the strategic affairs of the Persian Gulf.

CONCLUSION

The removal of the Soviet Union from the strategic calculations of the United States has significantly influenced its strategic behavior in the Persian Gulf. The Gulf War of 1991 was the first clear indication of how far the United States would go in the pursuit of its objectives. The dismantlement of Saddam's military power was carried out largely on the basis of what the Bush administration determined was warranted or proper. By the same token, the U.S. attitude toward Iran is also affected by the post–Cold War reality that there is no more USSR to woo Iran to its camp. That is the main reason underlying Washington's sustained policy of watchful neglect.

From the Iranian side, its activism in Muslim Central Asia and North Africa serves as an obstacle in the development of a rapprochement between Washington and Tehran. This is a difficult issue of negotiation. No nation-state could be asked to lower the level of its diplomatic activities because one or more of its competitors view it as a source of potential challenge. However, once the United States and Iran open a dialogue on issues of mutual concern, an understanding on the Iranian involvement in those regions could also be reached.

In the Persian Gulf, the United States wishes to see a more visible role for Saudi Arabia and the GCC. However, given the performance (or the lack thereof) of this organization in the wake of Saddam's military takeover of Kuwait, Washington might only be indulging in wishful thinking.

Now that President Bill Clinton is in office, there may not be any overriding reason to change this policy of watchful neglect. If the Clinton administration decides to stay the course, it is because the new foreign policy team will take its time to watch and learn from the institutional memory of the Bush administration. Besides, Iran has nowhere else to go but to deal with the United States sooner or later. One can also state the obverse of the preceding statement: Washington also has no choice but to deal with Iran, now or in the near future.

However, on economic affairs, Iran can deal with Europe and Japan. Given the fact that in the post–Cold War years, economic issues will be part of the "high politics," the United States may have to decide to deal with Iran sooner rather than later. On military affairs, as already noted, Iran has been doing business with the former Warsaw Pact and Communist countries. Its preference for Western military technology will be materialized, most probably, from France in the not-too-distant future. (The excessive reliance of the French defense industry on foreign military sales is a matter of historical record.) The buyers' arms market of the 1990s and beyond would enable Iran to continue its policy of not relying on just one or two sources, a that lesson was learned by that country during its war with Iraq.

In the post–Cold War world, U.S. foreign policy is heavily colored by its reliance on the use of airpower. In 1987, when the U.S. navy was confronting the Iranian navy, there appeared to be developing a new pattern of aggressiveness on the part of the United States, a sort of shedding of the Vietnam syndrome of eschewing military confrontations, as long as the human cost for such a confrontation was low. The Gulf War of 1991 epitomized this behavior. The air attacks on Iraq in the beginning of 1993 appeared to be a continuation of the same pattern. In the wake of this development, the "watchful" aspect of the U.S. policy toward Iran has the potential of creating military responses if and when the United States decides that Iran is becoming militarily too strong. The continued rebuilding of its military power and its hyperactivistic policies in Muslim Central Asia and North Africa are likely to serve as rationales for such responses on the part of Washington.

The preceding discussion begs the question of whether peace and stability can be established in the Persian Gulf by isolating or excluding Iran. The categorical answer is *no*. Iran is strategically too significant to be ignored in future security arrangements. In fact, logic compels one to state that only by including Iran in future security arrangements would the United States and other great powers be able to stabilize the Persian Gulf. The inclusion of Iran is also likely to result in a deescalation of the arms buildup.

No matter how much money Saudi Arabia spends on building its military capabilities, it will be a long time before that country would come even close to being a match for Iran. Arms purchases alone do not make a country a powerful military actor. The presence of scientifically trained manpower and equally sophisticated infrastructures play crucial roles. Beyond that, a country has to be economically powerful and largely self-sufficient in military and economic realms. On these variables, Iran is far ahead of Saudi Arabia. Therefore, why not build political stakes for Iran to become a part of an all-inclusive security system? Tehran has been more than willing to join such an arrangement.

The Saudi-Iranian rivalry has been fueled by excessive emphasis on the military aspects of U.S. foreign policy during the Cold War years. In the 1990s, such a policy is anachronistic, at best.

Countries of the Persian Gulf have more reasons to cooperate than to fight. On oil alone, both Saudi Arabia and Iran can cooperate with the West to pursue a policy of economic diversification. Under such an arrangement, the West would have guaranteed access to energy supplies; in return, these two oil countries (along with other sheikhdoms) could purchase technologies that would enable them to attain economic self-sufficiency. Saudi Arabia has already been involved in investing in petrochemicals and banking. Kuwait has also been quite active in these areas. A potential joint venture can be developed between Iran and Saudi Arabia in this field and could become a basis for the evolution of numerous other projects involving other states of the region.

NOTES

1. New York *Times*, January 14, 1993.
2. Bernard Lewis, "Rethinking the Middle East," *Foreign Affairs*, Fall 1992, pp. 99–119.
3. Anoushiravan Ehteshami, "Iranian Rearmament Strategy Under President Rafsanjani," *Jane's Intelligence Review*, July 1992, pp. 312–15.
4. Shirin Hunter, *Iran After Khomeini* (Westport, Conn.: Praeger, 1992), pp. 56–91.
5. "Iran Builds Its Strength," *Jane's Defense Weekly*, February 1992, pp. 158–59.
6. Ibid., p. 158.
7. Gordon Jacobs and Tim McCarthy, "China's Missile Sales — Few Changes for the Future," *Jane's Intelligence Review*, December 1992, pp. 559–63.
8. Ibid.; Joseph Bermudez, Jr., "Ballistic Missiles in the Third World — Iran's Medium-Range Missiles," *Jane's Intelligence Review*, April 1992, pp. 147–52.
9. David Albright and Mark Hibbs, "Spot-light Shifts to Iran," *The Bulletin of the Atomic Scientists*, March 1992, pp. 9–10.
10. Yosef Bodansky, "Radical States and Nuclear Proliferation: Racing on the Finish," *Defense and Foreign Affairs Strategic Policy*, Winter 1991–92, pp. 10–13.
11. Remy Leveau, "Algeria: Adversaries in Search of Uncertain Compromises," in *Chaillot Papers #4* (Paris: Institut D'etudes De Securite, September 1992).

4

Iraq and the Post–Cold War Order

Ahmad Hashim

In 25 years under the Ba'thist leadership of Saddam Hussein, Iraq's status as a regional actor in Middle Eastern and Persian Gulf affairs has undergone dramatic changes. In the mid-1970s, that country emerged from relative obscurity to become a regionally influential actor. In the 1980s and 1990s, it underwent two devastating wars: the Iran-Iraq War of 1980–88 and the Gulf War of January–March 1991.

Between the two wars, Iraq acquired the status of a major regional political-military power and then paled into relative military insignificance after the second war, which followed on the heels of Iraq's onslaught on its wealthy neighbor Kuwait. In grand strategic terms, Iraq's invasion and annexation of Kuwait was designed to "solve" the country's geopolitical vulnerabilities and acute financial insolvency in the wake of the Iran-Iraq War and enhance its status both as an Arab superpower and as a global actor whose wishes could not be easily ignored or overlooked by the great powers.

Iraq failed. Strategically, the country's vulnerability in the aftermath of the Gulf War stands at an all time high, but the availability of resources needed by Saddam's regime to ensure survival and to play a regional role remains at an all time low.

This chapter focuses on the role of Iraq in the strategic affairs of the post–Cold War Persian Gulf. The underlying theme of this chapter is that much of the country's "muscular" strategic and foreign security policy under the Ba'th stemmed from the ruling elite's evaluation of internal, regional, and global threats to their rule and to Iraq, on the one hand, and from a deep-rooted ambition or desire to make Iraq the paramount political, economic, technological, and military power in the Arab world and a leading actor in the

Middle East, on the other hand.[1] The central argument in this chapter is that contrary to the conventional wisdom regarding Iraqi threats to regional security in the post–Cold War Persian Gulf, its weakened status in the 1990s poses a serious threat to the very survival of Iraq as a state. The chaos from this troublesome reality does not bode well for the continued stability of the Persian Gulf region.

BACKGROUND

When the Ba'thists seized power in 1968, Iraq, despite its abundant oil, water, and agricultural resources, was a poor and backward state. It was one of the least stable countries in the region. Its military establishment had a deep-rooted tradition of involvement in the Iraqi political process and was responsible for violent changes of governmental systems or regimes.

Although Iraq is the center of one of the oldest civilizations and states in the Middle East, the modern state has not been able to overcome the "artificiality" of its origins. The British, who drew the political boundaries of the country in 1920 following the merging of three disparate *vilayets* (provinces) of the collapsed Ottoman Empire, managed to create a country that was a mosaic of competing and mutually antagonistic ethnic, religious and tribal groups. Of these, the most important were the Sunni Kurds in the north, the Sunni Arabs in the center, and the Shi'ite Arabs in the south. To cap it all, the British imposed an alien form of government — monarchy — and a foreign Arab Sunni family to rule Iraq.[2]

The manner in which modern Iraq was created rather than allowed to historically develop has had profound structural implications for its domestic affairs and, ultimately, its foreign role. The Sunni Arabs, who formed the political, cultural, economic, and military elites, evolved an Iraqi national identity that reflected mainstream values found in the rest of the Arab Sunni world. An all-embracing Iraqi political consciousness that all groups, particularly the leading three, could share did not emerge. The result was domestic political instability and outbreaks of civil strife or insurgencies, which drained the treasury and circumscribed the country's regional role, as Baghdad's energies were often directed inward.

Historically, Iraq's ability to play an influential and strategically important role has been stymied. Its desire to be a paramount Arab power has been hindered by both its domestic weaknesses and Egypt's position as *primus inter pares* in the Arab world because of the latter's military, cultural, and political ascendancy. Iraq's role in the Arab-Israeli conflict was marginal, because it was not geographically a confrontation state like Egypt, Syria, and Jordan.

Iraq's strategic role in the Persian Gulf was even more marginal. Ever since the revolution of 1958, it had been ruled by unstable republican-cum-military regimes whose elite followed radical policies, while the rest of the Gulf states were conservative monarchical systems, either allied with the West or under the protection of Britain, the paramount political-military power of the Persian Gulf at that time. Last, but not least, Iraq had less than 50 miles of coastline along the Persian Gulf. This extremely attenuated access to the sea was a major obstacle in Iraq's ability to play a decisive role in regional affairs. It also led that country into major political and military confrontations with Kuwait, at whose territorial expense Iraq wished to expand its access to the sea, and with Iran, which resented unilateral Iraqi possession of the strategic Shatt-al-Arab waterway on which Iraq's ports of Basra and Faw were located.

This was the situation faced by the new Ba'thist rulers in 1968. Yet, between 1968 and 1975, Iraq, under their helm, continued to be strategically and politically isolated in the Middle East and Persian Gulf. In short, five major structural obstacles, many of which were associated with the dynamics of the Ba'thist regime and its modus operandi internally and externally, contributed to this marginalization.

First, for many years the Ba'thist government fought a brutal battle against various domestic groups. The former's heavy-handedness, paranoia, and totalitarian methods, although seen as necessary by the elite groups, did not facilitate the process of consolidation.

Second, the regime was confronted by an ongoing Kurdish insurgency in the north of the country, which not only was a critical source of weakness for all Iraqi regimes but also drained the treasury. In March 1970, an agreement was reached that would have allowed the Kurds a measure of autonomy, but the accord collapsed in early 1974 because the mutual suspicions were too strong. Furthermore, there were too many outside parties interested in fomenting civil strife within Iraq in order to keep Baghdad preoccupied.

Third, the regime was involved in a bitter struggle with the West-owned Iraq Petroleum Company (IPC) for control of oil that was that country's primary source of wealth. The Ba'thists profoundly resented the control of Iraq's oil by the IPC and the fact that the company had the final say concerning the availability of the Iraqi oil in the world market. The regime was determined to end the last vestiges of Western "imperialism" in Iraq, which it saw as an obstacle to the ability of their country to plan its development and to play a wide-ranging role in foreign and economic affairs regionally and globally.

Fourth, the Ba'thist regime was deeply disturbed by what it saw as the country's military weakness and the unreliability of the military establishment. It was not the only geographical distance that marginalized Iraq in the Arab-Israeli conflict but also the lack of sufficient mobile mechanized and armored forces and the need to thinly spread forces to face the Kurds and hostile Iran. Ironically, for most of the 1950s and 1960s, Iraq was the most powerful state in the Persian Gulf subregion, but it was rapidly superseded by Iran from the late 1960s onward. Iran's patron, the United States, was most willing to fulfill the shah's requests for sophisticated arms, which the shah matched with an activist military presence and an anti-Soviet posture in the Persian Gulf. Iran also used its newfound might to overthrow the status quo on the Shatt-al-Arab when it took de facto control of half of the river. From the perspective of the Ba'thist civilian leadership of the late 1960s, for whom civilian party supremacy needed to be consolidated, the military was considered politically unreliable because of its coup-making propensities. Consequently, the regime moved with alacrity to purge and to "ba'thise" the officer corps. A precipitous decline in operational readiness was the result.

Fifth, the regime's ideological extremism between 1968 and 1975 isolated and alienated it from the rest of the Arab world, including the formerly "radical" and anti–status quo powers such as Egypt and Syria. These states, after their crushing defeat in the 1967 Six Day War, became more interested in regaining their occupied lands and in establishing a modus vivendi with the cash-rich and conservative states of the Persian Gulf. It was a pragmatic and effective trilateral alliance of the Arab world's most powerful and richest states — Egypt, Syria, and Saudi Arabia — that waged the politically successful October 1973 war. In the Persian Gulf itself, the radical pan-Arab ideology and socialist ideals of the Ba'thist regime, coupled with its aiding and abetting subversive forces, only heightened the perception of threat of the Gulf rulers.[3]

EMERGENCE OF IRAQ AS A MAJOR REGIONAL POWER

From the mid-1970s, Iraq emerged as a regional influential in the Middle East and Persian Gulf.[4] The Ba'thist regime consolidated its domestic power. With the dramatic rise in oil prices after the 1973 war, Iraq was able to engage in massive socioeconomic programs that changed the face of the country.[5] This oil wealth also enabled it to engage in one of the most accelerated arms buildups of any Middle Eastern country between 1975 and 1980. This process changed the Iraqi army from a largely counterinsurgency force into one dominated by armored and mechanized units.

Iraq improved relations with the European Economic Community and Japan and was able to purchase advanced technology, which it desperately needed. At the same time, it distanced itself from its patron, the USSR, which it accused of interference in Iraq's domestic affairs and of playing a subversive role in the region and the Horn of Africa.[6] Iraq reached an agreement with Iran in March 1975 over the contentious Shatt-al-Arab River; in return for Iraqi willingness to share the river, Iran offered to cease its logistical and material support of the Kurdish insurgency. Baghdad was then able to crush the insurgents with ease. The diminution of the cold war between the Persian Gulf's two major powers led to a general relaxation of regional tensions.

Three critical events between 1978 and 1980 provided Iraq's ambitious leaders with the opportunity to assume the mantle of leadership in the Arab Middle East. The 1973 Arab-Israeli War had decisively improved the political fortunes of Egypt and its president, Anwar Sadat, who utilized the war to build bridges with the United States. During that time, Iraq remained in the semidark corner of the Middle East as a rejectionist state. This changed dramatically with Sadat's visit to Jerusalem and then with the signing of the Camp David peace accords with Israel in 1979. This peace removed the militarily most powerful Arab state out of the confrontation with Israel and was met with anger on the part of the Arab world, which condemned this breaking of ranks. Iraq, which felt that the Camp David accord detracted from the Arabs' ability to face Israel militarily, took the diplomatic lead in opposing the agreement and offered its army in conjunction with Syria's to form a reconstituted and powerful eastern front to face Israel in the eventuality of war. This strategic scenario, which would have reoriented much of Iraq's strategic focus toward the Arab-Israeli conflict, never materialized, because of Iraqi-Syrian animosity and the outbreak of the Iranian revolution.

In late 1979, the Soviets invaded Afghanistan. The U.S. response — from the Carter Doctrine to the creation of the U.S. Central Command — resulted in its enhanced presence in the Persian Gulf. Iraq was less than thrilled by this development, for it perceived the increased U.S. presence as threatening to its national security as well as a potential obstacle to its aspirations in the region. It moved with alacrity to adopt a high profile in the nonaligned movement and enunciated its own doctrine or charter as guidelines for the Arab world to follow. The charter called upon the Arabs to rely on themselves, adopt a united stance, not to threaten each other, and to adopt a policy of neutrality vis-à-vis the great powers.

It was, however, the Iranian revolution of 1979 that changed the balance of power in the Persian Gulf and dramatically enhanced Iraq's strategic role. The military prowess that was so assiduously built throughout the 1970s by the shah was consumed by the fury of that revolution. The emergence of a stridently anti-U.S. Iran under Ayatollah Khomeini brought an abrupt end to the "twin-pillar" policy of the United States, in which Iran, with Saudi Arabia serving as a second, but "lesser," pillar acted as gendarme of Western interests in the Persian Gulf.

The rise of an Islamic revolutionary regime in Tehran signaled the return of a cold war in Iraqi-Iranian relations and heightened regional tensions. With the decline of Iran's army, Iraq saw an opportunity to regain unilateral control of the Shatt-al-Arab River. The revolution had severely destabilized relations between Iran and all of its neighbors. Khomeini and his followers saw the revolution as a blueprint for a political-religious renaissance throughout the Islamic world. The ideology emanating from Tehran represented an assault on the regional political order and the secular domestic structures of the Arab states, whether conservative or progressive. With a historical sensitivity to foreign interference in her delicate ethnosectarian structure, Iraq was particularly vulnerable to Iran's ideological exhortations. Violent polemics and military clashes culminated in a massive Iraqi invasion of Iran in September 1980.

Iraq's expectations that it would win its war easily and quickly were not met. Instead, it was faced with a grueling and bloody war that lasted eight years against a determined enemy. In the duration of this war, the external factor that weighed heavily in favor of Baghdad was the continued backing by the Gulf sheikhdoms, especially Saudi Arabia and Kuwait, which not only sold oil on Iraq's behalf but also provided it with billions of dollars in financial aid.

Another variable that favored Iraq in this war was that U.S. foreign policy was in search of an anchor in the Persian Gulf to provide stability and protect Western strategic and economic interests. Saudi Arabia was looked upon as a potential contender, but it lacked the intrinsic strategic status and power of an Iran. Iraq had the potential, but it had too many serious problems. To begin with, it was a leading rejectionist state. As such, there was little chance that Washington could rely on Baghdad for political support in its endeavors to find a solution to the Arab-Israeli conflict. Iraq was labeled by the United States as one of the radical states sponsoring "international terrorism." Also, Iraq was technically seen as the "aggressor" state against Iran. No matter how distasteful the regime in Tehran was from the perspective of the West, Iraq was not far behind.

Matters changed somewhat in 1982–83, when Iraq was thrown on the defensive when it was Iran's turn to invade Iraq. Faced with massive offensives by a demographically superior and fanatically determined enemy, it looked as if the Ba'thist regime would succumb. The exportability of the Iranian revolution to the neighboring states appeared more real and menacing, and if Iraq fell, the whole political-strategic picture in the Persian Gulf and the Middle East would change. Faced with an existential threat, Iraq achieved impressive levels of societal mobilization, built a huge military, and moved to solicit international aid for its war effort. The fears of the regional powers and the West of the consequences of an Iraqi defeat considerably facilitated Baghdad's quest for international help in the form of high-technology weapons and financial aid. For his part, Saddam skillfully exploited Iran's intransigence and seeming "fanaticism." Iraq was portrayed as the defender of the eastern flank of the Arab world against the allegedly "barbarous" and "fanatical" Persian hordes and the promoter of regional stability and security.[7] Saddam restored full diplomatic relations with the United States (broken in 1967), toned down his rhetoric against Israel, and moved to integrate an isolated Egypt into the Arab fold.[8]

The exigencies of this war as symbolized by the pressures on Iraq, the increased threats to the freedom of navigation on the sea as both Iraq and Iran took their war to the Persian Gulf, the dynamics of superpower competition, and the security concerns of friendly sheikhdoms forced the United States to make its naval presence felt in the area in 1987 at the invitation of Kuwait. What then emerged was a policy of turning the tide of the war against Iran. The Americans sided with what they saw as the lesser of two evils. The United States fought with Iran on a number of occasions. In the meantime, U.S. spy satellites were regularly providing Iraq with data on Iranian military movements, while U.S. analysts allegedly provided strategic targeting data for the Iraqi air force. In early 1988, armed with an impressive array of ballistic missiles to supplement its air force, Iraq intensified its attacks on Iranian cities, severely affecting Iranian morale. In the meantime, a reconstituted Iraqi army took the offensive and pushed Iranian troops back to the border, destroying in the process most of the combat potential of the Iranian military.[9] Iraq emerged as the relative victor in the Iran-Iraq War.

The end of the war saw Iraq reemerge as a central regional power with tremendous ambition buttressed by an impressive military capability.[10] The victory had greatly enhanced the military and political-strategic prestige of Iraq.[11] In concrete terms, the military power of the country was enormous: Baghdad had built the largest armed forces in the Middle East in terms of manpower and inventory, and it had one of the largest stocks of unconventional weaponry in the region and a burgeoning military-industrial complex that had been built from scratch during the war.[12]

As such, Saddam Hussein wanted to influence and shape the strategic realities of his neighborhood, and with its power and prestige, Iraq seemed well-placed to do so. Iran had to lick its wounds and focus its attention on rebuilding its ravaged economic infrastructure and military. Iraq, for its part, wanted long-term strategic superiority over Iran. What the Iraqis had learned from the Iran-Iraq War was that their smaller and demographically outnumbered country had to deal with Iran from a "position of strength." In Iraqi eyes, Khomeini had not ended the war because he wanted to but because he had been forced to do so because of the defeat of his army. Saudi Arabia did not have the manpower or military capability to fill the power vacuum in the Persian Gulf. The Gulf Cooperation Council, which was formed in 1981 by the Arab Gulf monarchies to coordinate their policies and defense in the wake of the strategic uncertainties brought about by the Iran-Iraq War, could not function as a military counterbalance to the huge Iraqi war machine. Saddam also involved himself in the "confessional" politics of Lebanon against Syria. Hafez al Assad had to pay for siding with Khomeini. Iraq also moved closer to its three staunchest regional allies, Egypt, Jordan, and North Yemen, when they agreed to establish the Arab Cooperation Council. It also reentered, or, more accurately, entered, the Arab-Israeli military arena with a vengeance. For a short time, Iraq's military power was a source of immense pride for the whole Arab world. For the first time, it seemed, there was a strategic deterrent against Israeli military and a chance for the Arabs to right the imbalance of power in Israel's favor.[13] It was in this context as the Arab world's strongest power that Iraq threatened to burn half of Israel if the latter dared attack Iraq's technological and military-industrial complexes.

On the negative side, however, the war had not solved any of Iraq's geopolitical vulnerabilities; indeed, it had accentuated them and created vulnerabilities, geopolitical or other, that had not existed before. With its seaports closed, Iraq was more dependent on the goodwill of its neighbors than ever before for the export of its oil and import of its industrial goods via the use of their ports and transportation network. The victory over Iran had solved nothing. Iraq's military might had made it the focus of unwanted global attention and an increase in covert attempts to attenuate or hinder any further growth in that power. Increasingly, Western countries were beginning to feel that Iraq had become too powerful for regional stability. Such Western views only enhanced the Iraqi perception of threat. She began to believe that Israel would be the instrument by which Iraq's military power would be sabotaged.[14] Furthermore, from late 1988, Iraq began to see the West as increasingly hostile, it attacked Iraq for its human rights record and its "totalitarian" system of government, and it wanted not only to shackle Arab military power but also to prevent the burgeoning of Arab science and technology. With the decline of the Soviet Union and its descent from superpower status, Iraq felt that the United States would become overly assertive globally and would attempt to shape the political dynamics of the Middle East to further its interests and those of its "surrogate," Israel.[15]

Finally, Iraq emerged from the war with a crushing debt burden. In 1980 Iraq had a high credit rating and virtually no debt, but by 1988, it owed billions to its creditors in the West, the Soviet bloc, and the Arab world. It demanded that the Arabs consider their loans as grants for the service Iraq had rendered by saving them from the Iranian "menace." Iraq's debt load hindered considerably its grandiose reconstruction and massive economic development plans. This was particularly galling to the Iraqi leadership, which wanted to see a return to normality and to end eight years of relative deprivation and hardship for its people.

Iraq's greatest problems were its geopolitical and financial vulnerabilities and difficulties. By mid-1990, Iraq felt that these were becoming unbearable. In searching for a solution, Saddam turned his might on one of his major benefactors but an increasingly obnoxious neighbor from Baghdad's perspective — Kuwait.

THE GULF WAR OF 1991 AND ITS AFTERMATH

The Iraqi invasion of Kuwait on August 2, 1990, and subsequent ejection from the emirate was a watershed event in that country's contemporary history. In less than a year, Iraq went from being a regional superpower to being a country with vastly diminished sovereignty over its affairs and struggling for survival. After the end of the war with Iran, Iraq had a new set of problems with Kuwait. Members of the Organization of Petroleum Exporting Countries (OPEC) agreed to abide by production quotas set by that organization. This was a decision collectively taken to firm up oil prices worldwide. Kuwait emerged as a regular violator of its quotas. Baghdad viewed the Kuwaiti overproduction as a deliberate attempt to create downward pressure on oil prices, a measure that a cash-needy country such as Iraq could ill afford. Another source of considerable irritation was the Kuwaiti refusal to cancel the billions of dollars of debt incurred by Iraq during the Iran-Iraq War. Iraq was of the view that it owed Kuwait nothing because it had saved the weak Arab states from the Iranian menace. The third source of quarrel was that emirate's alleged theft of oil from the Rumallah oil field straddling the Iraqi-Kuwaiti border.[16] Furthermore, Iraq also alleged that a conspiracy existed involving Kuwait, Saudi Arabia, and the United States to manipulate its economic woes in order to keep it weak and preoccupied with internal affairs.

Iraq's action precipitated the first post–Cold War crisis and united almost the entire international community against it. Through a series of UN resolutions (SCR 660, 661, and 678), the world community left little doubt that the Iraqi occupation of Kuwait would not go unpunished if Saddam's aggression was not vacated. As the crisis dragged on, the United States began to define the goals of the coalition of states that were gathered in Saudi Arabia. These goals included the defense of Saudi Arabia, the immediate, complete, and unconditional withdrawal of Iraq from Kuwait, and the restoration of security and stability in the region. Attempts by some parties to reach a negotiated settlement got nowhere because of U.S. insistence on unconditional Iraqi withdrawal. Iraq, on its part, insisted that Kuwait was an integral part of its territory. At the same time, Saddam Hussein wanted to link the settlement of the Kuwaiti crisis with a resolution of the Palestinian issue.

January 15, 1991, came and went without the Iraqi withdrawal. Seventeen hours later, on January 16, a massive aerial campaign was launched against a wide variety of targets in Iraq and Kuwait. Six weeks of punishing air attacks was followed by a lightning 100-hour ground assault on February 23 which routed the Iraqi forces with surprisingly low cost to the coalition. On February 27, President George Bush ordered a halt to the offensive that had liberated Kuwait and had captured a large swathe of Iraqi territory bounded by Saudi Arabia to the south and Kuwait to the east.

On March 3, Iraq accepted the cease-fire terms demanded by the coalition, which included rescinding the annexation of Kuwait and the immediate release of prisoners of war. A month later, on April 6, Baghdad accepted the terms for a permanent cease-fire in accordance with SCR 687, which stipulated continuation of an arms embargo for the indefinite future and UN-supervised destruction of all chemical and biological weapons, long-range ballistic missiles, and nuclear infrastructure. Iraq agreed to compensate Kuwait and other countries for damage incurred during the war. An unequal demilitarized zone was up on the border with Kuwait, extending ten kilometers into Iraq and five kilometers inside Kuwait, to be patrolled by UN observers. The UN was also to demarcate the border between the two countries. Iraq's compliance with these demands were to result in a gradual lifting of sanctions.

Baghdad also found itself opposed by an array of opposition groups based outside the country and spanning the political spectrum, including Islamic Fundamentalists, Kurdish autonomists, nationalists, dissident Ba'thists, Leftists, and liberals. Opposition to the regime was longstanding and had expanded considerably after 1979 when Saddam (then second in charge) edged out President Hasan al-Bakr and had himself "elected" to the presidency. However, Iraq continued to be a well-policed and "self-policing" society in which the populace had internalized "correct" patterns of conformity and norms of behavior. Severe weaknesses were exhibited by the opposition groups in the past; however, the Gulf Crisis of August 1990 saw dramatic changes in their fortunes. The mobilization of the world against Saddam inspired hope in the opposition groups that no longer would they be ignored by the international community.

Consequently, they redoubled their efforts to establish a common anti-Saddam platform, and they also began courting member states of the coalition. Some of these countries hoped for a popular uprising to occur at a time when the Saddam regime was facing a crisis characterized by a loss of control over society and disarray in the military. No one was prepared for the magnitude of insurrections that erupted in the Shi'ite south and Kurdish north after the cessation of the Gulf War.

Saddam controlled the Shi'ite population during the Iran-Iraq War by the twin policies of repression and bribes. Therefore, why did they rebel in the aftermath of the Gulf War of 1991? Details about their uprising are still sketchy. What follows are tentative observations.

First, there was a political and military vacuum in the southern part of the country following the Iraqi defeat. This was an unprecedented development. Even during the most desperate years of the Iran-Iraq War, when it seemed that the southern front might collapse, there was no political or military vacuum there; the Iraqi army retained its cohesion, and the Ba'thist party continued to exercise tight control. However, in the Gulf War of 1991, the transportation and communications networks had been devastated by the coalition bombings. The remote border regions with Iran were not being watched, and the military and security services were in disarray. This vacuum was fully exploited by the rebels. Second, the social contract between the populace and the government, in which the former had tacitly accepted an authoritarian system in return for economic development and largesse, had unravelled in the south. The region had suffered the most devastation in two wars, and the people had seen a disproportionate number of their sons, husbands, fathers, and brothers killed or wounded in ultimately worthless military adventures. At the same time, even before the August 1990 crisis, the bankrupt government of Iraq no longer had the financial and economic wherewithal to satisfy the material needs of the people. If we add to this the Shi'ite sense of political marginalization in a political system in which they were excluded from the top hierarchy of the ruling elite, it is not surprising that there existed a genuine sense of grievance among segments of the Shi'ite populace. Third, although the war with Iran may have enhanced the national consciousness of the Iraqi Shi'ite, this does not mean that a sense of loyalty toward Saddam's regime existed, despite the government's attempts to equate the two.

What are the reasons underlying the failure of the Shi'ite insurrection? To begin with, it was not a general insurrection. Initially, the revolt was an explosion of pent-up rage and revenge characterized by an orgy of looting and destruction and offered no ideological vision. It was more against the Saddam regime than for anything else. However, when it did achieve a semblance of organization and success as a result of leadership provided by units infiltrated from Iran, it attained an ideological hue that proved disastrous. Carried away by the euphoria, the rebels raised the green banner of Islam and portraits of Ayatollah Khomeini and Baqir Al-Hakim and called for Islamic rule in Iraq. This development considerably dismayed opposition groups outside Iraq. Even the Shi'ite fundamentalists went out of their way to deny that their agenda was to bring about Islamic rule. Member states of the coalition, which had made clear their desire to see Saddam overthrown, were thoroughly disconcerted by a rebellion that might result in the fragmentation of Iraq or bring to power a pro-Iranian fundamentalist regime. Their very neutrality during the revolt enabled the Iraqi military to move about freely and crush it.[17] Most important was the reaction of the Ba'thist party elite, the Sunni Arabs, and Shi'ite middle class. For these secular-minded segments of the population, the idea of a fundamentalist regime coming into power, aided by Iran, was a horrifying vision. Furthermore, the atrocities committed against government officials during the Shi'ite uprising were seen as a portent of the bloodbath to come if the rebels were to prevail. Finally, the political-military vacuum in the south in the aftermath of Iraqi defeat proved to be fleeting. The regime marshalled the considerable remaining military resources available to it (apart from isolated incidences of defections and desertions, the army remained loyal) and sent it into action against lightly armed rebels who could not match its firepower.

In contrast to the Shi'ites, the Kurdish insurrection proved to be an intractable problem. Traditionally, Kurds have always taken advantage of the government's preoccupation with other pressing domestic or foreign issues to bring up their demands for autonomy and to rise up in revolt if assured of foreign support. Between the end of the Iran-Iraq War and the Kuwait crisis, the Patriotic Union of Kurdistan (the Talabani group) and the Kurdish Democratic Party (KDP — the Barzani group), in order to better coordinate their activities, combined their forces with smaller Kurdish groups to form the Iraqi Kurdistan Front (IKF). In order to allay the hostility of other Iraqi opposition groups with whom they sought closer relations, they stressed that their objective was to seek autonomy for Kurdistan within a democratic Iraq. When Iraq was forced to move forces to the south, leaving only three combat-effective divisions in the north and a host of ill-motivated infantry troops, the Kurdish revolt erupted.

This revolt surpassed the most optimistic expectations of the Kurdish elements. Within days and for the first time in their history, the guerrillas took several major urban centers, including the oil center of Kirkuk, and captured immense quantities of military equipment. By mid-March, the IKF declared that 75 percent of Kurdistan was in rebel hands. The IKF rapidly moved to restore essential services and civil administration in the "liberated" areas.

After crushing the revolt in the south, Baghdad quickly moved its combat-effective forces to the north. These forces launched a lightning campaign resulting in the retaking of all urban centers by April 1. Neither the IKF nor the international community counted on what happened next. Within days of the collapse of the Kurdish revolt, hundreds of thousands of civilians began an exodus that was unprecedented in modern Iraqi Kurdish history. The refugee problem received enormous international coverage, prompting a massive humanitarian effort to provide the refugees with food, medicine, and shelter. On April 8, the European Community adopted a British proposal to create a "safe haven" on Iraqi territory north of the thirty-sixth parallel, protected by coalition military forces, to which Kurdish civilians were encouraged to return.

The events that followed these rebellions convinced the world community that given the magnitude of chaos that prevailed among various opposition groups an acceptable option would be the continuation of the status quo. No one is suggesting that Saddam should be allowed to stay in power, but even those who arduously seek an abrupt end to his brutal rule find themselves groping for alternatives to Saddam.

It is apparent that the Kurds wish to have their autonomy either legitimized by the present or future Iraqi government or guaranteed by one or more major powers. However, the problem is that neither Iran nor Turkey would endorse such a development, for they are wary of the implications of an autonomous state in Iraq for the Kurdish population in their own countries. Even Arab states would not endorse this option because it would result in a possible division of Iraq. When viewed from within, no future Iraqi government is likely to allow the creation of an autonomous Kurdistan. The Kurdish groups know only too well that Saddam bothered to have a dialogue along these lines only because he was in the weakest position of his entire career in the wake of his defeat in the Gulf War of 1991.

Saddam managed to retain control and enough support in the "center." This term not only underscores the important linkage between Sunni Arab heartland and the capital city of Baghdad but also makes a statement along socioeconomic and cultural lines. It includes urban areas of Iraq, where a vast majority of its large middle class, professionals, and intellectuals reside. These groups also enjoy the nation's highest standard of living.[18] Why the center held during the rebellions may be explained by a combination of several factors. First, there was the sense of hostility expressed toward the goals of the rebellions. The Kurds were viewed as putative separatists, and even if their quest for autonomy were genuine, they could not be allowed to control oil-rich At-Tamim province. The worst nightmare was the perceived desire of the rebels in the south to establish an Islamic Fundamentalist regime. Such a development would have permanently overturned the political and economic status of the center, including the Shi'ites, Kurds, and Christian Arabs. Second, the center might have held because of a genuine sense of loyalty among a core of the population wedded to the Ba'th Party's commitment to secularism, economic development, and the promotion of a distinct and nonsectarian Iraqi nationalism. The third reason underlying the survival of the center is what David Hirst describes as the "legitimacy of the worst alternative" among segments of the population.[19] This concept describes the belief that if Saddam goes, things would not get better but would get worse, and dramatically so. Not only might the regime unravel, but also, so might Iraq. Fourth, fear of the pervasive presence of the security and military apparatus in the center (for example, there is a Republican Guards division of 15,000 men permanently based near the capital), which the regime knows is the key to control of the country, might have also induced caution. In order to widen his base of support in the center, Saddam has resorted to a policy of mobilizing the Sunni Arab tribes. After two decades of being castigated as symbols of a feudal and reactionary past, these tribes are now considered an important pillar of Iraqi society.

The center does have its grievances and problems, the foremost of which are declining socioeconomic standards of living and spiralling prices (inflation is at 2,000 percent). Wages and salaries have not risen in real terms from 1990 to 1992. There is no job security in the stagnant economy, and unemployment has reached 20 percent. The level of poverty has increased. The middle class has seen its savings wiped out, and many are being forced to pawn their valuables or take second jobs, for example, driving a cab or hawking wares in the streets, while an increasing number of the poorer classes are relying more on the state for their basic needs. The rationed products provided by the government furnish only 55 percent of required calories, according to Minister of Commerce Mohammed Mahdi Salih. In comparison to the society at large, bitterness and humiliation over Iraq's erosion of national sovereignty and power is felt most acutely in the center. There is also considerable amount of resentment over the lack of political freedoms and lack of public accountability on the part of the government.[20]

The task of reconstruction is enormous. Iraqi officials claim the Kuwait affairs cost $200 billion, to which should be added another $200 billion spent on the Iran-Iraq War.[21] Long-term construction will depend upon foreign exchange, trade, and foreign technical expertise and a willingness on the part of the Iraqi private sector to take heed of the government's exhortation to play a more vigorous role in the economy. Iraqis know that their ability to engage in long-term reconstruction in the current climate, with sanctions in place, is not possible. Even if sanctions are lifted, the obstacles are formidable: indebtedness makes the country a terrible credit risk, and reparation payments will siphon off as much as 30 percent of Iraqi income for the indefinite future.[22] However, toward the end of 1992, reports from Iraq were portraying a very positive picture of the Saddam regime's ability to rebuild a substantial portion of that country. This account was especially surprising in view of the continued refusal of the UN to lift economic sanctions.[23]

IRAQ AND THE POST-COLD WAR WORLD: GLOBAL AND REGIONAL CONTEXTS

Iraq's relations with the outside world remain in deep freeze despite her persistent efforts to attenuate or break out of isolation. Currently, she sees herself under siege from, and threatened by, several enemy groupings that have continued with the tacit alliance established before the Gulf War. This list includes "colonialists" or "imperialists" (the West); the "reactionary" Arab states (Arab members of the war coalition) that were motivated by envy, injustice, and treachery; and the Zionists and the Iranians.[24]

Iraqis point out that given the deterioration in their relations with Washington and London, they are not surprised by the stance taken by the United States and Britain during the crisis. However, the French active participation in the coalition was an unpleasant surprise for them. France and Iraq had developed a special relationship over two decades.

In the Iraqi view, the West did not go to war over Kuwait but did so because it could not countenance the emergence of a militarily strong and politically influential Iraq. The West could not tolerate the emergence of a strong Arab state or leader. Iraq, with its accomplishments, had violated the limits imposed by the West upon scientific and technological development in the Third World.[25] Iraq's violation of these limits were a threat to the West's domination of the region as well as a danger to its illegitimate creation in the Middle East, the Zionist entity, Israel. Indeed, using this occasion, the Western imperialists, aided by their "reactionary stooges" in the region, finally carried out in a devastating manner the measures they had threatened to take against the Iraqi scientific and technological infrastructure from 1988 to 1990.

After the end of the Gulf War, however, Iraq expressed an interest in restoring political and economic relations with the Western powers, which were its main trading partners before the crisis. The West has not been forthcoming, however. Iraq's relations with that powerful group of countries are dictated by the latter's continued insistence that Saddam must be removed from power. A coup by the army or the party did not materialize. Even though it issued several statements calling on the Iraqi people to topple Saddam, Washington was not interested in helping the rebels during the insurrections because of its fears that Iraq might fragment or fall under the domination of Iran. As a tactical maneuver to overthrow Saddam, the United States and her allies maintained steady and unremitting pressure in the form of sanctions as mandated by SCR 661.

Iraq found no comfort in the position of the Soviet Union during the Gulf Crisis. Although the latter took a strong stance against Iraq diplomatically, it was not a member of the military coalition and did display considerable ambivalence about the possible use of force. However, it did little to prevent the slide toward war, and a last-minute effort by Soviet President Mikhail Gorbachev to avoid a ground assault was brushed aside by President George Bush. The Soviet role in this conflict symbolized for Iraq the irrelevance of the Soviet Union. After the war, Baghdad avoided criticizing the USSR, possibly in the hope that it might at some point attenuate Iraq's isolation. When Gorbachev was overthrown in the short-lived coup of August 1991, the Iraqi media launched into a scathing criticism of the harm that the Soviet leader had done to his country's global position by his policies and to Iraq by his role of passive spectator during the Kuwait crisis.[26]

Any Iraqi attempts to play a pan-Arab role (that is, support of Palestinians and opposition to the "imperialist" Western presence) in regional politics are now limited by that country's exhaustion, lack of resources, and growing contempt for the Arabs. Iraq continues to maintain good relations with those Arab countries that were sympathetic to it during the war: Algeria, Jordan, Sudan, Tunisia, and Libya. However, as early as April 1991, Iraq made clear its willingness to turn over a new leaf in its relations with the leading Arab members of the coalition, Egypt, and Saudi Arabia, declaring that ties cannot remain severed forever. Iraq even attended a summit of foreign ministers of the Arab League in Cairo in May. However, it continues to be viewed with utmost suspicion and fear by many countries.

Arab attempts in early March 1991 to guarantee Gulf security, which culminated in the "Damascus Declaration," foundered when Egypt, one of its major participants, withdrew its forces. Syria, the other major participant, also expressed its ambivalence toward this arrangement. It became clear that each member of the proposed security system had its own agenda. Egypt, cognizant of the extent of the Iraqi defeat and the imbalance in the region, wanted to focus on the Iranian threat to the Gulf. Indeed, Egyptian leaders and defense planners are increasingly worried by what they see as Iran's growing threat to the region and to Egypt. In a larger sense, Cairo remained equally concerned about the implications of the destruction of the Iraqi military power for the overall significance of Arab power in the region, especially in relation to Iran, Israel, and Turkey.[27]

Syria, for its part, has very few links with the Gulf countries. It cannot afford to keep significant forces in the region because of the Israeli threat. Moreover, Hafez Assad does not wish to alienate its powerful friend, Iran, which had been excluded from this all-Arab security system. The smaller Gulf Arab states, traumatized by Saddam's military action against Kuwait, have adopted the short-sighted policy of perceiving Iraq as a permanent threat and believe that their security can best be guaranteed by a permanent Western military presence. They were also uneasy over the exclusion of non-Arab Iran from the short-lived regional security structure that was supposed to be implemented after the Gulf War. However, how they hope to reconcile Iran to a permanent Western military presence is unclear.

Saudi Arabia is loath to rely on a permanent Western presence and has shown contempt for the Kuwaiti decision to sign a security agreement with the United States without contemplating the long-term impact of such a Western presence. Nor does Riyadh view Iraq as a permanent threat, although it is very keen on seeing Saddam toppled from power. However, in order to acquire an effective deterrent based on localized offensive military capabilities, it has embarked on a massive expansion of its currently ineffective ground forces.[28] However, despite growing Arab sympathy for Iraq's plight and concerns and dismay over the strategic consequences stemming from an excessive weakening of that country, little progress has been made in terms of mending fences with Baghdad as the Arabs continue to focus their attention on the Arab-Israeli negotiations.

Iraq's relations with its two powerful non-Arab neighbors, Iran and Turkey, were full of tensions through the summer and fall of 1991. Iranians greeted Iraq's invasion of Kuwait with glee because the latter had been one of Iraq's major benefactors during the Iran-Iraq War. This feeling was later tempered by the realization that Iraqi annexation of Kuwait was a significant strategic threat to Iranian interests in a variety of ways. First, Iraq had the potential of becoming the swing producer and a dominant force in OPEC (instead of more supple Saudi Arabia) if it were to continue the occupation of Kuwait. Second, Baghdad would have also acquired the financial wherewithal to engage in an even more massive buildup than the one during the Iran-Iraq War, thereby leaving Iran far behind in the arms race between the two. Third, Iraq's better access to the waters of the Persian Gulf — if it were to remain in Kuwait — would have enabled it to build up significant naval power in a body of water that Iran regards as a *mare nostrum*.

Iranian President Ali Hashemi Rafsanjani made it clear that Iran would not accept Iraqi annexation of Kuwait even if other countries did so. Saddam moved to resolve differences with Iran when in mid-August he announced that Iraq would accept Iranian conditions for a formal end to the war between them. Iraq withdrew from occupied Iranian territory and agreed to a joint ownership of the contentious Shatt-al-Arab River. By this surprise move, Saddam might have been trying to protect his back or enlist Iranian support.[29]

Iran maintained a studious neutrality throughout the war, however, despite calls by more radical political elements to join Iraq in a holy war against the presence of the infidel Westerners. Iran's top leadership expressed the view that the Gulf War was not being waged between right (that is, Iraq) or Islam and wrong (that is, the West) or blasphemy, as Saddam (who suddenly discovered religion) maintained. Rather, it was "between two evils." At the same time, Iran expressed deep solidarity for, and sympathy with, the Iraqi people's suffering during the air bombarment.[30] Rafsanjani also envisioned a situation, at some point during the crisis, when Tehran would be able to play a mediating role between the antagonists.[31] Iran allowed Iraqi air force planes to land at its air bases because it was presented with a fait accompli. However, it wasted no time in declaring that those aircraft would be impounded for the duration of the hostilities and Iraqi pilots treated as prisoners of war.[32]

Iran, nonetheless, saw the Western-led war against Iraq as a potential threat to its own national security, especially if the international coalition would have decided to dismember Iraq. Tehran perceived such a scenario as extremely disconcerting and quite unacceptable, because it would have created a destabilizing power vacuum in the region. Two related developments of such a scenario, as Iran envisioned it, would have been a potential decision of Turkey to grab oil-rich northern Iraq and a potential decision of Israel to intervene directly in the Gulf War. However, this worst-case scenario did not materialize. At the end of the Gulf War, Iran discovered that, with little direct cost to itself, its national security had been enhanced by the collapse of Iraqi military power and as a result of the destruction of much of its offensive capabilities.[33]

When viewed from the perspective of Baghdad, Tehran's behavior in the aftermath of the Gulf War reconfirmed the longstanding Iraqi perception that Iran was a dire threat to its national security. After the war, Iran's active and overt support for the rebels in the south stunned the Iraqis, who bitterly denounced the "betrayal" by Iran (for example, Saddam's frequent reference to Iran as a "poisoned dagger").[34] The barrage of anti-Iraqi propaganda — in which President Rafsanjani called upon Saddam to stop killing his people and give up power and spiritual leader Ayatollah Ali Khamenei characterized Saddam as "detrimental and dangerous to Islam" — was seen as interference in Iraqi domestic affairs and as throwback to Iranian behavior under Ayatollah Khomeini between 1979 and 1988. Iran's support for the rebels in the south was perceived as part and parcel of a longstanding global conspiracy to bring about instability and anarchy in Iraq and eventually fragmenting it into its constituent ethnosectarian parts.

Iran, which fought a bruising eight-year war with Iraq (which it believes it could have won), could not be expected not to take advantage of the difficulties experienced by the latter. In the aftermath of the Gulf War, the Saddam regime appeared to be on the verge of collapse. This was a golden opportunity for Iran to exploit fully, for this objective was an integral part of its unfinished business from its war with Iraq's Ba'thist rulers. The sudden adoption of Islamic rhetoric by Saddam during this war was not about to win sympathy from Iran. The latter saw Baghdad's tactics as mere ideological opportunism of a notoriously unreliable neighbor. What emerges from the preceding is that Saddam's overtures toward Iran in 1990 failed to persuade the ruling elite in Tehran of his peaceful intentions. By the same token, the ensuing Machiavellian behavior of Iran during and in the aftermath of the Gulf War convinced Baghdad to return to its original perception of its neighbor as the paramount regional existential threat to its territorial integrity and ideological values.

There are several variables that enhance the strategic significance of Iran in the Persian Gulf. In the 1990s, it appears to be in a secure geopolitical position. Its large oil reserves continue to serve as a major source of financing for future economic growth. It has a very large population base for the region — a population of approximately 56 million, more than the combined population of all Arab countries of the Gulf, including Iraq. Historically speaking, its leadership has continued to demonstrate its willingness to remain influential, if not dominant, in the region. The activist Islamic ideological posture of the present ruling elite is the most recent manifestation of this phenomenon. The dissolution of the Soviet Union has benefited Iran in two significant ways. First, the emergence of a number of independent Muslim republics in Central Asia has provided an enormous opportunity for Iran to create its strategic influence, using its economic, political, and religious potentials. In this area, Iran is in competition with Saudi Arabia and Turkey. Second, with the dissolution of the Soviet Union, Iran no longer has to concentrate major military units on its northern flank. Neither a weak Afghanistan (which is still fighting a civil war among various factions of Mujahedin) nor Pakistan (which has been a good neighbor of Iran but is in the grip of domestic instability and is also embroiled in an ongoing conflict with India over Kashmir) poses a threat to Iran. However, it was the crushing of Iraq in the Gulf War, coupled with the inherent weaknesses of the Peninsular states, that has enabled Iran to enhance its role in the Persian Gulf. It is now the dominant power in that region, having supplanted a defeated Iraq. Since the end of the war, Iran has engaged in a diplomatic "charm offensive" in the Gulf that is designed to show the conservative Arab states that they have nothing to fear from Iran.

Iraq, on its part, does not view Iran's resurgence in the Arab Gulf with any feeling of equanimity. Ba'thist Iraq had spent the better part of a decade trying to shut Iran out of the Arab side of the Gulf. Now, despite its claims that Iran represents a threat to the Arab nature of the Gulf and that Iraq must not be ignored in any future attempts to construct a regional security system, the Peninsular states, because of their current predilection for pursuing short-sighted and vindictive policies, are not paying much heed to the Iraqi position.

Iran's growing military power is another source of acute worry for Iraq as well as for the other Arab states. Currently, this power is not commensurate with Tehran's stature as a major power in the Middle East or, indeed, in the Gulf region itself. Despite the defeat of Iraq in the Gulf War, which removed a major source of security threat, Iran is proceeding with massive purchases of weaponry from the Commonwealth of Independent States and some Western sources.

Iran is rebuilding its conventional offensive capabilities that were dissipated in the bloody battles of 1987 but decimated as a result of the Iraqi offensive of April–July 1988.[35] The Iranian military is undergoing a process of major restructuring and reorganization. The Revolutionary Guards (*Pasdaran*), which formulated the bulk of Iran's infantry forces, and the regular army are being merged and will be under one joint chief of staff. This has been done to avoid the corruption, waste, and duplication of resources that had existed since the creation of the Islamic Republic. Iran is also in the process of implementing doctrinal changes and is engaging in new thinking about its style of warfare. Its defeat in 1988 by a better-equipped Iraq discredited its view that ideological fervor and spiritual commitment are major determinants in war. The Iraqi defeat in the Gulf War of 1991 by a better-trained and technologically superior enemy reinforced the trend in Iranian defense thinking that professionalism, technical expertise, extensive training, and, above all, technology are of paramount importance in modern war. Iran is also convinced that a truly effective military should achieve a synergistic relationship between the material and the human elements.[36]

Iran is putting more emphasis on its arms industry, and according to Shahram Chubin, it is not only routinely repairing and reverse-engineering its foreign weapons but is also capable of producing a wide variety of arms locally.[37] It is seeking joint production ventures with other Third World countries such as Pakistan and Syria. At a time when the Iraqi arms production capabilities are being destroyed by the UN Special Commission, Iran is also expanding its activities in unconventional arms production programs, which are designed to provide that country with indigenous chemical arms, ballistic missile production capabilities, and even nuclear weapons. The People's Republic of China, North Korea, and Pakistan are reportedly supplying Tehran with nuclear know-how. In the best of times, Baghdad would view Iran's military buildup with worry. Currently, in its weakened state, it must watch it with a growing sense of alarm and paranoia.

Relations between Turkey and Iraq went from bad to worse during the Gulf Crisis of 1990–91. Ankara was a strong supporter of Operation Desert Storm and allowed the coalition warplanes to hit Iraq from its Incirlik air base in southern Turkey. The flow of Iraqi oil was also stopped long before the initiation of hostilities. After the Gulf War, Baghdad made clear its intentions to restore normal relations with its neighbor to the north because the pipelines that run through Turkey are a crucial source of exporting oil. However, the Kurdish problem, which is of utmost security-related concern for these neighbors, continues to be major. This is also a conflict by means of which both Iraq and Turkey can increase or lower pressure on each other, because neither government is willing to allow much political power to Kurds residing in its contiguous territories. Turkey has its own running battle with the Kurdish Workers Party (PKK), which is Marxist in its orientation and aims to establish an independent state in all of Kurdistan.

In March 1991, Turkish President Turgut Ozal met with Iraqi Kurdish rebel leaders. After ascertaining that the Iraqi Kurds are not intent on creating an independent Kurdistan and thereby fragmenting Iraq, he endorsed their demand for autonomy with a democratic Iraq. Since then, the PKK has launched several attacks in Turkey. There are even reports that the Saddam regime was at least winking at the PKK in their military actions against Turkey. The Turkish government has retaliated by hitting the PKK bases within the Iraqi territory. This time, however, there emerged a strange alliance between Turkey and Barzani's KDP that are coordinating their attacks on PKK.[38] Turkey not only has allowed the allied use of its base for providing protection of Iraqi Kurds but also is supplying emergency food to them. This ongoing saga remains a major irritant between Iraq and Turkey and a conflict that may destabilize both countries.

LOOKING TOWARD THE FUTURE

The Gulf War of 1991 removed Iraq as a major military actor. That reality, instead of ensuring stability in the Persian Gulf, promises to lead to further turbulence and instabilities. Iraq is a major political actor. Its weakened status promises to intensify centrifugal and fissiparous tendencies that are so endemic to almost all countries of that area.

The continued rule of Saddam Hussein remains the single most important reason behind the UN refusal to lift economic sanctions on that country. Although the international community sympathizes with the continued sufferings and hardships experienced by the Iraqis, no country is likely to play a leading role in becoming a major source of economic assistance to, or be willing to do business with, Iraq, because it would only strengthen the position of the Ba'thist regime.

In the 1990s, one of the overarching questions about Iraq is, what would be the internal dynamics of that country after Saddam? No one has any reasonable solution or comforting answers. If Saddam Hussein were to be replaced by another member of the Ba'thist Party, the Iraqi people are not likely to be better off, because such a replacement might continue the ruthless governance of the Iraqi society with someone else at the helm. The Peninsular states would also continue to view such a ruler with utmost discomfort, and Iran is likely to sustain a high degree of hostility toward such a regime.

Would the rule of any one or more groups who are currently opposing Saddam from outside Iraq be a preferred option? Surely not. These groups come from a variety of ideological colorations. About the only issue that unites them is their opposition to the present government in Baghdad. None of them have any political experience to lead a complex and multiethnic society like Iraq.

Another important question regarding Iraq is whether the highly fissiparous nature of its politics would allow the possibility of some form of democratic rule. If the answer to this is yes, then which group (or person) is qualified to preside over its affairs after Saddam? This leads to another nettlesome question: whether political pluralism is indeed in the best national interest of Iraq, especially if it were to lead to some sort of autonomy for the Kurds. No ruler of Iraq would accept this reality without creating a strong feeling among the Arab part of its population that, somehow, the integrity of Iraq is not being compromised. If Kurds are not granted autonomy, could Iraq under a future regime still be called a society in which political pluralism prevails? At this point, one should also ask one of the unmentionable questions about Iraq: Might the Iraqi population be better off by replacing Saddam with a less brutal ruler but one who could sustain the territorial integrity of Iraq? As brutal as this question may sound, it may be a lot closer to the political reality of that country than one is willing to admit. Lest we forget, Iran, Turkey, and Syria are publicly opposed to allowing autonomy for the Kurds within their polities. Even if a future Iraqi ruler were to agree to the Kurdish autonomy (a highly unlikely happenstance), its spillover effects among the

Kurdish community residing in the neighboring states of that country are likely to be highly destabilizing.

The future of stability and peace in the Persian Gulf is linked with the political future of the post-Saddam Iraq in a substantial way. Saddam's successor is most likely to remain loyal to that part of his legacy that envisioned a major strategic role for Iraq in the Middle East and the Persian Gulf, but such a vision cannot be materialized without the expenditure of major national resources in rebuilding military infrastructures. One can only imagine how much consternation the resuscitation of militarism in Iraq might cause among its neighbors, who have not decelerated their own military buildups.

In the 1990s, the two highly active participants in an ongoing competition for the strategic influence and dominance of the Persian Gulf are Iran and Saudi Arabia. The latter has the nod from Washington; however, the U.S. assent is no guarantee for the materialization of the Saudi aspirations. Iran's strategic superiority cannot be denied, for it is based on its strategic location, large population, huge oil resources, considerable technical and technological know-how (compared with its neighbors), and, above all, the longstanding perception of its significance shared by all great powers. Therefore, in the 1990s, this competition may continue with its present intensity. However, the post-Saddam Iraq can play an important role in determining the future dynamics of the Saudi-Iranian competition. If Saddam's successor could assuage the Saudi fears, he might be welcomed back to the Arab fold, but whether such a development is going to harm the Iranian strategic interests is question that Saudi Arabia and post-Saddam Iraq must determine. One way to stabilize the Persian Gulf in the future may be to evolve security arrangements that are not aimed at excluding Iran or Iraq. Iran is too big and too important to be isolated or to be left out of any future security arrangements in the Gulf. Also, by including Iraq in future security arrangements, the Arab states of the Gulf may be able to create a balance between the Iranian and the Iraqi ambitions, ensuring that this balance promotes the interests of all nation-states of that area.

NOTES

1. For an assessment of the view that Iraq's pugnacious behavior is a function of both these distinct factors, see Jochen Hippler, "Iraq's Military Power: The German Connection," *Middle East Report*, January–February 1991, pp. 272–78; Ahmed Hashim, "The Strategic Culture of a Garrison State: Iraqi Views on Deterrence, Compellence and War-Fighting vis-à-vis Israel, 1988–1991," in *Regional Security in the Middle East: Arab and Israeli Concepts of Deterrence and Defense*, ed. David Wurmser (Washington, D.C.: United States Institute of Peace, 1993).

2. See R. D. McLaurin, Don Peretz, and Lewis W. Snider, *Middle East Foreign Policy: Issues and Process* (New York: Praeger, 1982), pp. 73–81; the classic study of the Iraqi policy, however, is Hanna Batatu, *The Old Social Classes and the Revolutionary Movements of Iraq* (Princeton: Princeton University Press, 1978).

3. On the Arab world's move from ideological to a more pragmatic subsystem in the early 1970s, see Paul Noble, "The Arab System: Opportunities, Constraints and Pressures," in *The Foreign Policies of Arab States*, eds. Bahgat Korany and Ali Hillal Dessouk. (Boulder, Colo.: Westview Press, 1984), pp. 41–78.

4. Iraq's rise as an influential regional power was the subject of a large number of analyses between 1978 and 1980; see, for example, *Christian Science Monitor*, April 10 and July 17, 1980; New York *Times*, February 8, April 13, and June 5 and 22, 1980; Philippe Rondot, "L'Irak: Une Puissance Regionale en Devenir," *Politiique Etrangere*, 1980; Claudia Wright, "Iraq — New Power in the Middle East," *Foreign Affairs* 58 (Winter 1979–80): 256–76.

5. "Focus on Iraq: Reaping the Harvest," *The Middle East*, February 1979.

6. *Newsweek*, July 17, 1978, pp. 24–25; Tewfik Mishlawi, "Crackdown on Communists in Iraq: Honeymoon Is Over," *The Middle East*, July 1978, pp. 29–30; Ralph Joseph, "Iraq: The Baath Settles In," *The Middle East*, August 1976, pp. 11–13; Sufyan Abdul Razzak, *Die Interessen und Konfliktkonstellationen in der Arabischen Golf-Region: Eine Studie zu den Abhangigkeitsstrukturen der Peripherien* (Hamburg: Verlag Burg GMBH, 1982), pp. 206–7.

7. For a representative Iraqi view of their role in the Gulf as the eastern flank of the Arab world during the Iran-Iraq War, see "Iraq: Defender of Peace in the Gulf," *Iraq: Views and News*, Iraq Press Office, Washington, D.C.

8. For an excellent summary of Iraqi foreign policy vis-à-vis the United States and the Arab-Israeli conflict during the Iran-Iraq War, see Frederick Axelgard, "The United States–Iraqi Rapprochement," in *Sources of Domestic and Foreign Policy in Iraq*, ed. Michael Szaz (Washington, D.C.: American Foreign Policy Institute, 1986), pp. 43–56.

9. John Antal, "Iraq's Mailed Fist," *Infantry*, January–February 1991, p. 27.

10. Ephraim Kam, "The Inter-Arab Scene: Key Strategic Developments," in *The Middle East Military Balance 1989–1990*, eds. Aharon Yariv and Joseph Alpher (Boulder, Colo.: Westview Press, 1990), pp. 23–24; Alain Gresh, "Ambitins Irakiennes," *Le Monde Diplomatique*, May 1990, p. 3.

11. It is unfortunate that prestige is an underdeveloped concept in the study of international relations, although it is the "everyday currency of international relations," as Robert Gilpin stated in one of his books in which he discusses the role of prestige in the conduct of international relations: Prestige has been defined as the reputation for power; it is gained as a result of victory in war and is a function of military and economic power in particular. See Robert Gilpin, *War and Change in World Politics* (Cambridge: Cambridge University Press, 1981), pp. 30–34.

12. Phebe Marr, "Iraq in the 90s: Its Role in Regional Politics," *Middle East Executive Reports*, July 1990, p. 16; "In the Crucible of the War: The Iraqi Arms Industry," *Mednews* 2 (May 8, 1989).

13. For example, see "al araq yuhtafal be'eid al jaysh: `ard `askari kabir dhama ahdath al muidat," (Iraq celebrates army day: Massive military parade including the most modern equipment), *al difa' al `arabi (Arab Defense Journal)* 14 (February 1990): 11; "Silah `araqi kiym`awi muzdawij wa tahwil israeli" (Iraq's binary chemicals and the Israeli riposte), *al difa' al `arabi (Arab Defense Journal)* 14 (May 1990): 11.

14. For example, see the interview with Taha Yasin Ramadhan, Deputy Prime Minister, in Foreign Broadcasting Information Service, Near East and South Asia, *Daily Report*, May 17, 1990, pp. 14–15.

15. Iraq's pre–Gulf War global and regional strategic *weltanschauung* and perception of threat is to be found in various analyses and in the speeches and interviews of Saddam Hussein; see *Wall Street Journal*, June 28, 1990, pp. A1, A10; Nadim Jaber, "The Iraq-West Confrontation: Background and Reaction," *Middle East International*, April 13, 1990, pp. 3–6. FBIS-NES, *Daily Report*, June 19, July 3 and 17, 1990.

16. For very good discussions of the historical and contemporary origins of the Iraq-Kuwait crisis, see Phebe Marr, "Iraq's Uncertain Future," *Current History* 90 (January 1991); Walid Khalidi, "The Gulf Crisis: Origins and Consequences," *Journal of Palestine Studies* 20 (Winter 1991); Henri Laurens, "Le Contentieux territorial entre l'Irak et Koweit," *Maghreb-Machrek*, October–December 1990, pp. 14–24; Beoit Parisot, "La situation economique et financiere de l'Irak a la mi-1990: Quelle influence sur la decision d'envahir le Koweit?" in *Maghreb-Machrek*, October–December 1990, pp. 36–44; Joe Stork and Ann M. Lesch, "Why War?" *Middle East Report*, November–December 1990, pp. 11–18; David Butter, "Baghdad Flexes Its Muscles," *Middle East Economic Digest*, August 3, 1990, pp. 4–5; Liesl Graz, "Iraqi Sabres Rattle in the Gulf," *Middle East International*, August 3, 1990. For the Iraqi perception of threat as presented by the Foreign Minister Tariq Aziz, see note from the Iraqi Minister of Foreign Affairs Tariq Aziz to the secretary-general of the Arab League, July 15, 1990, in Pierre Sallinger and Eric Laurent, *Secret Dossier: The Hidden Agenda behind the Gulf War* (New York: Penguin Books, 1991), Appendix I, pp. 223–34.

17. Gerald Butt, "Iraq: Ruthless Revenge," *Middle East International*, April 5, 1991, p. 4.

18. Phebe Marr, "Iraq's Future: Plus Ça Change . . . or Something Better?" p. 20. Mimeographed.

19. David Hirst, *The Guardian*, January 14, 1990; Philip Robins, "Middle East I: The Arabs Eye Eastern Europe Warily," *World Today*, August/September 1990.

20. This section is based on excellent first-hand accounts of the situation in Iraq in the summer and fall of 1991 by Trudy Rubin of the *Philadelphia Inquirer*; Tony Horowitz of the *Wall Street Journal*; Lamis Andoni of the *Christian Science Monitor* and the *Jordan Times*; and Francoise Chipaux of *Le Monde*.

21. *Financial Times*, March 4, 1991.

22. This is based on "Iraqi Reconstruction Fraught with Difficulties," *Middle East Report* 24 (May 5, 1991).

23. Trevor Rowe, "It Almost Seems as Though the War Never Happened . . . ," Washington *Post National Weekly Edition*, November 16–22, 1992, p. 18.

24. Saddam Hussein has expounded at length on this issue. See FBIS-NES, *Daily Report*, July 17, 1991, pp. 21–23. At first, it seems curious that one of these threats, Iran, is perceived as an instrument of the threats posed by the other groups and not as an actor who conducted the Iran-Iraq War on its own.

25. FBIS-NES, *Daily Report*, April 29, 1991, p. 16.

26. FBIS-NES, *Daily Report*, August 20 and 21, 1991, p. 191.

27. Egypt's concerns about the Iraqi military power are addressed in *Christian Science Monitor*, April 9, 1991. For an early and alarmist assessment by Egyptian officers, see Kamal Tohms, "Arabie Saodite, Turquie, Iran: Le Trangle de i'Equilibre," *Arabies*, March 1991, p. 25.

28. "Saudi Arabia: The New Gulf Cop?" *Issues: Perspectives on Middle East and World Affairs* 1 (January 1992): 6–7.

29. For an excellent analysis of Iran's response to the Kuwaiti crisis, see Shahram Chubin, "Iran and the Gulf Crisis," *Middle East Insight* 7 (December 1990): 30–35.

30. *Christian Science Monitor*, February 5, 1991.

31. Ibid.

32. Ibid. It is quite plausible that there may have been prior coordination between the Iraqi and Iranian governments over the aircraft and that Iran expressed its displeasure in order to maintain its neutrality. Whatever interpretation is correct, it is merely academic now, because Iran decided to keep those planes.

33. There was also the added bonus of the Iraqi aircraft, the return of Iranian territories that were under occupation by Iraqi forces, and the dropping of Iraqi claims to the unilateral ownership of the Shatt-al-Arab. For a similar assessment, see Walid Khalidi, *The Middle East Postwar Environment* (Washington, D.C.: Institute for Palestine Studies, 1991), pp. 17–18.

34. Quoted in FBIS-NES, *Daily Report*, July 29, 1991, p. 24.

35. Offensive capabilities are those weapons systems such as combat planes, tanks, ballistic missiles, and armored fighting vehicles that enhance a country's ability to project power beyond its borders and that are inherently destabilizing. See W. Seth Carus, "Weapons Technology and Regional Stability," in *Arms Control and Weapons Proliferation in the Middle East and South Asia*, eds. Shelley Stahl and Geoffrey Kemp (New York: St. Martin's Press, 1992), pp. 9–16. The 1992 military balance shows an Iranian order of battle (ORBAT) relatively unchanged from the figures given for 1989–90 and 1990–91 military balance: less than 700 tanks, a total of 70–800 armored personnel carriers and fighting vehicles, and less than 150 self-propelled artillery pieces. What this means is that the Iranian military suffers from low mobility and has little offensive capability. It must be assumed that the new purchases have not, as of yet, been integrated into the Iranian ORBAT; thus, they represent putative rather than actual power.

36. For an excellent and detailed analysis of changes in Iranian defense thinking occasioned by both the Iran-Iraq and Gulf wars, see Shahram Chubin, "Iran and the Lessons of the Gulf War," Los Alamos National Laboratory, Center for National Security Studies. Mimeographed.

37. Ibid., p. 107.

38. Hugh Pope, "Onslaught Against the PKK," *MEI*, October 23, 1992, pp. 11–12.

5

The Saudi Role in the New Middle East Order

Joseph Twinam

Obviously, Saddam Hussein caught the world by surprise on August 2, 1990, when he broke the rules of the game among the Arabs by invading Kuwait with intent to gobble it up. No one, except perhaps the Kuwaiti leaders, was more surprised than King Fahd of Saudi Arabia. He had labored to resolve the brewing conflict and had Saddam's word that it would not come to blows. Some weeks into the crisis, King Fahd spoke to the press about his disbelief and sense of betrayal when Iraqi forces blasted through Kuwait and then gathered menacingly on the Saudi border.[1]

The world felt threatened by Saddam's action, and, aside from Kuwait, no member of the international community was as threatened as Saudi Arabia. In one sense of the word, Saudi Arabia was not "prepared" to deal with this unexpected challenge in that on its own or in league with Gulf Cooperation Council (GCC) allies, it was not capable — perhaps could never be — of effectively resisting and, therefore, deterring the threat of land invasion by the massive force that Saddam Hussein had assembled. Indeed, there is no convincing evidence that the Arab or the wider Islamic worlds, both of which Saudi policy had courted so assiduously over the years, was "prepared" to come to the rescue of the threatened kingdom and of imprisoned Kuwait in an effective manner.[2]

Yet, in another sense, Saudi Arabia had carefully prepared over many years to handle such a crisis, however unexpected. It had developed a set of relations with the great powers, primarily the Western ones and particularly the United States, that caused them to see it in their interests to protect the kingdom. In Operations Desert Shield and Desert Storm, the world saw in an awesome way just how well "prepared" the United States and its Western allies were to deal (provided they had full Saudi and GCC cooperation) with the likes of Saddam's Iraq.

The experience was historic for the kingdom, that is, the Saudi perceptions of vulnerability, threat, assets, and foreign relationships were significantly altered in August 1990. It was clear that Saudi policy and the Saudi role in the Gulf would never be the same. What was not clear, however, and what is likely to remain in question for some time to come, is whether never being the same means being all that different. It is in that "fog" of post war that one must try to sort out — indeed, that the Saudi leadership is trying to work out — how the kingdom will act toward friend and cope with potential foe in order to find a safer future in one of the world's most strategic regions.

Moreover, like the other states of the region, Saudi Arabia is seeking to grapple with the formidable challenges in the Middle East in a dramatically altered global power context. Gone is the Cold War, which for over four decades heavily influenced the strategies of the outside great powers toward the region. Indeed, gone is the Soviet Union, long perceived by the Saudi leadership as a threat to the kingdom requiring a certain set of relations with the West. Thus, Saudi leaders must puzzle over the long-term significance of Russia to the Middle East, the scope for Saudi impact on the evolution of the Muslim republics of the former Soviet Union, and how close a relationship to seek with the United States and the other industrial democracies in a new world order.

THE OLD ORDER

One might usefully think of three different phases of Saudi policy — and Saudi national and economic development — up to the Gulf Crisis of 1990. In the 21 years of Ibn Saud's rule as king of Saudi Arabia (1932–53), the state and its institutions of governing and defense (and its oil industry) were just getting started, and so was the modern Arab world of independent states. The prestige of Abd al Aziz and his role as keeper of the holy cities gave Saudi Arabia some influence in the emerging Arab world, but it was a relatively poor and underdeveloped world in which the authority of colonial powers dominated.

The reign of King Saud bin Abd al Aziz (1953–64) and the first few years after the Al Saud deposed him in favor of Faisal bin Abd al Aziz were particularly troubled times for the kingdom. It faced the ideological onslaught of the revolutionary period in the Arab world and the direct military threat posed by Egyptian-Saudi confrontation in the Yemen civil war. The oil was beginning to flow in quantity, but prices were declining. The massive task of building a modern infrastructure in the harsh climate of a desolate subcontinent had only begun. The state treasury often experienced critical shortages. There was conflict within the ruling family. The loyalty of the officers of the relatively new army and air force was uncertain, and, thus, the development of a modern military was restrained by a regime that relied on the tribal national guard — the descendant of Ibn Saud's conquering Ikhwan warriors — as the ultimate support of its survival. There was not much money to spend on modernizing the military in any event, and the education base was still behind the curve in producing enough Saudis with the skills required in either a modern military or a modern civil sector. In this era, Saudi Arabia generally hunkered down and survived.[3]

The third, and most significant, era began sometime after the June 1967 Arab-Israeli War and came into full bloom in the wake of the 1973–74 Arab oil embargo. At the outset, the ruling family and the country were firmly in the control of King Faisal, who, since his assassination by a deranged young relative in 1975, has been increasingly revered as a leader of the stature of his father, the founding king. During the reign of the popular but ailing Khalid bin Abd al Aziz (1975–82), much of the day-to-day decision making was in the hands of Crown Prince Fahd bin Abd al Aziz, assisted by an inner circle of the surviving sons of Ibn Saud, notably National Guard Commander Prince Abdullah and Defense Minister Prince Sultan, with two sons of the late King Faisal, Foreign Minister Prince Saud and Intelligence Minister Prince Turki, impressively displaying abroad on behalf of the rising generation the "strength in depth" of the Al Saud leadership. With Fahd's ascension to the throne upon Khalid's death in 1982, his half-brother Abdullah became heir apparent and his full brother Sultan was clearly identified as third in the power structure. The point is that the Al Saud put dynastic squabbles behind them and presented to the world a richly experienced, cohesive group of senior leaders united in preserving the regime and the kingdom.

By 1970 Saudi oil income was beginning to flow quite amply, and by 1974 it was gushing — going from some $1 billion in 1970 to more than $100 billion by 1981. An almost incredible pace of economic development began, reaching its peak by the beginning of the 1980s. By the mid-1980s, the economic growth braked sharply as the Organization of Petroleum Exporting Countries (OPEC) oil producers came upon some lean years; soon, Saudi Arabia was running a poor second to the United States in the contest to have the world's biggest deficit in balance of payments. Yet, in the meantime, a huge and shabby underdeveloped country had been transformed into a gleaming modern one, and Saudis had reached a once-undreamed-of level of prosperity and educational opportunity. An important industrial-agricultural infrastructure had been developed to ease dependency on crude oil production.[4]

There were suddenly billions to spend on defense, and the Al Saud spent them. There was a massive modernization of the air force, army, and national guard, and a navy was created from scratch. Inevitably short on manpower, the Saudis opted for a "Cadillac style" military establishment — well-paid and -quartered, equipped with the best that money could buy, and sustained by a horde of foreign technicians and logistic support personnel. By 1990 the Saudi government had paid the U.S. government well over $50 billion for military equipment, training, and support services, including the impressive military construction program supervised by the U.S. Army Corps of Engineers. An additional tens of billions had been spent in France, Britain, and elsewhere, including the secret missile deal with China.

While spending freely at home, and thus becoming an important market for goods and services to industrial world governments, Saudi Arabia was able to accumulate by 1983 a surplus of some $160 billion in official assets invested abroad. Saudi investment became a key factor in recycling the petrodollar and in providing capital to Western economies ravaged by the "oil shocks" of the 1970s. By 1981, by its investment in U.S. Treasury instruments, the kingdom of Saudi Arabia owned 5 percent of the U.S. national debt. If there were something unhealthy in this, the Reagan administration certainly cured it, by tripling the national debt wile the Saudis were liquidating much of their holdings to cover balance of payments and budget deficits in the "oil glut" years.[5]

Thus, Saudi Arabia became a big player in the world of international finance and an important support of such multinational institutions as the International Monetary Fund and the World Bank. In addition, Saudi Arabia became a major foreign aid donor, concentrating on the Arab and Muslim worlds but, in general, playing a role that paralleled that of the key Western aid donors and, thus, sharing the burden. Most significantly, Saudi Arabia, by 1973 fully in control of price and production decisions in its oil industry and with at least a quarter of the world proven oil reserves, had become the major force — in both OPEC and the world — for trying to moderate the economically dangerous volatility of oil prices in the 1970s and 1980s.

Thus, as seen from Western, Arab, and other capitals, by the mid-1970s the kingdom of Saudi Arabia was an emerging world power. The United States and other Western governments were keenly aware of its clout in the worlds of oil, commerce, and foreign and international finance and of its critical diplomatic role in supporting the resolution of conflicts in the strife-torn Middle East. From the U.S. perspective the U.S.–Saudi relationship had become "world class." From Henry Kissinger on, when U.S. secretaries of state took off on Middle East peace shuttles, Saudi Arabia was usually a necessary stop on the tour. In the late 1970s, so many members of the U.S. Congress were hankering to visit the kingdom that it began to rival the "3-Is" of congressional voyaging — Ireland, Italy, and Israel. The kingdom, as seen from abroad, had become a place of considerable power and influence.[6]

THE SAUDI WAY

Therefore, Western observers for more than a decade prior to the 1990 crisis watched in constant fascination and occasional dismay at the way the Saudi leadership went about playing the role the world had assigned the kingdom. The Saudi leaders listened respectfully to a torrent of Western advice and exhortation about what they should do, but, in the end, they, of course, conducted Saudi policy on the basis of their own assessment of Saudi interests, strengths and weaknesses, and the kingdom's place in the world.

To a striking degree, the Saudi leadership seemed aware of the kingdom's weaknesses and vulnerabilities in a violent and envious neighborhood. Survival of the regime and the state was obviously the first priority. This involved a careful bridging of the conservative-modernist tendencies in the Saudi society. It required sustaining the regime's legitimacy in an Islamic context. It called for keeping the citizens passively prosperous while maintaining the loyalty of an expensively modernizing military establishment. Perhaps most of all, it required being safely in the middle of the mainstream of Arab opinion while helping to find and direct the course of that mainstream.[7]

Saudi leaders seemed exquisitely conscious of the demographic constraints on their military power, which was called on to defend a vast kingdom with fabulous oil riches. They were aware of their country's ongoing dependence on foreigners — Arab, Asian, African, and Western — for technical skills, services, and labor. They recognized their dependence on other states for military equipment and that the favored source, the United States, was not always reliable when specific Saudi requests to buy weapons systems such as the F-15s and AWACs ran into strong opposition from U.S. supporters of Israel. Most importantly, they realized that they must survive in an Arab and Islamic environment in which close ties to the West, and the United States in particular, were often a liability. Especially troublesome after the fall of the shah was how to coexist with a belligerent revolutionary Iran, which singled out Saudi links to the United States, the "Great Satan," as a relished point of attack on the kingdom.[8]

Within these formidable constraints, Saudi leaders took their oil power, their Western ties, their prestige in the world of Islam, and their considerable capacity for dispensing foreign aid and did the best they felt they could for the kingdom.

BEFORE THE MOMENT OF TRUTH

From these considerations emerged the unique foreign policy of Saudi Arabia in the Faisal-Fahd era up to August 1990. Observers would quibble about whether the slight shift in policy emphasis here or there might reflect the different personalities of Faisal and Fahd, an ebb and flow of Saudi self-confidence, the ups and downs of the U.S.–Saudi "special relationship," or the ever-shifting chessboard of Middle East power politics. Yet, the broad parameters of Saudi policy were in time rather clearly etched, even if the view of what was going on within those boundaries was sometimes dusty.

In its oil policy, Saudi Arabia, as a relatively "low-absorber," enjoys the luxury of being able to lead the so-called price doves of OPEC. With vast reserves and production capacity, it has the capability (within limits) to fight the market as the "swing producer" of OPEC. Saudi Arabia has garnered enormous prestige in the international community (and in the Arab world) from this power. It has clearly demonstrated a sense of enlightened self-interest in seeking an order in world oil markets protecting both producer and consumer interests — and long-term Saudi share of the world energy market. In the rising market of the 1970s, Saudi Arabia was willing to sacrifice billions in potential oil income in an effort to restrain the rise in prices. Yet, ultimately, Saudi decision makers felt compelled to follow the market price upward. In the 1980s Saudi Arabia lost billions of possible oil income by reducing production in an effort to sustain the OPEC market price but eventually felt the financial need to regain market share. In between, the Saudi government sometimes seemed to adjust its oil policy for political reasons, especially to try to stay at peace with Iran or to demonstrate its irritation at Iranian provocations. When the UN embargoed some 4 million barrels a day of oil production from Iraq and occupied Kuwait, Saudi Arabia moved quickly to make up most of the shortfall, thereby bringing world oil prices back down to their preinvasion level by the end of 1990.[9]

It is in the oil arena that Saudi policy has tended to be boldest, from the 1973–74 Arab oil embargo right through the present. This is not surprising, because oil is Saudi Arabia's strong suit, the area in which it feels the most power and the most leeway for taking risks in policy choices. In the post-war Gulf environment, Saudi oil policy is likely to continue to reflect both a regard for consumer country concerns and an obligation toward OPEC goals but, above all, a fine reading of the kingdom's own economic and political interests.

By contrast, it was in what Americans perceive as the Middle East diplomatic arena (basically, the various aspects of trying to resolve the Arab-Israeli conflict) that Saudi policy seemed most tentative. It was, of course, in this area that Saudi Arabia felt most vulnerable to Arab nationalist pressures, and it was this problem that caused the most strains in the Saudi–U.S. relationship over the years.

The broad outlines of Saudi policy up to August 1990 were fairly clear. For years the kingdom put a lot of money into supporting those Arab states — and the Palestine Liberation Organization (PLO) — in a direct territorial conflict with Israel. Yet, it consistently maintained the position of not being a "direct party" to the conflict. It refused to recognize or deal with Israel, yet, it accepted UN Security Council Resolution 242 — the "territory for peace" cornerstone of the Middle East peace process — with the implication that Arab states would establish normal relations with Israel once territorial disputes are resolved. From its perspective of Islamic responsibilities, Saudi Arabia had special concerns about the future status of Jerusalem, but it went along with the international negotiating strategy of keeping this most explosive of Arab-Israeli (indeed, Jewish-Muslim-Christian) issues on the back burner. Otherwise, Saudi Arabia tended to let the "direct party" Arabs call the shots on the Arab-Israeli peace question. It usually supported, often prodded, and sometimes made useful interventions in the seemingly endless effort to get Arabs and Israelis together to talk peace. Yet, it never tried to take the lead on this issue by using its formidable money power to dictate an Arab position.

The specifics are as follows. King Faisal was not consulted when his prime tormenter, Gamal Abdel Nasser of Egypt, postured his way into being attacked by Israel in June 1967. In the wake of the disastrous Arab defeat, Saudi Arabia supported Arab positions and financed Arab cause, yet, rather early on, accepted UN Security Council Resolution 242 as the basis for negotiations. Saudi leaders talked endlessly with would-be U.S. peacemakers, but, having restored the Saudi-Egyptian relationship, King Faisal gave full political support — notably, the Arab oil embargo — to Anwar Sadat's launching of the October 1973 Yom Kippur War. Thereafter, Saudi Arabia gave encouragement to the Kissinger and Carter-Vance efforts to move the peace process. Crown Prince Fahd made a significant contribution at the 1976 Taif Conference by firming an evolving Arab consensus on how to resurrect the Geneva Conference. The Saudis tried unsuccessfully to get PLO Chairman Arafat to say the magic words about accepting Resolution 242 that would meet the U.S. conditions for negotiating with the PLO. The Saudis were not informed about Sadat's historic decision to travel to Jerusalem in

November 1977 and were sorely offended. They continued, however, to voice support for U.S. efforts to promote Middle East peace right up to the convening of the Camp David meeting in late August 1978. However, the Saudi leadership, after some agonizing deliberation, backed off supporting the Camp David agreements. Saudi Arabia, however reluctantly, caved in to the Iraqi-Syrian led "rejectionist front" in ostracizing Egypt from the Arab world in the wake of Camp David and the March 1979 Egyptian-Israeli "separate peace."[10]

In the 1980s Saudi Arabia continued to play a limited game, carefully supporting mainstream Arab positions but bringing forth the generally constructive "Fahd eight points" for Middle East peace in 1981 and pushing them through, with minor modification, as the agreed Arab position at the 1982 Fez Summit. Outraged by the June 1982 Israeli invasion of Lebanon, Saudi Arabia, nevertheless, continued to work closely with the United States in resolving the Lebanese crisis (integrally related to the overall Arab-Israeli problem). Yet, in the crunch, both the Saudis and the Americans seemed to have failed to deliver what the other had expected as the Lebanon situation plunged further into disaster in 1983-84. Thereafter, the Saudis, although never out of touch from the background, seemed content to leave King Hussein, President Mubarak, and Chairman Arafat up front in the intricate and ultimately futile Arab efforts to approach Middle East peace at a time when neither the United States nor Israel seemed able or willing to make the tough political choices necessary to move the process. By 1988, however, the Saudis, in the protective wrapping of the Arab League, were playing a critical role in trying to bring order out of chaos in Lebanon.

On this critical front of Middle East stability, there was a general pattern to Saudi conduct. The Saudi leadership was usually quick and often skillful in promoting consensus where it was forming in the Arab world. They remained a crucial link between the United States and the West and the Arabs. They were generally supportive of Middle East peace but unwilling to truly stick their necks out in its pursuit. They sought to influence the Arab world, not to lead or dominate it. They were quick to spend that which came easy — money — in pursuit of conflict resolution but slow to fork over the dear currency of political commitment.[11]

By mid-1978, in both Iran and Yemen, the Saudi neighborhood was in turmoil, and Saudi Arabia had some good reasons for feeling insecure. By September 1980 revolutionary Iran and Saddam's Iraq were locked in what would be long and deadly combat, with the constant threat of spilling over to threaten the kingdom. In these circumstances, the Saudi leadership pursued what was perceived, in Washington at least, as an "ambiguous" course. They probed by fall 1978 about the extent of U.S. commitment to Saudi security but carefully avoided involvement in what might be perceived as a strategic relationship with the United States. They welcomed the deployment of U.S. Air Force F-15s in late 1978 at the height of the Iranian revolution and of U.S. AWACs in early 1979 during the dust-up between South and North Yemen. When Iraq invaded Iran in September 1980, the Saudi government requested, undoubtedly with considerable U.S. urging, the deployment of U.S. AWACs to bolster the air defense of the eastern province oil fields. Yet, throughout, the Saudi leadership seemed reluctant to acknowledge a security link with the United States. As the Iran-Iraq War heated up, Saudi Arabia refused to pick up repeated U.S. offers of closer military cooperation, while the U.S. AWACs continued to circle the skies over the eastern province. When the Kuwaitis lured the U.S. Navy into the Gulf in force in 1987 with the "reflagging" caper, Saudi Arabia rendered significant cooperation with the U.S.–Western mine sweeping and escort effort, but ever so quietly.[12]

In sum, until August 1990, there was a dusty ambiguity about Saudi policy. The commitment to Arab causes was clear, but Saudi policy seemed to ask — and to get — limited return on its money in terms of influencing those Arabs to whom the kingdom was giving lavish financial support. The posture toward revolutionary Iran had fluctuated between accommodation and truculence. Although pouring billions into warring Iraq, Saudi Arabia seemed either unable or unwilling to insist that Iraq refrain from those war-widening activities that brought direct Iranian retaliation against the kingdom and its GCC partners. Perhaps most important, the Saudi leadership wobbled between inviting in U.S. and other Western military support *in extremis* and denying any commitment to military cooperation with the West.

From Riyadh's perspective, this flexible Saudi approach obviously made sense; Saudi policy makers were choosing as best they could in the light of national interests in quite difficult circumstances. From Washington's perspective, however, there was frequent frustration (despite years of experience in dealing with a variety of mutual problems) at the often tentative, "soft," conciliatory, "ambiguous," and diffident Saudi approach to coping with life in a threatening neighborhood.

When Saddam Hussein began to threaten Kuwait in the summer of 1990, the Saudis played their accustomed role, by the accepted Arab rules. They were active in seeking reconciliation, a peaceful settlement, an outcome that would shuffle the conflicts among the Arabs once more beneath the table without inviting the United States, the West, and the world in to view the dirty laundry. At the end of July 1990 the lead players of traditional Saudi repertoire took to the stage with a finesse bred in many a performance. Then — to the surprise of the players — the curtain rang down. On August 2, 1990, Saddam Hussein's Iraq invaded Kuwait.[13]

THE MOMENT OF TRUTH

In the Saudi scheme of things, it is hard to exaggerate the historic importance of that moment in August 1990 when King Fahd, sitting with U.S. Secretary of Defense Dick Cheney, asked for U.S. armed forces to come to the kingdom to defend it from the Iraqi threat. What followed is recent and familiar history, as one-half million U.S., British, French, Egyptian, Syrian, and other military personnel poured into the Peninsula and the Gulf for the dramatic experiences of Desert Shield and Desert Storm, which would eventually relieve Saudi Arabia from threat and set Kuwait free. In the process, Saudi Arabia and the United States had formed an informal alliance far stronger than anything involved in the once dangerously controversial Baghdad Pact. Saudi Arabia and its GCC allies and newfound allies Egypt and Syria went to war alongside the United States and other Western and world members of the "coalition" against a renegade Arab state.[14]

Throughout the episode, Saudi Arabia played a new role in a new way in what seemed to be a new era in the history of the kingdom. It openly welcomed the massive influx of foreign defenders, cooperated exhaustively with their deployments, worked out joint command arrangements with them, and then fought side-by-side with them in crushing Iraq's military might in order to liberate Kuwait. In the process there emerged the prospect of a "new Saudi Arabia" — outspoken, calling on its citizens to sacrifice, challenging the assumptions or modus operandi of the old Arab order, openly declaring its intent to wipe out a neighboring Arab leader, and comfortable in its alliance with Western "crusaders" come to liberate good Muslims from bad ones.

In the immediate wake of the coalition victory, the Saudi-led GCC states, their solidarity reinforced from the seven-month crisis, met with their new allies Egypt and Syria on March 6, 1991, to set forth the Damascus Declaration. It was the charter for an alliance among the "Damascus Eight" (The "GCC plus two"), yet, it invited other Arab states, few of whom were at the time in the good graces of the anti-Saddam coalition, to join with them. It spoke of a new effort to promote peace, economic progress, and security in the Gulf and Arab world. Basically, however, it was the framework for a new Gulf security regime in which Egypt and Syria, amply rewarded with foreign aid for their contributions, would station significant military force in the GCC countries.[15]

Four days after the Damascus Declaration, the foreign ministers of the Damascus Eight met with U.S. Secretary of State Baker in Riyadh, expressing their appreciation for President Bush's March 6 "victory speech" to the U.S. Congress in which he had enunciated a four-point strategy for building security in the Middle East, including creating "shared security arrangements." What seemed to be in formation was a GCC initiative to build a security framework — at one level with Egypt and Syria, which would station a significant number of armed forces in the Peninsula, at another level with the United States and other Western members of the coalition involving arrangements for pre-positioning of equipment and frequent deployment of U.S. air and ground forces for joint exercises with GCC contingents. A new era of Western-Arab alliance seemed at hand.[16] From the beginning however, there was a question of what role Iran would play in such a Gulf security setup and of how an excluded Iran would react to it.

NEW ORDER OR OLD?

Having invested so much in the preservation of Saudi Arabia, the international community has understandably been intently, and sometimes rather critically, focused on whether Saudi policy post–Desert Storm would sustain a new boldness or slip back to "business-as-usual."

UNFINISHED BUSINESS

In trying to sort out the evidence to date, the first question to consider is whether Desert Storm is really over. Almost two years after the crushing coalition victory, Saddam, however weakened, still controls Iraq (or, at least, most of it). After the traumatic experience of August 1990, how to cope with Iraq has to be the top priority for Saudi policy makers. To date, the Saudi role has been rather assertive. Saudi Arabia has led the GCC and the Islamic Conference in pushing for implementation of all of the requirements of the UN Security Council cease-fire resolution.[17] It has been quite visible in its support of Iraqi opposition groups seeking to overthrow the Saddam regime. Obviously, Saudi Arabia, within the constraints of the internationally recognized norms of denying involvement in "covert operations," is firm in its policy of seeking a friendlier regime in an Iraq still intact with respect to its territory.[18]

Some ambivalence has appeared in the Saudi approach, involving the prospect that revolution against Saddam might produce a breakaway state in the overwhelmingly Shi'ite south of Iraq subject to Iranian influence. This possibility was precisely what drove Saudi Arabia and its GCC allies, as well as the United States, to tilt toward Iraq in the long war with Iran. Having invested tens of billions in supporting Iraq and having suffered considerable Iranian reprisal for so doing, Saudi Arabia was understandably alarmed by the apparent early success of the antiregime uprising in the south of Iraq in the immediate wake of Desert Storm. It is widely believed that the Saudi leadership helped influence President Bush's decision not to provide military support to the revolt in the south, a choice that virtually assured that forces loyal to Saddam would crush it brutally.[19]

Since then, the Saudi leadership has been remarkably firm in keeping its GCC allies more or less in lockstep with the United States and the European members of the coalition in the quest for a new regime in Iraq. As long as Saddam hangs on (and the failure of the July 1992 attempt to eliminate him once again suggests that might be for awhile), this basic consensus is likely to hold. If and when Saddam falls, however, there is ample room for difference of views about whether and how much to support a successor regime — possibly a series of successor regimes. For the Saudis, this will likely involve an exquisite balancing of interests, including not just the central question of promoting a nonthreatening government in Baghdad but also a mix of U.S. and Western, Arab, and GCC and Iranian attitudes. This aspect of future Saudi policy is a question mark — as is the future of Iraq.

THE FORMER SOVIET FACTOR

There is another great unknown. Before the Gulf Crisis of 1990, the Saudi leadership had begun to respond, ever so cautiously, to the signals of the Gorbachev policy toward the Middle East. Slowly, lagging behind most of its GCC allies, Saudi Arabia began to make contact with the Soviet Union. Clearly, the days when King Faisal equated communism with Zionism were well behind. The Saudis began to see Gorbachev's Soviet Union as a state to do business with rather than a threat to be feared, and, ironically, as the Cold War vanished, Washington watched this transformation with satisfaction rather than alarm. Indeed, by the advent of the Gulf Crisis, the Saudi leadership regarded the Soviet Union as a tottering giant in need of support and eventually pledged up to $3 billion in this regard.

Saudi Arabia, at the height of the Gulf Crisis, took the plunge of restoring formal diplomatic relations with the Soviet Union in September 1990; however, within a year or so, the Soviet Union had ceased to exist. Saudi policy must, therefore respond to another imponderable, globally far more significant than the question of whither Iraq and obviously farther beyond Saudi influence — that is, whither the pieces of the former Soviet Union.

Indications to date are that Saudi Arabia will pursue a proper state-to-state relationship with Yeltsin's Russia, which has every reason to see Saudi Arabia as a place to borrow sorely needed money and perhaps even as a growing market for Russian goods. Of course, the most attractive Russian product, other than crude oil hardly needed in the Gulf, is military equipment. Given the Kuwait example with respect to Soviet missiles and the subsequent Saudi one regarding Chinese missiles, it should not be too shocking in Washington if someday Saudi Arabia bought from Russia arms it was having difficulty getting from the United States. However, for the foreseeable future, this is not the sort of worry as is the prospect of Russian military "fire sales" elsewhere in the Gulf and Middle East and is, in any event, a problem of controlling worldwide arms proliferation rather than the riveting sort of geopolitical challenge characteristic of the Cold War years. History teaches that Russia will be a long-term factor in the Middle East, but for the moment, noncommunist Russia from the Saudi perspective is becoming just another important European country with which to deal.

With some reason, Saudi Arabia is more alarmed about the evolution of the Muslim republics of the former Soviet Union. Here, the world is witnessing a scramble for outside influence, with the Saudis actively at work playing their Islamic card. Their main protagonist is Iran, also exerting influence on an Islamic basis. Ironically, the country more or less in league with Saudi Arabia is Turkey, a society of Muslims but a state of strictly secular nature.[20] This alliance underscores another dilemma facing Saudi policy — the political aspect of Islam.

THE ISLAMIC FACTOR

The political significance of Islam seems hard enough for Muslims to deal with at present and almost impossible for non-Muslim Westerners to understand. Some of the confusion stems from the Western addiction to the misnomer "Islamic Fundamentalism."

The entire history of the Saudi regime and state is intertwined with Islam — an austere, reformist brand that others call "Wahhabism." By any standards, Saudi Arabia is a strict Muslim state. Certainly, Hijazis and other Arabians who faced Ibn Saud's Wahhabi forces during the conquests that created the kingdom would have considered the Saudi brand of Islam both "political" and "militant." Since the conquest, the Al Saud have derived great influence at home and throughout the Islamic world as host of the Hajj, and today, King Fahd prefers to be referred to as "Keeper of the Two Holy Places." King Faisal was founder of the Islamic Conference, in which Saudi influence remains quite strong. The Saudi government has long been known as a financial supporter of a variety of Islamic causes, including political movements.

Yet, what the West generally recognizes as Islamic Fundamentalism, perhaps more accurately described as "militant political Islam," has become a threat to the Middle East order that Saudi Arabia seeks. In the heyday of secular Arab nationalism, it was one thing for the Saudis to promote Islam as a political buffer against the revolutionary onslaught of Nasserism and Ba'thism. Since then, however, things have changed. Khomeini's brand of militant Shi'ite Islam was a clear threat to the Saudi regime, and the Iranian-backed Hezbollah has been a thorn in the side of Saudi efforts to foster the restoration of Lebanon. The Sunni Islamic forces in Jordan and Syria, in Egypt and Sudan, and in the Maghreb — notably in Algeria — have become a threat to the sort of Arab order Saudi Arabia seeks.[21] Indeed, virtually all of the Sunni Islamic political movements cheered for Saddam Hussein during the Gulf Crisis.

Thus, in its foreign policy, Saudi Arabia faces a complex problem of whether to support political Islam in the region and what kind of political Islam to support. It is a problem that also plays on the Saudi domestic scene.

THE DOMESTIC FRONT

The wrenching experience of the Iraqi threat and the coalition response impacted on the traditional Al Saud balancing act between modernist and traditionalist forces within the kingdom. The modernists saw this trauma as a catalyst for long-awaited political and social reform. The religious conservatives, including some younger elements tending toward the classification "militant fundamentalist," exerted counterpressure. The king, who had first advocated a consultative assembly and constitution more than two decades before, well before he even became crown prince, and had promised these reforms on several occasions over the intervening years, moved with the "deliberate speed" customary of the Saudi system of decision by consensus building. Finally, in March 1992, he decreed the establishment of a "basic law" or constitution and of an appointed consultative assembly. On the way to this decision, he had publicly warned the more militant of the traditionalist elements to mind their manners.

Although these reforms seem modest enough in a world hurtling toward democracy, it was a giant, if long-delayed, step in the Saudi context. Some weeks later, back into the Al Saud balancing act, the king pronounced that representative democracy is not appropriate to a society like Saudi Arabia.[22] It was a message clearly heard in other GCC countries, torn between the Kuwaiti public's drive for democracy and the Saudi pull against the tide.

THE GULF SECURITY ORDER

In the wake of Desert Storm, there was felt need to establish a set of relationships among the coalition partners and arrangements for cooperation that would prevent the recurrence of something like

Iraq's August 1990 invasion of Kuwait. The initial road plan laid out a "Damascus Eight" structure intertwined with U.S. and other Western security roles.

The establishment of a new security order for the Gulf ran into problems quickly. During U.S. Defense Secretary Cheney's late spring 1991 visits to the region, it became apparent that the GCC was in some disarray about what, if any, role it would play as an institution in enhancing the region's security. Reportedly, there were differing views among member states about how, or whether, to cooperate with Iran in this endeavor. By May 1991 the Saudis appeared to have lost interest in building a significant GCC force and were going their own way, with talk of doubling the size of the Saudi military establishment.[23]

The Egyptian-Syrian roles in Peninsula security quickly became uncertain. There were reports that King Fahd had decided against permitting any foreign troops to be stationed permanently in the kingdom.[24] On May 8, 1991, President Mubarak abruptly announced that Egypt would withdraw all of its troops from the Peninsula.[25] After meeting with visiting Secretary Cheney, however, he apparently agreed to leave a token Egyptian force, alongside a similar Syrian one, in Kuwait.[26] By the beginning of 1992, it seemed reasonably clear that there is to be no Egyptian or Syrian military presence in Saudi Arabia — or elsewhere in the Peninsula as far as the Saudis have a say. Longstanding precrisis Saudi concerns on this score had been rekindled and reinforced by Iranian objections to any "outside" military presence in the Gulf.[27]

On April 28, 1991, Lieutenant General Prince Khalid bin Sultan, who had been the senior Saudi commander in Desert Shield and Desert Storm, indicated in a press interview that there was no need for a U.S. military presence in the region larger than that existing prior to August 1990 and that the idea of pre-positioning U.S. equipment in Saudi Arabia had not even been considered.[28] Were the Saudis slipping back into their precrisis ambiguity? In any event, by summer 1991, the Bush administration seemed to have abandoned hope of helping erect a grand design for security in the region (its aspirations in that regard had never been all that grand) and was back in the familiar pattern of quietly cajoling Saudi Arabia into some quiet, modest, even ad hoc level of military cooperation. The United States, having worked out security agreements with Kuwait, Bahrain, and Qatar, is still negotiating arrangements with Saudi Arabia and other GCC states.

Since Desert Storm, Saudi Arabia has firmly supported President Bush's stated goal of controlling the proliferation of weapons of mass destruction in the Middle East. Saudi Arabia and the United States are as one in wanting to get rid of Iraq's weapons of mass destruction. Saudi Arabia, of course, is also interested in seeing Israel's nuclear capability dismantled, but voices in the United States note that Saudi Arabia is among those Middle East states possessing missiles, acquired (in this case) from China, capable of delivering weapons of mass destruction. Moreover, Saudi Arabia is very eager to acquire more conventional weapons. Early in the 1990 Gulf Crisis, the kingdom had requested, and the Bush administration had agreed to, the purchase of some $21 billion worth of U.S. military equipment. The U.S. Congress had rapidly agreed to providing a $7 billion package of the most urgently needed arms but had blown the whistle on the rest.[29] Since then, much of the remaining $14 billion request has been met, including, finally, the key element — 72 F-15 Eagle aircraft.

Although special election-eve factors permitted the F-15 sale to slip through Congress without controversy, voices in Congress and beyond are likely to keep contending — in addition to the familiar argument that selling certain U.S. arms to Saudi Arabia poses a threat to Israel or at least increases Israel's need for more U.S. military assistance — that if the United States has to protect Saudi Arabia in any event, why can the Saudis not spend their money on better things than fueling the Middle East arms race. The old days when presidents and Congress fell into mortal combat about whether to sell certain arms to Saudi Arabia, and when the Saudis reacted with understandable doubts about the U.S. connection, may still be with us, survivor of the awesome momentum of Desert Storm.[30]

Since Desert Storm, the U.S. and Saudi governments have clearly been in a cordial battle of diplomatic nerves involving the trade-offs on Saudi military cooperation and U.S. arms supply.

THE BOTTOM LINE

How the Saudis spend their money (and how much they have to spend) may indeed be the key to how effective the Saudi role will be in shaping a safer and more harmonious Gulf and Middle East. Secretary Baker, in congressional testimony in the midst of Desert Storm, and President Bush, in his "victory speech" at its end, spoke of the need to bring greater prosperity to the Middle East in order to relieve tension there.[31] There was the thought that the gap between the "haves" and "have nots" should be narrowed and that the region possessed sufficient oil wealth to take on this burden essentially by itself. Certainly the U.S. Treasury is in no shape — and the U.S. taxpayer in no mood — to take on a bigger share of that task, given the fact that a huge percentage of U.S. foreign aid, roughly $5 billion per year, has long gone to Israel and Egypt to rent "partners in peace."

There is no question that the vat oil wealth around the Persian Gulf assures the economic survival of its denizens well into the next century. However, in terms of who can lend and who must borrow in the short term, the picture is more complex. Iran, in the wake of the revolution and the long war with Iraq, is an economic basket case. It is into borrowing for a long time, and that is why its revolutionary leadership is edging away from fanaticism toward pragmatism. Iraq, of course, is a self-made disaster area. What it owes the world for its misdeeds exceeds five years of average oil income before 1990. What it needs to survive and rebuild in the wake of the devastation of Desert Storm at least equals that amount. Certainly, into the twenty-first century, Iraq is not going to be a lender; it is likely to be a nonperforming loan. Kuwait is slowly coming back to oil production, having survived the crisis financially by prudently husbanding "surplus" oil income abroad over many years. By the beginning of the twenty-first century — hopefully, well before — Kuwait will be able to resume its longstanding role of sharing a significant level of its riches with the poorer states of the Middle East. However, that day is obviously some years off, even assuming that Iraq pays anything beyond token reparations for its crimes in Kuwait.

That leaves Saudi Arabia — assisted by the United Arab Emirates (meaning Abu Dhabi) as a junior partner — to bear the burden of balancing the needs of the "have-nots" in the Middle East with the largesse of the "haves." The Saudis, of course, have a long record of being generous foreign aid donors. Prior to the 1990 Gulf Crisis, it looked as if Saudi Arabia needed to produce about 5 million barrels per day of oil worth about $20 per barrel to make ends meet. Making ends meet meant sustaining the welfare state (including subsidies to the "private sector welfare state") at home, a continued heavy expenditure on the military, and a modest amount of aid to poorer neighbors. By one account, Saudi foreign aid had fallen from $5.7 billion in 1980 to $1.2 billion in 1989, although it rose sharply — if temporarily — to some $3.7 billion in the crisis year 1990.[32] Prior to the August 1990 crisis (and since), there was little prospect of Saudi Arabia's fully achieving this needed level of some $36 billion in oil export earnings under normal conditions in the early part of the 1990s. Moreover, official Saudi foreign holdings had, over the "oil glut" years, been drawn down from a peak of some $160 billion to a fairly illiquid level of about $40 billion.[33] In short, the Saudis were in rather tight financial straits (by their plush standards) when Saddam invaded Kuwait.

The Gulf Crisis of August 1990 caused a sharp "spike" in oil prices. Saudi Arabia raised production to near capacity and, thus, in time brought prices back down to their pre-August level. In the process, Saudi Arabia made a huge windfall profit on increased production and temporarily increased prices, but it is well-documented that the kingdom spent more on sustaining Desert Shield and Desert Storm than it gained from the windfall.[34] By early

1991 Saudi Arabia was in the world financial markets, for the first time in about two decades, borrowing money to meet temporary cash flow problems.[35] If there is to be any kind of stability in the Gulf, Kuwait and Iraq will have to come back into the oil export market sooner rather than later, and Saudi Arabia will have to make market-share room for them. This would put Saudi Arabia back in the 5-million-barrel-per-day-at-roughly-$20-per-barrel league, with only a limited potential (after buying both lots of butter and some guns at home) for helping the needy in the Middle East.

Thus, the Saudis are looking in the early 1990s at an annual oil income, once Kuwaiti and Iraqi exports return to the precrisis level, of some $36 billion. However, they want to buy $14 billion in weapons from the United States (and much more from whatever source if they double the size of the armed forces). They have pledged more than $2 billion in economic aid to Syria and perhaps even more to Egypt. They have committed $3 billion to the remnants of the Soviet Union and are now heavily into wooing the Muslim Asian republics of the former Soviet empire. Saudi Arabia can do some of this — keep the citizens prosperous, buy military equipment and services, and finance a diplomacy based on lending money — but there are limits! Egypt and Syria have huge appetites as aid recipients. There is the prospect of renting the friendship of a devastated Iran. Pakistan, Bangladesh, and Turkey, supporters of the coalition, are high on the list of aid supplicants. Then, there are those currently out of favor but long on the dole — Jordan, the PLO, Yemen, Sudan, and the Maghreb states. In light of its recent domestic turmoil, Algeria is of particular and growing concern to Saudi leaders. There is obviously a limit to Saudi ability to buy happiness in the Middle East.

THE RAY OF SUNSHINE

In the wake of Desert Storm, President Bush, prodded obviously by both his Arab and his European allies in the coalition, sent his secretary of state on a serial odyssey to the Middle East in search of Arab-Israeli peace. Early on, the Saudis made clear their traditional position — that they are not direct party to the conflict and, thus, would not participate directly in any peace conference that their new Desert Storm ally might arrange. Subsequently, however, the Saudis stood rather tall. They clearly were the force behind the GCC's decision in mid-May 1991 to send an observer to the proposed Middle East peace conference and to participate on a state-by-state basis in any side talks on such issues as arms control and water resources.[36] Later, in an effort to create confidence building measures on the road to peace negotiations, Saudi Arabia supported the Egyptian proposal to suspend the Arab economic boycott of Israel in return for suspension of Israeli settlements in the occupied territories. In an area in which the kingdom had characteristically been the most cautious, Saudi Arabia was showing a remarkable boldness in helping the United States ensnare Israel and the Arabs in the quest for peace.[37] During the historic Madrid conference and since, including its participation in the January 1992 "regional" peace discussions in Moscow and follow-on sessions, Saudi Arabia has been uncharacteristically bold in assisting the peril-ridden Middle East peace process. It is unclear where this will lead, but certainly the success of the Rabin-led Labour Party in the June 1992 Israeli elections has given renewed hope that the peace process might make real progress in 1993 and beyond.

THE SAUDI ROLE

Therefore, where does Saudi Arabia fit in as the world contemplates how to make the Gulf and the Middle East a more peaceful and better place in the wake of Saddam's folly? Certainly, the end of the Cold War creates a more constructive global environment, but the Middle East has a long history of creating problems locally.

Saudi Arabia is obviously the leader in the GCC, which has a new level of importance after recent events. There is no question that the GCC is a useful vehicle for Saudi cooperation with five smaller neighbors and that the kingdom is dedicated to both the security and welfare of its GCC partners and the viability of the GCC as an institution for encouraging cooperation among the monarchies on the Arab side of the Gulf. What is in question is whether Saudi Arabia — inevitably the preponderate force in the GCC — will have the patience to work through the GCC and thus enhance it as an institutional force for stability in the Gulf or will tend to go its own way while using the GCC as an applauding Greek chorus. The signals in the year since Desert Storm suggest that the kingdom is inclined to focus on a massive increase in its own defense capability first and worry about a common GCC defense capability later.[38]

In any event, Saudi Arabia can count on more or less leading the GCC coalition as it faces the tough questions of future relations with Iran and Iraq. In this endeavor it certainly has — even in tight financial times — enough petrodollar power to keep Egypt and Syria in its corner in this sorting out of the Gulf balance of power. Saudi Arabia, backed by GCC allies Egypt and Syria and the West, led by the United States, is a more than credible contestant in this tricornered game of Gulf tranquility. However, the Saudis obviously face numerous complexities in the quest.

The first present imponderable is whither Iraq. The survival of the Saddam regime is obviously intolerable to Saudi Arabia, its GCC allies, the United States, the West, and, perhaps, Iran. However, well over two years after his violation of the rules of the Arab game, and the new world order, Saddam is still around. What the Saudis do in the future in the Gulf obviously is very dependent on who is ruling Iraq and how they relate to that regime. In this connection, the Saudi conduct at the February 1992 OPEC meeting is interesting, recalling that since the Gulf Crisis, Saudi Arabia had been producing oil at roughly the precrisis levels of the kingdom, Kuwait, and Iraq combined. At the February session the Saudis agreed to cut their production only by 500,000 barrels per day, roughly equal to the recovery of Kuwait's production post Desert Storm. Thus, Saudi Arabia is still producing "Iraq's share" of OPEC production at a time when market share is dear. This constitutes an important form of leverage over the future conduct of Iraq, whoever may be in control there.

Inextricably tied to that question is the future of Saudi-Iranian relations. In turn, the Iranian factor has great weight in how, how much, and how openly Saudi Arabia is willing to cooperate — especially in the military sphere — with the West in general and the "Satanic" Americans in particular. The pragmatic tendencies of President Rafsanjani's faction in Iran do not extend to gracious acceptance of U.S. military power in the Gulf. In addition, since Desert Storm, an entirely new issue has emerged — the Saudi-Iranian competition to influence trends in the Muslim Asian republics of the former Soviet Union. Moreover, the crisis in Algeria spotlights the question of whether Iran or Saudi Arabia will be more influential on Islamic political movements in the Arab world.

Thus, the future of the Saudi role in the Gulf is far from clear. Yet, several things seem assertable. The GCC, whether or not it fulfills the aspirations of early 1991, is stronger than it was before the August 1990 crisis, and Saudi Arabia is committed to the security of its members and to making the institution effective to some degree. (The boundary dust-up between Saudi Arabia and Qatar does not fundamentally change this trend.) There is growing evidence, despite the Abu Musa dispute, that Saudi Arabia and Iran have more or less concluded that it serves their mutual interests to get along, particularly in trying to cope with the uncertainty that is the future Iraq. Obviously, the quality of the Saudi relationship with Egypt and Syria impacts on these regional power relationships.

At another, and even more complicated, level, the Saudi relationship with the West — and the United States in particular — is being calibrated. In the wake of Desert Shield and Desert Storm, there simply can be no question that a great additional bond of trust has been forged between the Saudi kingdom and the West, especially the United States. The relationship may well deteriorate from the peaks of Desert Storm. The Saudis, among other things, have to square the circle of getting along with Iran and the United States at the same time. Yet, the fact that the United States has demonstrated (notably, in the Gulf in 1987–88, then, overwhelmingly, in Desert Shield and Desert Storm) a willingness to come in to defend the kingdom and then to withdraw as quickly as possible has built confidence among Saudi leaders about the basic nature of the relationship. Saudi actions in support of the Middle East peace process over the past year or so (1991–93) are perhaps the most convincing indication of the quality of this new relationship.

One should not expect Saudi Arabia to change its personality overnight. Yet, there are clear signs that the kingdom is beginning to play a more assertive role — indeed, something of a leadership role — in the emerging post-war Middle East. Within limitations, it has the financial clout to do so, and it has a special tie with the United States and the West that enhances its weight in Middle East circles. As always, however, how Saudi Arabia deals with Arabs and with the United States will be heavily influenced by the state of the quest for Arab-Israeli peace, and that issue, of course, is one in which Saudi Arabia, although clearly capable of playing a constructive role, has only a limited ability to determine events.

NOTES

1. James LeMoyne, New York *Times*, November 29, 1990.
2. See, for example, the August 8, 1990, speech of President Mubarak of Egypt, reported by the Associated Press, in which he chided the Arab world for dithering while the great powers and the United Nations responded to the crisis.
3. The early history of the kingdom is well set forth in a number of books, including (succinctly, if somewhat blandly) Ismail I. Nawwab, Peter C. Speers, and Paul F. Hoye, eds., *Aramco and Its World: Arabia and The Middle East* (Washington, D.C.: Arabian American Oil Company, 1980); in more detail, Nadav Safran, *Saudi Arabia: The Ceaseless Quest for Security* (Cambridge, Mass.: Harvard University Press, 1985); very readably, Robert Lacey, *The Kingdom: Arabia and the House of Saud* (New York: Harcourt Brace Jovanovich, 1981).
4. A good account of Saudi economic development through the 1970s is in John A. Shaw and David E. Long, *Saudi Arabian Modernization: The Impact of Change on Stability* (New York: Praeger, 1981).
5. Odeh Aburdene, "U.S. Economic and Financial Relations with Saudi Arabia, Kuwait and the United Arab Emirates," *American-Arab Affairs*, Winter 1983–84.
6. For a discussion of the U.S.–Saudi relationship in this period, see Joseph Twinam, "America and the Gulf Arabs," Part I, *American-Arab Affairs*, Summer 1988, pp. 145–56.
7. For an insight into Saudi policy from the U.S. perspective from the vantage point of the beginning of the 1980s, see William B. Quandt, *Saudi Arabia in the 1980s: Foreign Policy, Security and Oil* (Washington, D.C.: Brookings Institution, 1981).
8. For an analysis of factors in Saudi policy making, see David E. Long, "Saudi Arabia in the 1990's: Plus ça Change . . . ," in *The Gulf, Energy and Global Security: Political and Economic Issues*, eds. Charles F. Doran and Stephen W. Buck (Boulder, Colo.: Lynne Rienner, 1991); see also Twinam, "America and the Gulf Arabs."

9. For an interesting discussion of the world oil market in this period and the Saudi role, see Daniel Yergin, *The Prize: The Epic Quest for Oil, Money and Power* (New York: Simon and Schuster, 1991), Chaps. 31–34.
10. Quandt, *Saudi Arabia in the 1980s*, Chaps. 2 and 7.
11. Twinam, "America and the Gulf Arabs," Part I, pp. 154–56.
12. Joseph Twinam, "America and the Gulf Arabs," Part II, *American-Arab Affairs*, Fall 1988, pp. 120–21; see also the statement of Assistant Secretary of State Richard Murphy before the Senate Foreign Relations Committee, May 29, 1987.
13. *Middle East International*, August 3, 1990, pp. 3–6.
14. *Middle East International*, August 31, 1990, p. 6.
15. FBIS-NES-91-049-7, March 1991, pp. 1–2.
16. U.S. Department of State, *Dispatch* 2 (March 11, 1991); FBIS-NES-91-047-11, March 1991, p. 18.
17. See the communique of the Thirty-Ninth Ministerial Council meeting in Riyadh, June 4, 1991, FBIS-NES-91-107-4, June 1991, and the "Kuwait Declaration" issued by the Twelfth Supreme Council meeting in Kuwait, December 23–25, 1991.
18. Mushahid Hussein, *Middle East International*, April 3, 1992.
19. Gerald Butt, *Middle East International*, March 8, 1991, and May 3, 1991.
20. Cherif J. Cordahi, *Middle East International*, April 3, 1992.
21. Youssef M. Ibrahim, New York *Times*, March 30, 1992.
22. Ibid.
23. Patrick Tyler, New York *Times*, May 4, 1991; David Ottaway, Washington *Post National Weekly Edition*, April 29–May 5, 1991.
24. Associated Press, Riyadh, May 11, 1991.
25. Patrick Tyler, Washington *Post*, May 11, 1991.
26. Jeffrey Smith, Washington *Post*, June 2, 1991.
27. Nadim Jaber, *Middle East International*, November 22, 1991, and May 1, 1992.
28. Judith Miller, New York *Times*, April 29, 1991.
29. Thomas Friedman, New York *Times*, September 15, 1990; Michael Gordon, New York *Times*, September 27, 1990.
30. Eric Schmitt, New York *Times*, June 9, 1991.
31. U.S. Department of State, *Dispatch* 2 (February 11, 1991 and March 11, 1991).
32. Don Phillips, Washington *Post*, June 17, 1991.
33. U.S. Department of Commerce, FET for Saudi Arabia, October 1989.
34. Judith Miller, New York *Times*, January 11, 1991.
35. Edward Cody and Steven Mufson, Washington *Post National Weekly Edition*, February 18–24, 1991.
36. FBIS-NES-91-092-13, May 1991, p. 1.
37. Jim Muir and Donald Neff, *Middle East International*, July 26, 1991; Thomas Friedman, New York *Times*, July 19–August 2, 1991.
38. The Saudi role in the GCC is discussed extensively in Joseph Twinam, *The Gulf, Cooperation and the Council: An American Perspective* (Washington, D.C.: Middle East Policy Council, 1993), esp. Chap. 11.

III

Strategic Issues and Prospects

6

Gulf Oil: Geo-Economic and Geo-Strategic Realities in the Post–Cold War and Post–Gulf War Era

David Winterford and Robert E. Looney

The end of the Cold War has unleashed powerful new forces that continually threaten to undermine prospects for unfettered global peace and prosperity. Ambitious leaders, economic grievances, ethnic animosities, ancient rivalries, and competing claims to choice territories all promise to rattle global geo-economic and geo-strategic calculations for years to come. In this unfolding post–Cold War recalibration of the international order, national agendas — especially the calculus of national power — are increasingly driven by economic imperatives. Throughout the world, contemporary political leaders are reinventing a linkage that ancient strategists never forgot: powerful nations are built on powerful economies.

The Gulf War, the first post–Cold War crisis of global significance, provided an unmistakable harbinger of the determination with which calculating political leaders may seek to redress economic difficulties and grievances at home while pursuing leadership aspirations abroad. Given the centrality of one commodity in the Gulf — oil — Iraq's invasion of Kuwait, and the response of the United States and its coalition partners to that invasion, must be seen in terms of the geo-economic and geo-strategic importance of oil. This was a war fought for decisive influence over global oil markets and for a determining influence over the post–Cold War realignment of power in the Gulf region.

The Gulf War and its aftermath have radically changed the contours of regional and global oil politics. The tripolar regional contest for leadership in the Gulf — and in the Organization of Petroleum Exporting Countries (OPEC) — among Iran, Iraq, and Saudi Arabia has been unexpectedly jarred by the war and some of its unintended geo-strategic consequences. On one somewhat obvious level, the crisis tilted the balance between Iran and Iraq, which had been heavily in Baghdad's favor, toward Tehran. Clearly, defeat in the war means that Iraq's prospects of becoming the first populous state in the Middle East to achieve a fully industrialized and diversified economic base with a matching advanced military capability are dashed for the foreseeable future.[1] However, the blows administered to Baghdad have not solidified Tehran's position of regional dominance. Fearing invasion by Iraq, then fearing Iran's potentially dominant postwar role, Saudi Arabia converted its swing role in OPEC into a swing role in regional politics. Determined to keep the United States fully engaged in the region despite the collapse of a Soviet threat, Riyadh may, thus, be seen to have utilized successfully the incomplete status of the Gulf War to buttress its alignment with Washington and, thereby, check both Iraq and Iran.

Post-war strategic,, military, and national development imperatives confronting Iran, Iraq, and Saudi Arabia indicate that all of these countries face a compelling need to enhance national revenue. Here, the ramifications of the Gulf War for long-run oil prices are much less obvious. Not since the early 1970s has there been more uncertainty concerning the economic fate of these nations and the other Gulf countries. Already, many Gulf states have undertaken radical restructuring of their development plans, together with accompanying social and political strains. Whether many of these countries will be ale to maintain stability will depend on future developments in world petroleum markets.

Both the Gulf War and the ongoing post-war reordering of the Gulf region are inextricably linked to the pricing and production of oil. On the most vital level, strategic imperatives, military capabilities, and political ambitions in the region are directly related to the amount of national treasury to be derived from oil. For regional (and extraregional) actors, the price of oil is, thus, central; seeking to influence, if not control, that price is a critical and enduring challenge. Several key questions emphasize the evolving post-war link between the geo-economic and geo-strategic dimensions of oil: What is the likelihood of cooperation between Iran and Saudi Arabia on pricing and production issues in the coming years? Can OPEC cope with security-related problems that appear to be recurring among its members (for example, the Iran-Iraq War of the 1980s, Iraq's invasion of Kuwait, and the Gulf War of 1990–91)? How has Operation Desert Storm affected the pricing and production policies of OPEC?

The main purpose of this chapter is to gain some perspective on these issues by assessing likely movements in world oil markets in the unfolding post–Cold War and post–Gulf War period. To do so, several issues are examined: first, key economic patterns and longer run trends that characterized oil market prior to Iraq's invasion of Kuwait; second, the impact developments since the liberation of Kuwait have had on these fundamental market dynamics; third, key emerging regional security considerations that are likely to have a decisive impact on oil price and protection policies; and, finally, based on these factors, several conclusions concerning the geo-economic and geo-strategic dimensions of oil, especially future oil prices and the distribution of economic power in the Gulf region, and the changing geo-strategic realities confronting OPEC.

PRE-GULF WAR: KEY FACTORS AFFECTING THE PRICE OF OIL[2]

After more than two decades[3] of experience in forecasting prices and production levels, analysts have developed several general principles concerning the function of oil markets. One notable advance is that energy is no longer thought of as exempt from the laws of supply and demand. It was not very long ago that energy was viewed as a necessity and, as such, was unresponsive to price. Similarly, supply was thought to depend more on the whims of nature than on the ability to find and extract the mineral.[4]

The demand for oil just prior to Iraq's invasion of Kuwait contrasted sharply with the situation at the beginning of the 1980s. In the first quarter of 1981, world oil consumption was about 56 million barrels per day (bpd), and the price of oil was over $48.64 per barrel (in 1988 dollars). In the first quarter of 1988, world oil consumption was again about 56 million bpd, but the price of oil had dropped to below $12 per barrel, despite worldwide economic expansion.

To gain insight into the likely market response to oil in the post–Gulf War period (specifically, the balance of the 1990s), it is instructive to recall the events, market responses, and adjustments that contributed to patterns characteristic of the 1980s.[5]

First, the Iranian revolution and the onset of the Iran-Iraq War reduced world oil production between 1979 and 1981. Because short-run oil demand is very inelastic (relatively price insensitive), the reduction in supply pushed prices sharply higher.

Second, the oil consumption and price combination that prevailed in the first quarter of 1981 could not be sustained in the longer run. In the absence of economic growth, a sustained price of $48.64 per barrel would eventually have reduced consumption by the world's largest oil consumer, the United States, about 40 percent, from 16.5 to 10.2 million bpd. On the other hand, for U.S. consumers to continue to absorb 16.5 million bpd without economic growth eventually would have required an estimated price of only about $20.61 per barrel.

Third, experience in the 1980s indicates that U.S. consumers require nearly a decade to adjust fully to changes in oil prices. Oil consumption responds slowly to price changes because substantial changes in the ratio of oil consumption to output require new capital investment.

Fourth, as short-run demand adjusted to prices during the 1980s, the market price and quantity of oil consumed were pushed down. Non-OPEC oil producers added to the downward pressure on price as their production increased. Beginning in 1981, however, OPEC moderated downward pressure on prices by reducing its own production.

Fifth, short-run demand nevertheless continued to decline, and non-OPEC oil production continued to rise. OPEC's continued attempts to support prices reduced its production to about 14 million bpd by mid-1985, less than 50 percent of its total capacity.

Finally, OPEC's attempts to support prices ended in a well-publicized failure. Excess capacity and the incentive for OPEC members to cheat on quotas led to a surge in OPEC production. With demand being inelastic in the short run, that surge in production caused a price break in late 1985 and early 1986. Thereafter, OPEC was unable to restrain its production sufficiently to drive prices back up to earlier levels.

The above analysis indicates that consumption responds symmetrically to rising and falling oil prices. Given this adjustment mechanism, the price of $15.47 per barrel in early 1989 would have eventually increased U.S. oil consumption by an estimated 35 percent, from 17 to 23 million bpd. On the other hand, for U.S. consumption to remain at 17 million bpd, in the long run, prices must rise to an estimated $26.63 even without economic growth.

Although longer-run movements in oil price can be explained in terms of market responses and adjustments over time, shorter-run movements are still difficult to predict. In fact, it is fair to say that analysts have only begun to understand the mechanisms controlling month-to-month (or even year-to-year) changes in price. Even the dramatic fourfold increases in oil prices in 1974 and the three-fold increase in 1979 during a period of stable supply appear to defy the normal laws of supply and demand. It is now clear that inventory demand fluctuations set off by supply interruptions can contribute a great deal more to the shortage in the market and to the severity of the price shock than can the initial supply reduction. Of course, supply disruptions themselves may stem from a variety of political acts, ranging from war to an attempt by national decision makers to determine the price of oil by national or cartel production decisions.

Similarly, the explanation of the price declines in January 1986 remains unclear. It is not surprising that oil prices fell; the surprise is why it took so long to happen and why prices fell so far. The downward pressure had been enormous for years, as worldwide consumption declined by 23 percent between 1979 and 1985 and remained steady through 1985. Even the futures market anticipated a price decline for nearly three years before it occurred, as suggested by the discounts on long-term contracts relative to shorter maturities during most of that time. Indications now exist that the market was also surprised by new information in January 1986. Saudi Arabia announced its intention to increase production three months before the price drop, and OPEC failed to reach a new accord in light of the Saudi action one month before.

The most popular explanation of recent oil price movements is that, beginning in 1972, OPEC began exerting its market power to control the world oil price.[6] Certainly, OPEC possessed potential market power to control the price of oil during most of the 1970s. OPEC countries produced more than two-thirds of total noncommunist output and accounted for nearly 90 percent of all oil involved in international trade. Nevertheless, little evidence exists that OPEC exercised its market power. Political events, not OPEC decision making, were the catalysts that initiated the two oil price shocks, and, as noted, reductions in supply do not explain the price shock that occurred.

OPEC production slowed slightly during the first three months of 1974 and again during the first three months of 1979.[7] However, total OPEC production for 1974 matched that for 1973, and total production for 1979 exceeded that for 1978. What production figures from these two events do not reveal is the extent of the shortages caused by the demand side of the market, in particular, surges in inventory demand. Unfortunately, the extent of the inventory demand shock cannot be fully described, because the only available inventory data refer to primary stocks in Organization for Economic Cooperation and Development (OECD) countries, and nearly all stocks held outside the OECD countries are unknown. Still, more than just anecdotal evidence exists to indicate that considerable hoarding occurred downstream from refineries. Immediately after the Iranian revolution began in October 1978, refined product stocks fell sharply in all OECD countries even though crude oil supplies and refinery throughout continued unabated.

Deliveries from refineries to downstream markets continued at an unusually rapid pace through the first three months of 1979 (indeed, too rapid a pace to be explained by a consumption increase) until the process finally slowed in mid-1979 and refiners began to rebuild their stocks. By this time, most of the price increase had already occurred. Refiners continued to build their stocks to record levels over the next 12 months and to offset in prices the slowdown in consumption that would soon dominate the market.

In short, past forecasting errors can be blamed partly on the one- to two-year lag in acquiring accurate data and the inventory adjustments underway in the oil market during this period. Long-term trends are difficult to identify, much less to quantify. Clearly, projecting oil prices, particularly figures for a specific year, is highly speculative. More realistically, it is better to view oil price movements as cyclical. In this regard, the rise and fall of oil prices from 1969 to 1986 is unlikely to be repeated in the extreme.[8] The depths to which prices sank during the 1960s drove out most competing fuels.[9] When prices ascended a few years later, most fuel-using equipment was designed to burn only a narrow range of petroleum products. In the short term, consumers had little choice other than to pay higher fuel prices. As time went on, however, consumers learned to conserve energy. Worldwide, coal and gas consumption expanded while oil demand contracted. If historical experience is any guide to future behavior in global energy markets, the active presence of competing fuels again will tend to hold down the oil price cycle. In this event, competition among fuels will most likely prevent a complete collapse of oil prices.

In world energy markets, oil penetrates very rapidly into the bulk fuel market when its price is less that $10 per barrel. Under such circumstances, global oil consumption could increase by 2–3 million bpd within a few months, largely at the expense of coal, and could continue to grow by as much as 5 percent per year as oil captures virtually the entire increment in world energy demand. Thus, oil prices below $10 are stable only if very substantial oil reserve discoveries occur, such as those that took place during the 1950s and 1960s. On the other hand, competition among fuels prevents oil prices from sustaining a level much above $20 per barrel. In the longer term, coal from Australia, Canada, South Africa, the United States, and other producing areas can easily be delivered into major European and Asian markets for $20 to $25 per barrel equivalent. Natural gas is an even-stronger competitor.

One final fact deserves particular attention: past experience indicates that day-to-day oil price changes are driven by Saudi Arabian production decisions more than by anything else, and those decisions reflect political and economic calculations made in Riyadh. Since the drop in demand and price peak of 1981, oil prices could stabilize above their earlier levels only because the Saudis and a few other OPEC members were willing to decrease production to balance the market. In the summer of 1985, however, Saudi production had fallen to 2.5 million bpd — about one-half of the country's OPEC production quota and over a 500 percent drop from the production levels of the summer before.

The only way that the Saudis could restore their production and stem the erosion of their export revenues was to retreat on price. They did so through a set of complicated netback agreements that guaranteed profit margins to refiners buying Saudi crude oil. As they executed these agreements, Saudi officials warned that they were no longer willing to act as swing producer. Simply stated, the Saudis lost control of the marginal barrel of crude oil and, thus, the ability to set prices. Oil prices were falling in the late 1980s and early in 1990, just as Iraq's ambitious leader was crafting his plans for Iraqi preeminence in the Gulf region. Global oil geo-economics had begun to seriously threaten Iraq's regional geo-strategic plans.

OIL AND IRAQ'S DECISION TO INVADE KUWAIT

Just prior to Iraq's invasion of Kuwait, the general economic considerations raised in the foregoing analysis lead to a likely price scenario in which oil markets were assumed to continue the adjustments that began in the early 1980s. This scenario assumed that oil markets had not yet completely adjusted to worldwide excess capacity in the producing countries, with the net result that prices and/or production levels were projected to continue to fall in the early 1990s.[10] However, by the mid-1990s, short-run demand was expected to increase from the unsustainable combination of oil consumption and price that characterized the late 1980s and early 1990s.

With a growing world economy, and low initial prices, the general expectation in the early 1990s was for strong growth in oil demand from the mid-1990s onward. Given the low prices in the late 1980s, the growth rate in consumption was anticipated to increase from around 2 percent per annum in the early 1980s to 9.5 percent by the end of the century. This rate of consumption could not be sustained throughout the 1990s, however, because it would result in levels of demand greater that the world capacity to produce oil — little capacity is likely to be added with the low oil prices projected to bring about the rapid growth in oil consumption. Clearly, given the likely demand stimulated by relatively low 1989 prices, those prices could not be sustained throughout the 1990s. Previous experience had shown that oil prices rise as OPEC is pushed to full capacity, and nearly all excess capacity to produce oil is in OPEC.

Over a wide range of consumption scenarios, OPEC was expected to come close to full capacity between late 1992 and early 1993. At or below a price of $25 per barrel, OPEC could reach full capacity no later than early 1993. By that year a price of $25 per barrel could prove too low, if world capacity did not rise. Similarly, with world economic growth rates between 2 percent and 3 percent, oil prices could reach $30 to $40 per barrel by the year 2000.

The critical point from this analysis is that OPEC's decision makers should have been looking forward to a revival of OPEC as its share of world oil production increased during the mid- to late-1990s. Market forces alone indicated that rising production and rising prices heralded an era of substantial growth in national revenues for oil-producing nations.

Of course, these price forecasts are dependent upon a number of assumptions. *If* world capacity to produce oil is decreased, *if* OPEC restricts its production, *if* oil supplies are disrupted, or *if* economic growth is stronger, oil prices and national revenues will be higher. On the other hand, *if* world capacity to produce oil is increased, *if* economic growth is weaker, or *if* energy taxation is increased, oil prices will be lower than those forecast above.

All of these calculations indicate the inherent short-run uncertainty of global oil markets and, therefore, the uncertainty of national revenues derived from oil. When critical markets (and prices) are uncertain, national decision makers are often tempted to bring order and predictability to chaotic and seemingly capricious market forces. The temptation to control, and the political rationale to act, is almost irresistible when urgent needs confront seemingly volatile forces.

This was exactly the situation challenging Iraq. The central issue confronting authorities in Baghdad on the eve of the invasion was a critical need for substantial new amounts of cash. Although the analysis presented above suggest that a revival of OPEC and, thus, the fortunes of its members would have occurred just down the road, in 1990, hard-pressed national decision makers in Baghdad confronted an immediate need for money. In three different ways, oil played a critical role in Iraq's decision to invade Kuwait. First, Iraq was in a dangerous financial situation, with oil revenues far below the regime's ambitious plans for military power and economic industrialization. Legitimacy and stability at home required continued high levels of state spending, and building Iraq's military capability demanded huge resources. Second, Kuwait was pursuing an oil production policy at sharp variance with Baghdad's national interests. Through its production policies, Kuwait was exacerbating the fall in oil prices of the late 1980s, while Iraq required higher prices to boost its revenues. Third, Iraq alleged that Kuwait was pumping oil from the Rumallah oil field, a field that lies mainly within Iraq but that straddles the Iraq-Kuwait border.[11]

The most important factor was Baghdad's perilous financial situation. During the long war with Iran in the 1980s, Iraqi authorities consolidated power at home through a "guns and butter" strategy, paying for $52 billion worth of imported weapons and a similar volume of civilian-sector imports with a combination of running down financial reserves, oil revenues, commercial loans from industrialized countries, and loans from Arab states, principally Saudi Arabia and Kuwait.[12] At the end of the war with Iran, Iraq had changed from a prosperous oil-exporting country to one with over $70 billion in debt.[13] In mid-1990, Iraq's potential revenues were only $16–17 billion a year, and it needed either substantial new loans or a sharp increase in oil prices. Without new funds, the regime faced Hobson's choice: either it would need to scale back sharply its regional ambitions, thereby remaining in the shadow of Iran and Saudi Arabia, or it would need to clamp down on civilian consumption, thereby running the risk of further internal trouble. Saudi Arabia and the United Arab Emirates (UAE) forgave their share of the $30 billion Iraq owed to its Arab neighbors after its war with Iran, but Kuwait did not.

Iraq could not increase production to raise revenues because it had been unsuccessful in attracting sufficient new foreign investment. Unable to increase production, Iraq's only option was coercive attempts to secure an increase in revenues through price maximization. Baghdad's strategy was to secure a minimum price of $25 a barrel for oil — $8 a barrel more than prevailing global prices. At that level, Iraqi revenues would increase about $6 billion per year and the regime would not have to make the politically unpalatable and inherently difficult decision between guns and butter.

Iraq's threatening actions toward Kuwait in 1990 were having somewhat the desired effect. During the summer of 1990, Kuwait reduced its production, thus, contributing to a hardening of oil prices.[14] Although OPEC, in turn, adopted a $21 target reference price, Kuwait, Saudi Arabia, and the UAE refused to accept Iraq's $25 target. Although the new OPEC target of $21 was helpful to Iraq, it was still far too low to meet the costs of the domestic and regional agenda set by Baghdad. It is in the context of the regime's desperate need for cash that analysts should also see Iraq's demand for nearly $2.5 billion from Kuwait for Iraqi oil allegedly stolen from the Rumallah oil field.

The invasion of Kuwait was viewed by Baghdad as a quick means of addressing both its immediate cash needs and its regional ambitions. By occupying Kuwait, Iraq was provided with secure access to another 100 billion barrels of reserves.[15] Combined with its own reserves, Iraqi authorities would then at last be in a position to challenge Saudi short- and long-term influence over oil prices. Although the impact on Iraqi revenues remained a central consideration, core geo-strategic factors remained critical in Iraqi calculations. Iraq's preeminent strategist, Saddam Hussein saw the invasion as part of consolidating Iraq's economic foundations, a process necessary for reinforcing Iraqi national power. With an ambitious leader and a mighty military capability, incorporating Kuwaiti oil would thus establish Iraq as the premier regional power, able to challenge both Saudi Arabia and Iran for dominance in the Gulf.

In terms of global oil markets, because Kuwait contains one-tenth of the world's proven oil reserves and accounts for 2.5 percent of global production, the geo-economic payoff for Baghdad of annexation would have been an ability to pressure, if not coerce, Saudi Arabia into following Iraqi oil policies. As the other smaller Gulf states fell into line, Iraq would then also have come to dominate OPEC and be a determining influence on OPEC pricing and production policies. As the single most significant player in the geo-economics and geo-politics of global oil, Iraq would have been in a strategic position to direct and benefit from a likely trend toward higher oil prices.

Ironically, as the analysis presented earlier indicated, Iraq's $25 (or even higher) per barrel for oil would likely have been met by market forces two to three years later. By waiting, Iraq would have achieved its financial goals while retaining intact its diversifying economic infrastructure and its threatening military capability. Had there been no war, and helped by unfolding market forces, Iraq was well on its way to achieving Baghdad's goal of being the preeminent regional power. With the war, devastation ensued, eliminating much of Iraqi industry and military capability while denying Iraq the fruits of its abundant oil.

OPEC AND POST–GULF WAR OIL: GEO-ECONOMIC ISSUES

The first obvious result of the Gulf War for global oil markets is that for many years, Iraq will be unable to play a role in global oil politics or economics commensurate with its position as the holder of the world's second largest oil reserves. The destruction unleashed by the coalition forces has left Iraq's oil refining and export capacities in ruins. After two major wars, Iraq has debts of around $80 billion and demands for reparations in excess of $100 billion. Reconstruction of domestic infrastructure could readily pose a burden of another $100 billion. Indeed, with no capital, and confronting these magnitudes of bills, it is very hard to see Iraq maintaining full state control of its oil resources. In short, under prevailing conditions, Iraq's ambition to dominate the Gulf and OPEC looks unattainable for some time.

OPEC was unraveling at the time of the Kuwaiti invasion, its discipline undermined by evaded quotas, declining output, and international strife. Pre–Gulf War, OPEC had reason to look forward to a revival of the organization as its share of world oil production increased during the mid- to late-1990s. For several reasons, the invasion of Kuwait and its aftermath have now made this scenario more doubtful.[16] First, developed countries will increasingly favor supplies form outside the Gulf. The Iraqi action is thus likely to give a boost to non-OPEC exploration. Second, conservation will also become more attractive, depressing demand. Even prior to the invasion, worries about global warming and environmental damage implied that demand would be less than consensus forecast. Third, OPEC producers have ambitious plans to increase production. Before the invasion, Cambridge Energy Research Associates had predicted that OPEC's large producers would add about 7 billion bpd of extra capacity over the next five years, roughly matching the increase in expected demand. Unless producers cut their investment, the world may again find that capacity in the gulf outstrips demand. If so, discipline over production would look, once again, to be a futile ambition. Fourth, similar to Iraq, Saudi Arabia and Iran are also pressed for cash. Iran needs money to repair war damage from the 1980s and to finance its regional power ambitions. Saudi Arabia's falling oil earnings caused it to run up budget deficits totaling more than $90 billion from 1983 to 1989. On the other hand, a price war seems unlikely, because none of these three big Gulf producers can afford a collapse in the price of oil.

The crisis vividly demonstrated that Saudi security is entwined with the West. The Saudis' strategy is not much different from that of most other exporters who have much greater respect for the power of the marketplace and for Western military power today than in the pre–Gulf War era of nationalism. They have learned that their primary customers will act, and they want to demonstrate that they are reliable suppliers. Even Iran is showing some stirrings in that direction.

The economic imperatives of the 1990s also are pushing oil exporters toward a new flexibility. With the question of sovereignty over oil resources resolved in their favor, they are now preoccupied with more pragmatic and acute needs — chiefly, foreign capital and technology. They need more income from oil just to keep up with their rapidly growing populations. Because they are unlikely to gain more revenue from much higher prices (because they will lose customers), they need to pump more oil. Enhanced production requires new investment in exploration and capacity. How will they pay for it? There is a general expectation of a capital shortage in the 1990s. One place oil exporters may look for investment funds is in the once-banished foreign oil companies. As a result, doors that slammed shut with nationalization in the 1970s will swing open again in the 1990s, and companies will find themselves exploring and producing in territories they never expected to see again. Certainly for post-war Iraq, there may be very little choice but to cede large segments of state control of oil resources to foreign oil interests.

Finally, events outside the Gulf are creating potential new competitors for OPEC. In the aftermath of the Gulf Crisis, attention has shifted away from the Middle Eat toward Russia, which will become a more important, if uncertain, factor in international oil markets. If a secure contractual basis can be established with Western oil companies, Russia may, to some degree, balance the world's dependence on oil. Indeed, active efforts are now underway on the part of Western leaders in effect to use Russia and the former

Communist countries to bypass or even ignore OPEC in designing their future energy policies.

The new interest in Russia is most evident in several oil agreements under discussion.[17] These agreements do not even mention the OPEC countries. If all goes according to plan, in 1992, approximately 50 countries will sign an energy treaty that will define market conditions for trade in oil and gas between the former Communist bloc and the rest of the Western industrialized world. The proposed treaty does not ask the OPEC countries to join. The accord and protocols will cover issues from investment protection to exploration rights, trade dispute settlement, repatriation of profits, and the environment.

At the insistence of the United States and Germany, the main thrust of the draft text is the legal protection of foreign investments. Although the will is obviously there, most Western oil companies have been cautious about rushing to invest in the republics of the former Soviet Union because of the political uncertainty. The main thrust of the draft treaty currently on the table is the legal protection of foreign investment, including safeguards in the event of war or renationalization programs. In the short term, one of the most important geopolitical effects of the charter will be to rule out the likelihood of any of the producing republics joining OPEC. The market access clause of the text under discussion specifically rules out any price fixing or production quotas.

Clearly a significant factor for the future is the likelihood that Russia and several of the former Soviet republics may, with the aid of foreign investment and technology, reverse their downward trend in production to become significant exporters.[18] The old Soviet Union's oil problems never really involved lack of reserves: low investment, poor technology, and inefficiency were the main constraints on output.[19] These may be overcome quickly once the expected post–Cold War/Gulf War boom in foreign investment begins.

As the world's largest oil exporter, what might all these geoeconomic factors indicate about future Saudi policy regarding prices or output? As rational actors, Saudi leaders should price their energy just below the costs of their closest competitors. In the short run, that competition is from other sources of energy, such as from natural gas in North America and Europe, where the long-distance transmission infrastructure is more than adequate to meet current demand. In the longer run, the competition is from new sources of additional supply, such as Russia, and from coal and new natural gas supplies. Thus, the most important economic determinant of oil prices in both the short and the long run should be competition among fuels in the bulk fuel market. Because the Saudi reserves are unlikely ever to be worth more than the value of substitute bulk fuels, the Saudis have little economic incentive to restrain development of their fields.

In short, Saudi Arabia has both the economic incentive and the ability to meet the world's incremental energy demand through the rest of the century and at prices comparable to those that prevailed in mid-1986. As noted below, the realignment of strategic forces in the Gulf after the war serves to reinforce a complementary political incentive for Saudi Arabia to adopt pricing policies that address the needs of the world's largest oil consumer, the United States.

OPEC AND POST–GULF WAR OIL: GEO-STRATEGIC ISSUES

Post–Gulf War regional security dynamics are also contributing to a weakening of OPEC's resilience and a strengthening of downward pressure on oil prices. The Gulf War has stimulated a surge in defense spending in the Middle East. Although other parts of the world may be anticipating a post–Cold War peace dividend, fears, insecurities, and rivalries have been further exacerbated in the Gulf, resulting in an expensive post–Gulf War regional arms buildup. Several key aspects of this arms race bear directly on the issue of OPEC cohesion and the future direction of oil prices.

First, continuing Iraqi claims to Kuwait are ominous, and the constant brinkmanship throughout 1992 with the UN and the United States may indicate an Iraqi intention to frustrate and eventually break the UN-mandated arms embargo. The Iraqi leadership may be gambling that the West does not have the staying power to sustain the embargo indefinitely or the collective will to mount another massive ground campaign. Reports suggest that by 1992, Baghdad had reduced its 1 million-strong Gulf War military to 400,000 men, organized into 22–27 divisions, including at least 4 divisions of Republican Guards.[20] This move may be designed to strengthen the Iraqi military in the aftermath of Desert Storm, when the huge but logistically unsupportable army fell apart under the pressure of the allied air campaign. In the event of renewed hostilities, a smaller army of higher quality could be much more effective. If Iraq can break the embargo and acquire needed spare parts for its estimated 250 intact aircraft, then the Iraqi military could again pose a credible threat to neighboring countries.

Second, Iran, rather than Iraq, is currently viewed by some as the most serious long-term threat to Saudi Arabia and other states on the western side of the Gulf because of the rapid growth of its population, its impressive military building program, and the continuing contest for ascendancy between Shi'ite fundamentalism and Sunni conservatism. Although Iranian hostility toward the Gulf monarchies was tempered somewhat during the Gulf War, the Iranians are not likely to forgive or forget the substantial support lent to their Iraqi enemies by the Gulf Cooperation Council (GCC) states in the 1980s during the Iran-Iraq War.

Iranian armed forces are in the process of rebuilding from the substantial losses occurred in that war. Tehran is rearming on a scale that dwarfs current Iraqi efforts, with $50 billion in military expenditures planned for the next five years in addition to the estimated $19 billion spent in 1991 alone.[21] Indeed, the U.S. military foresees a much stronger Iran, and U.S. intelligence officials reportedly fear that Iran's military rebuilding program could threaten regional peace as early as 1996. As one U.S. intelligence analyst commented, "There is also cause for concern that Iran is conspiring to build a strategic strike capability.... It could include nuclear weapons, long-range delivery systems and missiles."[22] So far, major purchases have reportedly included modern jet aircraft and tanks from China and Russia, including a squadron of MIG-29s, as well as advanced Scud missiles from North Korea.[23]

The Iranian navy is also in the process of rebuilding. Among other items, Iran is putting together a naval force of amphibious ships and support ships (including a replenishment ship).[24] These acquisitions indicate that Iran is developing a navy capable of sustained at-sea operations and having a power projection role. Of further concern is the purchase in 1991 of three kilo class submarines from Russia for delivery sometime in 1992. *Jane's* reports that the submarines will be based at Chah Bahar on the Gulf of Oman, some 70 miles west of Pakistan and 250 miles east of the Straits of Hormuz.[25] The kilos might be useful in tanker interdiction and/or in a role aimed at blocking the entrance to the Gulf. Speculation that Iran also acquired two tactical nuclear warheads from Kazakhstan in 1991, although steadfastly denied by Moscow, further deepens Saudi and regional concern about Iranian intentions.[26]

With the breakup of the Soviet Union, Saudi-Iranian rivalry has taken new forms as each seeks influence in the new Central Asian republics.[27] This newly emerging arena concentrates the central issues in the Saudi-Iranian contest: access to the new republics promises advancement of religiously based geopolitical interests, and those republics could be a source of nuclear technology, nuclear weapons, and advanced weapons systems.

These post–Cold War/Gulf War fears and challenges have prompted Saudi Arabia, in turn, to plan for expanding the size of its armed forces to 200,000 men in eight divisions, a substantial increase from the 70,000-man force existing in August 1990. Whether the Saudis can achieve this goal with a military manpower pool of only 6.7 million is questionable unless it intends to rely on foreign troops to fill in the ranks of its units.[28] An all-Saudi force of this size also competes for manpower with government plans to reduce reliance on a large foreign work force by encouraging more Saudi nationals to work in domestic industry. Also, the high-tech equipment employed by the United States and its allies in the war required well-trained servicemen to operate effectively, training that takes several years to acquire.

Even more serious problems confront the Kuwaitis, whose orders for new aircraft and armored vehicles contrast sharply with the critical manpower shortage facing their armed forces. The military has shrunk from a preinvasion force of 21,000 to around 10,000 by 1992, in part due to the dismissal of about 10,000 Bedouins and Palestinians from its ranks in the aftermath of the war.[29]

Given the pressing need for money to pay for this regional arms buildup and given that security threats are derived from rivalries between OPEC members themselves, prospects look to be quite dim for coordinated political management by OPEC of production/prices in defiance of underlying geo-economic realities. Indeed, the strain imposed by the war and the renewed post-war rivalry between Iran and Saudi Arabia for dominant influence, first in the Gulf and then in the new Central Asian republics, bode ill for OPEC cohesion.

Of utmost importance in evaluating these unfolding trends is the central role now played by the United States in preserving security in the Gulf. Despite considerable post-war attention to planned major arms purchases and evolving collective security arrangements, little has been accomplished that substantially improves the defensive capabilities of Saudi Arabia and the smaller GCC states, other than the continuing presence of U.S. warships and aircraft in the region. There does not appear to be much progress toward the regional collective security pact proposed at the end of the war as the cornerstone of Gulf security. Fears of complete Saudi domination of a formal military arrangement by the other GCC countries and Saudi discomfort at the prospective presence of large numbers of troops from traditional rivals are some of the stubborn obstacles hampering regional security arrangements.

Confronted by evolving security challenges yet unable to handle them autonomously, Saudi Arabia and the other GCC states must rely ever more on a U.S. security shield. The Gulf War itself unmistakably demonstrated U.S. commitment to the region in general and Saudi Arabia in particular. The quid pro quo is equally unmistakable. Riyadh understands very clearly that having risked thousands of U.S. lives and continuing to provide a vital security shield, Washington, in return, expects a high level of Saudi oil output. The Saudis, Kuwaitis, and others benefiting from a significant U.S. military presence in the Gulf know they cannot reduce production drastically if that should result in a major surge in oil prices.

The factors now at work in the Gulf region suggest that the net effect of all these geo-economic and geo-strategic forces will be to usher in an era of relative price stability for the foreseeable future. Now that the United States, along with some coalition partners, has assumed an explicit role in assuring the secure flow of oil, the external orientation of key Gulf oil exporters, especially Saudi Arabia and the other GCC states, has been decisively altered. OPEC, as always, reflects the balance of interests and power among its members. Saudi Arabia is more dominant among the exporters than ever, and Saudi Arabia is more tied to the United States than ever. Committed to moderate prices and stable supplies, it has no doubt that its fortunes depend on a Western, specifically U.S., security umbrella and on Western economies. Saudi authorities want to be assured of their long-term survival and, with a quarter of proven world reserves, assured of Saudi access to a long-term market.

OPEC AND GLOBAL OIL: NEW POST-COLD WAR/GULF WAR DIRECTIONS

Against the external geo-economic and geo-strategic trends indicated in the above analysis, recent developments within OPEC are further straining unity. OPEC last formally agreed to quotas at its July 1990 meeting, right on the eve of the Iraqi invasion of Kuwait. As a result of the cessation of exports from Kuwait and Iraq during the Gulf War, the other members of OPEC decided to increase production to make up for the shortfall. At its meeting in Vienna in November 1991, the organization agreed to permit its members to continue lifting as much crude as they could produce. The notional ceiling of 23.5 million bpd agreed upon at the September ministerial meeting was simply rolled over. It seemed a sensible arrangement at the time, because oil prices were averaging $23 a barrel, Kuwaiti production was only just beginning to trickle back onto the market, and no compromise seemed in sight on allowing Iraq to resume exports.[30]

Unfortunately for OPEC, for several reasons, prices started to fall in late 1991 through early 1992. The winter growth in demand for OPEC oil peaked too soon as the oil companies built up inventories quicker than needed. The recession in the Western industrialized world turned out to be deeper than expected, resulting in a depressed demand for oil, dampened all the more because of a relatively mild winter. Kuwait started to resume production faster than was believed possible. Even Iraq was edging its way slowly toward an agreement for the resumption of oil exports at a value of $1.6 billion a year to pay for humanitarian needs.[31]

It is little wonder that OPEC members who rely for their oil revenues more on the price than on the volume of crude they export were worried. Even before the end of 1991, Algeria and other members were agitating for an emergency meeting of the organization. Saudi Arabia resolutely rejected the idea. The fact that Algeria, Libya, Nigeria, and Venezuela began reducing output unilaterally indicated that the kingdom had the correct negotiating stance.[32] Clearly, Saudi Arabia was unwilling to relinquish its 35 percent share of OPEC's overall market for crude exports. It boosted production from 5.4 million bpd before the Gulf War to 8.5 million bpd at considerable expense and would not make a deal that did not permit the maximum degree of flexibility.

The first real glimpse into the medium-term future was provided at the mid-February 1992 OPEC meeting.[33] This meeting satisfied none of the members. At that time, a fragile consensus on output was reached, only to be instantly denounced by its two strongest signatories, Iran and Saudi Arabia. Oil prices continued their seasonal slide as the market continued to remain unimpressed by the proposed cutbacks. The price weakness reflected a number of problems stemming from oversupply and the worldwide recession. In contrast to the 1980s, however, these difficulties were exaggerated by Saudi Arabia's reluctance to make short-term output adjustments.

The February 1992 OPEC agreement and its aftermath are very important because they set the tone (apparently for some time) of Saudi Arabia's approach toward pricing.[34] Under the agreement, Saudi Arabia would have to cut production to 7.9 million bpd as part of an overall ceiling of 22.5–22.7 million bpd. However, Saudi Arabia spent $5 billion during the Gulf War to boost its production from 5.4 million bpd to close to 9 million bpd in January 1992. The kingdom is clearly unwilling to relinquish its hard-won market share. Riyadh faces a budget deficit of some $8 billion, which restricts its ability to maneuver. Saudi authorities also understand the nature of the implicit bargain on prices, production, and security now existing between Washington and Riyadh. Thus, the Saudis plan to violate the OPEC agreement by staying with their 8 million bpd.

The kingdom's insistence on maintaining its large share of overall output will inevitably bring it into conflict with other smaller producers. All OPEC member nations are suffering the effects of low oil prices, and most have budget deficits. Some members, such as Algeria, which is under emergency rule, and Venezuela, which recently suffered an attempted government overthrow, are pressed by political unrest at home, partially caused by lower oil revenues.

In spite of paying lip service to smaller producers' concerns, Saudi Arabia has reasserted its dominance over the discordant producers' club. Its assertive role is increasingly mapping out a future for OPEC. One significant achievement at the February meeting long sought by the Saudis was a move away from production quotas to allocate output more closely in line with individual countries' capacity. However, this presents an opportunity for new disagreements. The danger of using production capacity as a basis for allocating output levels is that countries have a tendency to be overly optimistic in their assessments of their ability to produce oil. In addition, the new system will formalize Saudi Arabia's increased clout within OPEC. Arch-rival Iran and several other producers are already fighting to reverse the move and return to the quotas that were in place before the Gulf War. Tehran has called for a return to the quotas as soon as Iraq is able to reenter the export market. If the return of both Iraq and Kuwait to full production is not to plunge the oil market into crisis, other members, including Saudi Arabia, will have to agree to significant cuts. These decisions are bound to be inherently conflictual.

There are also a number of indicators of what the longer term may hold for OPEC. The Geneva meeting made clear that Saudi Arabia will demand that any agreement on overall quotas must take into account its need for a 35 percent market share and minimum of 8 million bpd. Saudi Arabia's aim at the OPEC meeting was to eradicate the last vestiges of the 1990 agreement and the quota shares, especially the kingdom's 22.45 percent share implied in the agreement. It is clear that the Saudis were trying to establish new principles to run the organization: if there are to be future production cuts, then they must be prorated for all members. The Saudis also want to get such a system in place before Iraq resumes exports and Kuwaiti production recovers to its pre-war level. It appears that the Saudis hope that no matter how low current prices sink, the relatively low prices will help the U.S. economy and, indeed, the world economy toward recovery and lead eventually to a stronger demand for oil.[35]

Time is on the Saudi side. Capacity utilization in early 1992 was running at close to 90 percent, and as output declines in the United States and in Russia, the kingdom is the only one of the world's three biggest producers that is expanding production. Saudi production capacity will probably increase to 10 million bpd by 1995 under the current Saudi Aramco development program and bolster the kingdom's clout within OPEC. At the same time, capacity enhancement programs in Abu Dhabi, Iran, and, possibly, Kuwait are far less ambitious or advanced. In several other large producers, cash concerns intensified by low oil prices are constraining the pace of development and transforming attitudes toward foreign oil companies. Algeria, Iran, and Iraq are all seeking foreign investment in upstream development, overturning a long tradition of avoiding outside advances in their need for development capital.

For most observers, the change in oil market attitudes is proving to be of far greater interest than the latest disagreement between

OPEC members over precise production levels. The market is starting to reflect a new psychology. It is now starting to focus on underlying geo-economic realities, including potentially large new production in Russia, rather than reacting to developments on the basis of fears about the security of supplies. On the basis of these underlying realities, events are not moving OPEC's way over the short term. Moreover, oil production quotas are a thing of the past. They were never strictly observed, anyway, and even if OPEC reintroduces them, quotas will be no more than a cosmetic cover to disguise the policy differences that have divided the member countries since the mid-1980s.[36]

In sum, if OPEC states have a shared interest at present, it is their common need for cash. However, hopes of securing higher prices are being undermined by the collective reluctance to consider deeper cuts in production and by new rivalries and fears within the organization unleashed by the end of the Cold War and the Gulf War. Saudi Arabia, in particular, is determined to set the tone for OPEC's future and will not trim output again, only to see others reap the rewards of higher prices while Saudi Arabia ends up paying the price in terms of its relations with Washington.

CONCLUSIONS

Before drawing conclusions concerning future developments in oil markets or the stability of OPEC and its members, one should heed the advice of Daniel Yergin:

> Recent history shows that just when calm is taken for granted, some new surprise, mixing politics, and economics, comes along and shakes all assumptions. Even now one can see the possible elements of a surprise during the next two or three years. The world is producing oil near the limits of capacity, meaning that there is little room for error.[37]

From the vantage point of autumn 1992, it is interesting to note that the preinvasion geo-economic and postinvasion geo-strategic trends outlined above still seem to be in effect. If anything, the end of the Cold War and the aftermath of the Gulf War appear to have both strengthened the economic trends[38] and sharpened regional fears and rivalries, thus postponing the time when OPEC will likely regain some control over oil prices. The Gulf War has accelerated the trend away from oil and further undermined OPEC cohesion. Germany, Japan, and, to a minor extent, the United States have increased taxes on petroleum products, which will tend to restrain demand. The growing strength of the environmental movement has spurred greater energy efficiency and the replacement of oil with abundant natural gas. The postinvasion mini-oil shock reinforced the determination of oil buyers to seek supplies from less volatile areas, that is, outside the Middle East. The pace of oil (and gas) exploration in the North Sea is at an all-time peak, and similar activities are taking place in West Africa, South America, and other parts of the Third World. Over time, joint ventures between Western oil companies and Russian producers should reverse the downward trend in that country's production that began in 1988.[39]

Overall, probably the single most important factor depressing oil prices will be the financial troubles of the major Middle Eastern oil exporting countries. The extensive loans Saudi Arabia has contracted from international and regional banks reflects the financial predicament faced by its government. Even before Iraq's invasion of Kuwait, Saudi Arabia's military budget was huge — the equivalent of about 16 percent of its GNP in 1984–88.[40] The war added enormously to military outlays. Saudi Arabia's request for billions of dollars of U.S. military equipment and its plans to expand its armed forces presage a major increase in its military outlays in the coming years. Riyadh fears that higher prices will trigger strong countervailing forces that will, in a few years, depress prices, thus repeating the boom and bust of the 1980s — thus, the Saudi policy of attempting to enhance its oil revenues not by higher prices but by exporting a larger volume of oil. Riyadh is well aware that this policy also suits its chief security partner and guarantor, the United States.[41]

Iran, with its economy shattered by the revolution and its eight-year war with Iraq, has undertaken ambitious economic and military goals. Higher oil exports are essential to generate the revenues needed to finance its national and regional aspirations. Moreover, looming on the horizon is the reentry of Kuwait and Iraq into the oil markets. Both countries have vast petroleum reserves and pressing financial needs. They are even less likely than before the war to adhere to OPEC quotas. Kuwait, in particular, is lobbying for a much-larger oil production quota.[42] Kuwait's determination will most certainly clash with Saudi Arabia's high level of production and with Iraq's eventual return to world oil markets as an exporting nation. Kuwaiti authorities claim the emirate badly needs the money to make up the losses from the war, which cost it $65 billion and cut deeply into its assets of nearly $100 billion. The Kuwaitis also state that with planned expenditures of $8–10 billion, they will raise output to 2 million bpd by the end of 1992, thus restoring output to levels prevailing just prior to Iraq's invasion of Kuwait in August 1990. Abu Dhabi, Iran, Venezuela, and Nigeria have all announced expansion of capacity, and there are prospects of sizable oil deposits in Yemen.[43]

Overall, for OPEC, the demands of regional and global geo-economic and geo-strategic events and trends will surely add to downward pressure on oil prices in the post–Cold War and post–Gulf

War era. These events and trends indicate that OPEC is in danger of losing its credibility as a crisis-management organization by failing to anticipate and handle economic and security challenges confronting the organization.

In the post–Cold War and post–Gulf War environment of the Persian Gulf, oil affairs continue to cause uncertainty. This uncertainty, aside from the fact that it stems from the sustained downward trends in oil prices, is also exacerbated by the continued competition between Iran and Saudi Arabia for the strategic domination of the Persian Gulf.

NOTES

1. John Roberts, *A War for Oil? Energy Issues and the Gulf War of 1991* (Boulder, Colo.: International Research Center for Energy and Economic Development, Occasional Papers No. 13, 1991), p. 1.
2. The following section draws heavily on Robert Looney, "World Oil Market Outlook: Implications for Stability in the Gulf States," *Middle East Review*, Winter 1989–90, pp. 30–39.
3. For an excellent overview and assessment of OPEC's attempts at coordinating policy and resolving conflicts, see M. E. Ahrari, "Conflict Management of the OPEC States," *Mediterranean Quarterly*, Summer 1991, pp. 86–109.
4. Douglas Bohi, "Evolution of the Oil Market and Energy Security Policy," *Contemporary Policy Issues*, July 1987, p. 21.
5. See, for example, Samuel A. Van Vactor and Arlon R. Tussing, "Perspective on Oil Prices," *Contemporary Policy Issues*, July 1987, pp. 1–19; Stephen P. A. Brown and Keith R. Phillips, "Oil Demand and Prices in the 1990s," *Federal Reserve Bank of Dallas Economic Review*, January 1989, pp. 1–10; Michael Olorunfemi and Maria Knoble, "OPEC's Experience in the 1980s: Shaping Its Strategies for the 1990s," *OPEC Review*, Spring 1991, pp. 1–12; Cyrus Bina, "Limits of OPEC Pricing: OPEC Profits and the Nature of Global Oil Accumulation," *OPEC Review*, Spring 1990, pp. 55–74; Robert Bacon, "Modelling the Price of Oil," *Oxford Review of Economic Policy*, Summer 1991, pp. 17–34; and Klaus Matthies, "The OPEC after Thirty Years," *Intereconomics*, September–October 1990, pp. 253–56.
6. This interpretation is at best misleading and at worst simply incorrect; see, for example, Mohammed Ahrari, *OPEC: The Falling Giant* (Lexington: University of Kentucky Press, 1986).
7. Bohi, "Evolution of the Oil Market and Energy Security Policy," pp. 23–25.
8. A view also put forth in George C. Georgiou, "Oil Market Instability and a New OPEC," *World Policy Journal*, Spring 1987, pp. 295–312; see also Arlon Tussing, "An OPEC Obituary," *Public Interest*, Winter 1983, pp. 3–21; Jahangir Amuzegar, "A World without OPEC," Washington *Quarterly*, Autumn 1982, pp. 60–70.
9. The following is based on Van Vactor and Tussing, "Perspective on Oil Prices," pp. 15–18; Walter J. Mead, "The OPEC Cartel Thesis Reexamined: Price Constraints from Oil Substitutes," *Journal of Energy and Development*, Spring 1986, pp. 239–42.
10. Following Brown and Phillips, "Oil Demand and Prices in the 1990s," pp. 4–6.

11. The Rumailah oil field is a banana-shaped oil field that lies deep below the desert in southern Iraq and northern Kuwait. With more than 90 percent of the field in Iraqi territory, the Rumailah oil field is reported to be one of the largest oil fields in the world, with estimated reserves of 30 billion barrels. Thomas C. Hayes, "Big Oilfield Is at the Heart of Iraq-Kuwait Dispute," New York *Times*, September 3, 1990, p. 11.

12. Roberts, *A War for Oil?*

13. Marry E. Morris, "Regional Dynamics of the Gulf Crisis," in *The Rand Library Collection* no. P7700 (Santa Monica, Calif.: Rand Corporation, 1991), p. 2.

14. In any event, oil prices were gradually increasing from the level in the mid-1980s. In 1986–87, benchmark West Texas International crude was $12–16 a barrel; as Iraq applied increasing pressure on Kuwait, oil prices responded. Thus, just before the invasion in mid-summer 1990, the range for crude oil had risen to $18–23 a barrel. For a pre-war analysis, see Edward L. Morse, "The Coming Oil Revolution," *Foreign Affairs*, Winter 1990–91, p. 41.

15. Thomas Allen, Clifton F. Berry, and Norman Polmar, *CNN War in the Gulf* (Atlanta: Turner, 1991), p. 29.

16. "The End of OPEC," *The Economist*, August 18, 1990, pp. 55–56.

17. Hillary Clarke, "Oil, Bypassing OPEC," *Middle East*, March 1992, pp. 30–31.

18. Leyla Boulton, "The Lure of Oil's Final Frontier," *Financial Times*, March 6, 1992, p. 15.

19. Despite proven reserves of almost 60 billion barrels, outdated technology combined with a lack of new wells and equipment is expected to drive production to less than 450 million metric tons in 1992, from 510 million in 1991. This is a 12 percent decline in just one year and drops Russia to nearly the same level as second-ranked Saudi Arabia. See Thomas Ginsburg, "Russian Oil Rush: Riches, Risks and Red Tape," San Francisco *Chronicle*, August 2, 1992, p. 4c. For data on global, regional, and national oil production reserves, imports, and exports, see American Petroleum Institute, *Basic Petroleum Data Book*, 12 (May 1992).

20. "How Saddam Is Picking up the Pieces a Year after 'Storm,'" *Jane's Defence Weekly*, February 22, 1992, p. 284.

21. "Iran Builds Its Strength," *Jane's Defence Weekly*, February 22, 1992, p. 158.

22. "Fear of Flying," *Newsweek*, February 17, 1992, p. 6.

23. "Iran Builds Its Strength."

24. *Jane's Fighting Ships, 1991–92* (Alexandria, Va.: Jane's Information Group Ltd., 1992), pp. 286–91.

25. Ibid., p. 286.

26. Douglas Waller, "Sneaking in the Scuds," *Newsweek* June 22, 1992, p. 44.

27. Martha Brill Olcott, "Central Asia's Catapult to Independence," *Foreign Affairs*, Summer 1992, pp. 108–29.

28. Peace Is Still in the Balance," *Jane's Defence Weekly*, March 28, 1992, p. 528.

29. "Picking up the Pieces," *Jane's Defence Weekly*, March 28, 1992, p. 531.

30. "OPEC: Saudi Arabia Takes Charge," *Middle East*, February 1992, pp. 24–25.

31. Ibid.

32. Ibid.

33. Peter Kemp, "Saudis Stand Firm as Oil Prices Slide," *Middle East Economic Digest*, April 3, 1992, pp. 9–10.

34. Deborah Hargreaves, "A Deal That Fails to Heal Divisions," *Financial Times*, February 18, 1992, p. 17.

35. Kemp. "Saudis Stand Firm as Oil Prices Slide."

36. "OPEC: Saudi Arabia Takes Charge," p. 25.
37. Daniel Yergin, "Less Oil Politics and More Oil Business," *International Herald Tribune*, August 5, 1991.
38. Eliyanu Kanovsky, "Don't Prop up the OPEC Cartel," *Wall Street Journal*, June 18, 1991, p. A20.
39. Boulton, "The Lure of Oil's Final Frontier," p. 15.
40. United States Arms Control and Disarmament Agency, *World Military Expenditures and Arms Transfers, 1990* (Washington, D.C.:United States Arms Control and Disarmament Agency, 1990), p. 39.
41. At least as long as prices do not fall too far (for example, to $15 per barrel).
42. Youssef M. Ibrahim, "Kuwait Seeks to Raise Oil Output," New York *Times*, April 20, 1992, p. C2.
43. Erick Watkins, "Yemen's Oil Fired Optimism," *Financial Times*, January 28, 1992, p. 27.

7

Arms Race in the Persian Gulf: The Post–Cold War Dynamics

M. E. Ahrari

Historically speaking, conflicts between and among nations, when blown out of proportion, led to wars. A region where conflicts are ample is also characterized by violent flareups and wars. The recurrence of armed clashes and wars prompts arms buildups and arms races. The Middle East, in general, has all the preceding characteristics; consequently, it has, at times, led all other regions of the world in an arms race, and at others, it has sustained a dubious distinction of remaining a close second after Europe.

Arms races in different areas of the world are driven by criteria that are idiosyncratic of a region. There are international variables that also affect their dynamics. This is especially true of the Persian Gulf. A realistic assessment of the nature of the arms race in the Persian Gulf can be made only by couching it in the general dynamics of the Middle Eastern arms race.

The first striking characteristic of the politics of this region is a pervasive feeling of insecurity — real or imagined — experienced by the authoritarian Arab regime and by Israel.[1] All Arab governments preside over authoritarian regimes of one sort or another. Under such rule, according to Adeed Dawisha, legitimacy flows from the ruler toward the political system, but in Western democracy, rulers draw legitimacy from the political system.[2] This point is quite significant in explaining the feeling of insecurity among rulers in the authoritarian systems. In a democracy, about the only challenge to those who exercise power stems from the disenchantment of the people — through the ballot box. When a ruler is perceived as incompetent, that person is ousted as a result of elections and can move on to a "life after the public service." On the contrary, because authoritarian regimes provide virtually no avenues for the expression of political dissent, the opposing groups must be dealt with decisively and often ruthlessly, sustaining a credible deterrence against domestic dissent.

For Israel, this feeling of insecurity stems from the fact that since its creation, that state has been technically at war with all its neighbors except Egypt. Thus, sustaining a military edge, both qualitatively and quantitatively, has become a sine qua non of the Israeli security policy.

The second reason for an arms race appears to be the low level of tolerance stemming from the conflicting foreign policy objectives of various countries. Of course, this reason is not idiosyncratic to those regions alone. Nation-states all over the world utilize this as a rationale for arming themselves. Because the politics of the Middle East has such a low tolerance for conflicting foreign policy objectives, more often than not, threats to these objectives become crucial reasons not only for the arms race but also for violent clashes.

The third reason for the continued escalated pace of the arms race is the "praetorian" nature of the armed forces in the Arab Middle East and the Persian Gulf. The military in almost all countries of those regions plays a two-pronged role of a praetorian guard as well as an institutional interest group. Because it is expected to protect the regime of rulers with shaky (or, at best, questionable) legitimacy, as a quid pro quo, it is expected to be appeased through the regular purchases of modern armaments.

In the 1950s, a number of Middle Eastern states were winning independence from the colonial powers — largely from Great Britain but also from France. Their independence found a forceful expression in the idea of Arab nationalism. It so happened that the republican states found nationalism more suitable to their aspirations for unifying the Arab masses that were living in countries whose borders, as they perceived it, were artificially drawn by their former colonial rulers. For the monarchies, however, these borders were almost sacred symbols of sovereignty. Such differences between the republican and monarchical states only intensified with the passage of time. The pan-Arabic nature of Arab nationalism also became a powerful source of friction between the two camps.

When the Cold War entered the Middle East, both superpowers found a receptive audience in different Arab camps. The success of the North Atlantic Treaty Organization (NATO) as an alliance to deter Soviet expansionism in Europe persuaded the United States that it should be emulated in the Middle East as well as in other regions of the world. Gamal Abdel Nasser, president of Egypt, was not at all interested in joining the U.S. camp, especially because he was one of the chief protagonists of the nonaligned movement of the 1950s. The seeds of dissension and mistrust were, thus, sown between the United States and the Arab republican camp, and the latter was to drift closer to the Soviet Union in the ensuing years. The monarchical camp, although it did not join the U.S. alliance arrangement en masse, was quite receptive to the Washington (and to the overall Western) perspective related to the Cold War.

The creation of Israel in 1948 emerged as one of the major sources of conflict in the Middle East. Because Great Britain, as the occupying power of Palestine, played a crucial role in the establishment of the Jewish state, it also became a chief target of Arab discontentment in the region. Furthermore, the Arab states did not forget the enthusiastic support that was provided by the United States, even during the presidency of Woodrow Wilson, to the notion of a Jewish homeland in Palestine. Of course, by the time Israel was created, the United States was emerging as the only superpower and an heir to the British legacy of domination in the Middle East.

In the early- to mid-1950s, it was becoming apparent that the United States was going to replace Great Britain as a dominant power in the Middle East. The USSR, which was coming out of a phase of focused attention on eastern Europe during the Stalinist era, was also becoming involved in this region. The U.S.–Soviet increased involvement was the beginning of the jelling of the Cold War in the Middle East. As a dominant power, the United States remained a firm political supporter, although not yet a military supplier, of Israel, a state whose destruction had already become one of the major political objectives of Arab nationalism. As can be seen from the preceding, there were too many conflicts brewing in the Middle East in the 1950s — inter-Arab, Arab-Israeli, and Arab-Western — and consequently, there were ample reasons for military competition and attendant arms race.

The Arab-Israeli War of 1948 and the combined attack by Great Britain, France, and Israel on Egypt in 1956 had already provided full justification for military preparedness on the part of Egypt. Because the destruction of Israel emerged as an "Arab" objective, this conflict also became a basis for military preparedness for other Arab states such as Syria, Jordan, and Iraq. Similarly, the much-touted Arab resolve to destroy Israel convinced the latter, once and for all, that the ultimate guaranty for its survival was its decisive military superiority. The quantitative disadvantage of the Jewish state of its small population base was to be compensated by institutionalizing the qualitative edge over its Arab adversaries.

The political conflict between the Nasserite and monarchist forces of the 1950s was the chief reason fueling the need for the arms buildup in the Persian Gulf. The main thrust of this conflict was in the fertile crescent, specifically in Iraq and Jordan; however, after the elimination of the Hashemite dynasty from Iraq in 1958, its scope expanded to the Arabian Peninsula. The Yemeni civil war of 1962 was an occasion for the unsheathing of the fury of this conflict in that area. It also became a classic example of the intermingling of the traditional Saudi security-related fears, Nasser's strategic ambitions regarding the Arabian Peninsula, and the Cold War–related involvement of both superpowers in the Middle East, in general.[3] This war, which lasted seven years, became one more reason for the heightened military expenditures by Egypt. Saudi Arabia also utilized this occasion to build its own military muscle, a development that was in harmony with its ambitions to dominate the Arabian Peninsula. The significance of the arms race in the 1960s for almost all the major Middle Eastern actors is underscored by the fact that of the 13 countries that were reported to have spent more than 10 percent of their GNP on military expenditures between 1963 and 1973, 10 were from the Middle East; of these, the prominent nations were Egypt, Israel, Saudi Arabia, Iran, Iraq, and Syria.[4]

The Arab-Israeli War of 1967 was a watershed event from the perspective of the arms race in the Middle East. The humiliating defeat of Arab forces militarized the region to an unprecedented dimension. The "front-line" Arab states wanted to become militarily strong to avenge their crushing defeat and to regain the substantial amount of territory they lost in this war. The other Arab states also wanted to become militarily powerful in order to make their own contribution to the liberation of their Palestinian brethren (or so they proclaimed).[5] Figures on military expenditures in Table 7.1 underscore the escalated pace of militarization of a number of Middle Eastern states (especially examine the column labelled "MILEX/GNP [%]").

The fueling of the arms race in the Persian Gulf from 1970 on had a lot to do with the complementarity between the Iranian strategic ambitions and the U.S. strategic need to find a regional hegemon. The British withdrawal from the Persian Gulf created a power vacuum. The United States, the natural heir to fill this gap, was embroiled in a war in Vietnam that had become highly unpopular at home. A natural spillover effect of this phenomenon was the categorical rejection of the U.S. people of any further involvement in the potential trouble spots in Asia, and the Persian Gulf certainly stood out as one such spot. However, as a superpower, the United States could not afford to allow this power vacuum to remain, because its natural beneficiary, as Washington envisioned it, was the Soviet Union. The Nixon administration, in its pursuit of a "second-best" option, decided to rely on regional hegemonies. Iran under the shah was ideally suited for this role. In the 1970s, the abundance of petrodollars became the chief source to realize the shah's hegemonic ambitions in the region. Because his ambitions paralleled the U.S. need for a reliable regional gendarme, it appeared that nothing could go wrong in the pursuit of this policy from the perspectives of Tehran

TABLE 7.1
Military Expenditures (MILEX) in Constant Dollars and as Percentage of GNP: Selected Middle Eastern Countries

Country	Year	Constant Dollars (millions)	MILEX GNP (%)
Egypt	1963	483.72	8.61
	1964	511.77	8.56
	1965	586.73	9.20
	1966	457.55	7.13
	1967	422.00	6.67
	1968	573.60	8.94
	1969	655.66	9.59
	1970	933.14	12.96
	1971	1,016.86	13.70
	1972	1,136.15	14.62
	1973	N.A.[a]	15.06
Iran	1963	268.82	4.16
	1964	314.98	4.47
	1965	429.38	5.48
	1966	483.38	5.58
	1967	659.29	6.85
	1968	791.95	7.44
	1969	956.30	8.26
	1970	1,051.04	8.21
	1971	1,347.12	9.41
	1972	1,704.69	10.61
	1973	2,158.57	11.45
Iraq	1963	217.59	10.22
	1964	295.71	12.49
	1965	304.16	11.36
	1966	295.21	10.46
	1967	279.03	10.25
	1968	382.38	12.34
	1969	476.97	14.76
	1970	452.54	13.60
	1971	489.50	13.44
	1972	474.31	12.77
	1973	N.A.	N.A.
Israel	1963	285.59	8.58
	1964	362.12	9.91
	1965	357.30	8.96
	1966	429.01	10.64
	1967	672.12	16.32
	1968	837.85	17.70
	1969	1,135.94	21.35
	1970	1,484.03	25.92
	1971	1,491.25	23.75
	1972	1,490.95	21.62
	1973	3,255.72	45.41

Table 7.1, continued

Country	Year	Constant Dollars (millions)	MILEX GNP (%)
Saudi Arabia	1963	145.87	7.48
	1964	154.11	7.08
	1965	139.35	5.70
	1966	168.42	6.29
	1967	336.34	11.33
	1968	205.27	6.50
	1969	233.69	6.88
	1970	220.91	6.02
	1971	259.54	6.43
	1972	650.97	14.67
	1973	N.A.	N.A.
Syria	1963	101.37	8.71
	1964	92.43	7.28
	1965	91.43	7.01
	1966	88.67	6.96
	1967	94.74	7.07
	1968	154.71	11.02
	1969	158.29	9.73
	1970	194.79	11.77
	1971	171.28	9.10
	1972	249.31	12.25
	1973	N.A.	N.A.

[a]N.A. = not available

Source: United States Arms Control and Disarmament Agency, *World Military Expenditures and Arms Trade 1963–1973* (Washington, D.C.: United States Arms Control and Disarmament Agency, 1974).

and Washington. Table 7.2 provides an overview of the spiralling nature of Iranian military expenditures. The last column of this table (MILEX/GNP [%]) underscores the fact that between 1967 and 1970 (the year of the enunciation of the Nixon Doctrine), the percentage of the Iranian military expenditure as part of its GNP went up by 2 percent, not a significant increase. However, the same figures show an increase of more than 5 percent between 1970 and 1975. One should also keep in mind that this was also the time when the intermittent and unrealistic price escalations introduced by the Organization of Petroleum Exporting Countries (OPEC) states were causing considerable turbulences in the international economy.[6] The Saudi military expenditure is another item of interest in this table. Looking at the MILEX/GNP (%) column of the same table for Saudi Arabia, the percentage increase between 1970 (6.27 percent) and 1975 (17.4 percent) is considerably larger than that of Iran. Taken together, the military expenditures of Iran and Saudi Arabia

TABLE 7.2
Military Expenditures (MILEX), GNP, and Percentages of MILEX in Relation to GNP: Iran and Saudi Arabia

Country	Year	MILEX (Constant Dollars [millions])	GNP (Constant Dollars [millions])	MILEX GNP (%)
Iran	1966	662	18,300	5.58
	1967	905	20,400	6.85
	1968	1,090	22,500	7.44
	1969	1,320	24,500	8.26
	1970	1,470	27,300	8.21
	1971	4,524	54,143	8.40
	1972	5,365	62,870	8.50
	1973	6,103	73,545	8.30
	1974	9,447	79,965	11.80
	1975	11,828	82,483	14.30
	1976	12,377	91,657	13.50
	1977	10,747	92,461	11.60
	1978	12,320	84,131	14.60
	1979	N.A.[a]	73,203	N.A.
	1980	N.A.	65,875	N.A.
Saudi Arabia	1966	228	9,720	6.29
	1967	459	10,800	11.40
	1968	286	11,700	6.39
	1969	332	12,600	6.84
	1970	326	13,600	6.27
	1971	981	9,739	10.10
	1972	1,301	11,767	11.10
	1973	1,845	13,943	13.20
	1974	3,792	34,860	10.90
	1975	8,448	48,449	17.40
	1976	11,623	60,801	19.10
	1977	11,053	72,018	15.30
	1978	11,678	73,579	15.90
	1979	13,831	76,380	18.10
	1980	15,176	105,744	14.40

[a]N.A. = not available

Source: United States Arms Control and Disarmament Agency, *World Military Expenditures and Arms Trade 1963–1973* (Washington, D.C.: United States Arms Control and Disarmament Agency); United States Arms Control and Disarmament Agency, *World Military Expenditures and Arms Transfers 1971–1980* (Washington, D.C.: United States Arms Control and Disarmament Agency).

underscore the so-called twin-pillars policy pursued by the Nixon administration in the Persian Gulf.[7] It should be noted, however, that a significant slant of this policy remained in favor of Iran until the fall of the shah in 1978.

The end of the 1970s will go down in the history of the arms race in the Persian Gulf as the beginning of an unprecedented scale of military buildup. The triggering events were the Iranian revolution of 1978–79 that replaced a pro-Western monarchy with the staunchly anti-U.S. regime of Ayatollah Rouhollah Khomeini. The second crucial development was the Soviet invasion of Afghanistan in December 1979. As if the loss of a friendly regime were not bad enough from the U.S. perspective, its replacement not only was devoted to the strengthening of an Islamic regime in Iran but also soon made obvious its intentions of exporting this revolution to neighboring states, almost all of which were monarchies. There were two additional troublesome variables related to the Islamic revolution. First was the fact that the change of regime through the Islamic revolutionary turmoil was an unprecedented one in the post–World War II nation-state system. Therefore, neither the Western nations nor their regional counterparts in the Gulf (nor the Soviet Union, for that matter) knew how to come to grips with the developments in Iran. Second, the Islamic internationalism that was so heavily emphasized by the Khomeini regime during the months and years after its establishment was viewed with much alarm by the monar-chies. This Islamic internationalism was perceived as a threat to regional stability by Peninsular states in the mold of Arab nationalism of the 1950s and the 1960s. However, this time, the superpower whose strategic dominance was clearly at stake — the United States — appeared intent on at least sustaining the political status quo on the Arabian Peninsula. This resolve was further strengthened by an equally unprecedented Soviet military takeover of a non-Communist (and a Muslim) state. U.S. strategic thinking had to face these challenges. The most obvious and immediate response to these threats, which were perceived as being radical in nature and causing potentially irreversible damage to the U.S. national security interests, had to be of a military nature.

To make matters worse, the Iran-Iraq War started in September 1980. Even though this event diverted the attention of the Khomeini regime from focusing on exporting the Islamic revolution (assuming that it was, indeed, serious on this issue), the Peninsular states were in no mood to remain passive. Their response to the Iranian threat came in February 1981 in the form of the creation of the Gulf Cooperation Council (GCC). Economic integration and collective security were cited as its raison d'être; however, the charged environment of that time left no doubt about the fact that the security-related threats stemming from the Islamic revolution served as a catalyst for its creation. These issues were also to capture much of the attention and resources of the top decision makers of the GCC in the coming years.

As is obvious from the preceding, the politically charged environment of the Persian Gulf in the 1980s was most suitable for spiralling the arms race. The Iranian revolution was only one of the most significant reasons underlying it. The Soviet Union's continued occupation of Afghanistan refreshed the memory of brutal incorporation of the Central Asian Muslim states into the Russian and Soviet empires in the past. Even though it was quite apparent that any amount of militarization of the Persian Gulf could have created no more than a "tripwire" effect for potential Soviet aggression, the Peninsular monarchies could not have afforded to remain passive. Moreover, for these states, any potential aggressive moves on the part of Tehran appeared more feasible than a potential Soviet expansionism stemming from its occupation of Afghanistan, especially in the second half of the 1980s, when the Iran-Iraq War was escalating. The "carrot and stick" policy of these sheikhdoms, whereby they were urging Iran to seek a political solution while at the same time siding with Iraq in the military conflict, was not working. The Kuwaiti invitation to both superpowers to escort or reflag its ships was a deft move to deter Iran. Even though both superpowers responded, it was the U.S. naval presence and its famous "tilt" toward Baghdad during that time that played a crucial role in turning the tide against Iran. Ultimately, this policy persuaded Khomeini to accept the UN-sponsored cease-fire, a decision that was characterized by him as "more deadly than taking poison."

There are some additional criteria for understanding the arms race in the Persian Gulf and the Middle East. One such variable is the heavy reliance of ruling groups on worst-case scenarios of military threats. Such scenarios necessitate a predilection for overinsurance in the form of over-arming oneself. For instance, a sustained Israeli preference for a qualitative edge over Arab forces requires it to focus its attention on potential multifrontal and all-out attacks by the combined Arab forces; this characteristic has become the chief reason for inordinate Israeli expenditure on arms buildup. Similarly, Hafez Assad's near-obsession of gaining strategic parity with Israel has been the chief reason for an equally large Syrian military expenditure.[8] It should be noted, however, that this particular reason for military buildup is universal in its application.

Two additional reasons promoting the arms race in the Middle East are the availability of petrodollars to absorb the exorbitant costs for sophisticated weaponry and the strategic value attached by both superpowers to the region during the Cold War years. Of course, the petrodollar variable is more applicable to the Persian Gulf region, but the same actors also bankrolled the Egyptian and Syrian arms buildups, especially since the Arab-Israeli War of 1973.[9] Funds provided by the Gulf states also played a crucial role in the emergence of Iraq as a major military power before the Gulf War of 1991. The strategic significance of the Middle East also remains a relevant and a very significant variable even after the conclusion of the Cold War.

In fact, this significance has been one of the primary causes underlying the long-standing U.S. commitment to Israel. The strategic value of the Gulf states that was related to oil was responsible for the U.S. decision to go to war against Iraq in 1991.

To the preceding, regional ambitions of a ruler should be added as one of the crucial reasons underlying the continued arms race in the Middle East. Shah Mohammed Reza Pahlavi of Iran was the most obvious example of such an ambition. Saddam Hussein's military buildup during the Iran-Iraq War might have been one of the chief motivating factors underlying his decision to militarily occupy Kuwait in August 1991 (another example). Assad's continued presence in Lebanon may also be seen as a direct outcome of Syria's hegemonic ambition on that troubled country.

DIMENSIONS OF ARMS RACE: CONVENTIONAL WEAPONS, MISSILE PROLIFERATION, AND NUCLEAR, CHEMICAL, AND BIOLOGICAL WEAPONS

Like most analyses that subsume the discussion of the Persian Gulf region under the general rubric of the Middle East, the thrust of analysis in this section will follow the same line. The Middle East as a region remained the largest market for arms. Between 1983 and 1986, it accounted for more than 61 percent of the total value of all Third World arms transfer agreement. This number slightly declined to 55.7 percent during 1987–90.[10] Of the total U.S. arms transfer to Third World countries, 64.8 percent went to the Middle East between 1983 and 1986. For the years 1986–90, this share was 76.3 percent, as presented in Table 7.3. This table also makes it obvious that although the People's Republic of China (PRC) gained most profits through its arms sales to the Middle East between 1983 and 1986, after the cessation of the Iran-Iraq War (which lasted from 1980 to 1988), the U.S. share of arms agreements went up (from 64.8 percent during 1983–86 to 76.3 percent during 1987–90). By the same token, almost all major industrial arms suppliers maintained a high level of activity related to arms sales in the Middle East.

Not only was the Iran-Iraq War extremely costly in terms of damages absorbed by both belligerents to their oil and other infrastructures, but also it was responsible for skyrocketing the arms buildup on the part of both states.[11] One of the arms suppliers whose role became extremely significant in the future dynamics of the arms race in the Middle East and the Persian Gulf was the emergence of the PRC during this war. Although the share of arms transfers of the PRC between 1987 and 1990 remained 14 percent (Figure 7.1), this amount is considerably larger when one examines percentages of arms deliveries to Iran and Iraq during 1983–90, which was 14 percent (Figure 7.2). (Also see Appendix A and Appendix B; these

TABLE 7.3
Percentage of Each Supplier's Agreement Value in the Middle East, 1983-90

Suppliers	1983-86	1987-90
United States	64.80	76.30
Soviet Union	46.23	28.35
France	82.60	83.24
United Kingdom	86.25	73.62
China	89.61	66.36
Germany	29.80	52.64
Italy	67.38	22.22
All Other European	73.23	81.95
All Others	60.31	60.97
Major West European[a]	78.17	74.99
Total	61.06	55.66

[a]Major West European category includes France, United Kingdom, Germany, and Italy.

Source: Richard F. Grimmett, *Conventional Arms Transfer to the Third World, 1983-1990*, Congressional Research Service, August 2, 1991, p. CRS 20.

FIGURE 7.1
Arms Transfer Agreements, 1984-90, with the Near East
(Supplier Percentage)

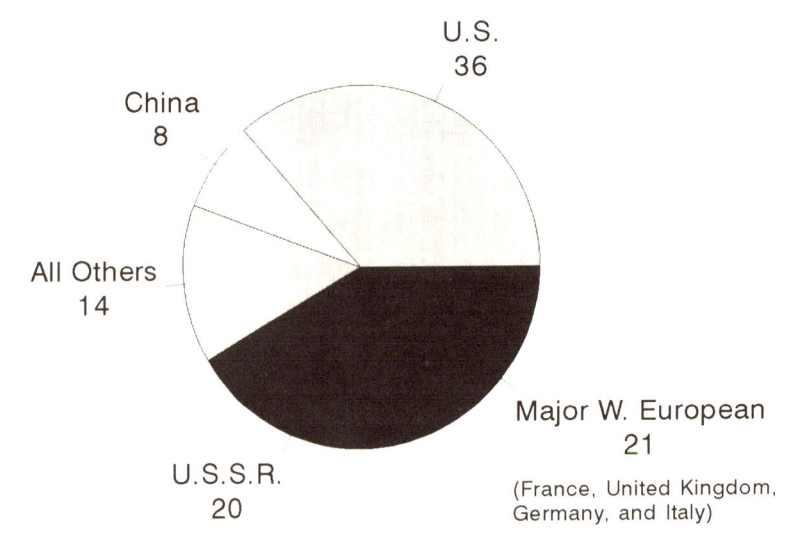

- U.S. 36
- China 8
- All Others 14
- U.S.S.R. 20
- Major W. European 21 (France, United Kingdom, Germany, and Italy)

Source: Richard F. Grimmett, *Conventional Arms Transfer to the Third World, 1983-1990*, Congressional Research Service, August 2, 1991, p. CRS 20.

FIGURE 7.2
Arms Deliveries to Iran and Iraq Collectively, 1983–90
(Supplier Percentage)

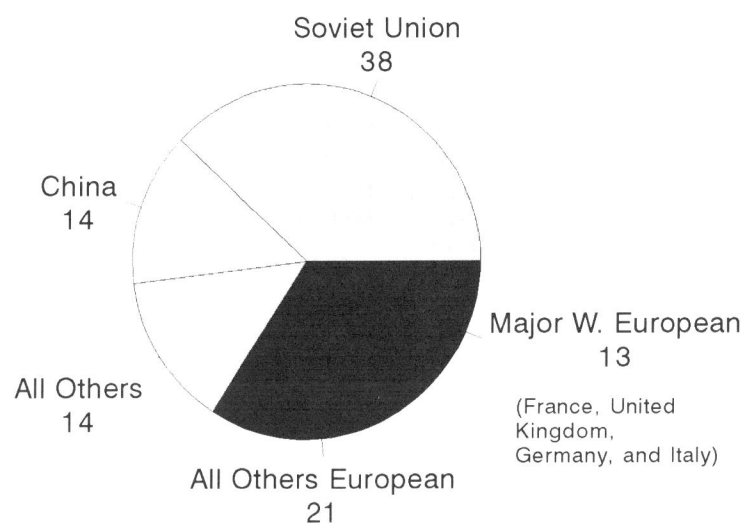

- Soviet Union: 38
- China: 14
- All Others: 14
- All Others European: 21
- Major W. European: 13 (France, United Kingdom, Germany, and Italy)

Source: Richard F. Grimmett, *Conventional Arms Transfer to the Third World, 1983–1990*, Congressional Research Service, August 2, 1991, p. CRS 20.

tables also provide an overview of the extent of involvement of major arms suppliers with Iraq and Iran between 1983 and 1990).

All major conflicts in the Middle East led to a higher level of militarization of significant regional states. The Iran-Iraq War was no exception to this rule. One disturbing offshoot of this war was an increase in domestic production of arms on the part of Iran. According to official estimates reported by the Stockholm International Peace Research Institute (SIPRI), Iran produced 70–80 percent of all its ammunition needs. The same source also notes that Iran "is self-sufficient in bullets and mortar shells; produces anti-tank missiles and is on its way to manufacturing sophisticated missile technology in the form of surface-to-air missiles (SAMs) and scud surface-to-surface missiles (SSMs)."[12]

Four significant issues of the Middle Eastern arms race will be discussed in the remainder of this chapter: ballistic missile proliferation, development of the nuclear option, and acquisition of chemical and of biological weapons.

BALLISTIC MISSILE PROLIFERATION

There are a number of variables related to missile proliferation that have provided an urgency to control it, especially from the perspective of the United States and other great powers. First, the purchase of missiles by a country that is not capable of producing them is an initial step toward its inevitable acquisition of indigenous know-how. Such a capability also enables the countries that have acquired missile technology to take independent military actions against their adversaries during conflict. Second, because the possession of missiles can be very effective in a situation of preemption, it has been argued that missile proliferation also increases instability in time of crisis and, thus, the risk of war because of the need to strike preemptively to eliminate a capability that, if used first by the other side, may result in your own annihilation. Third, the proximity of conflicting states in the Middle East makes these missiles even deadlier in terms of damage potential and kill ratio.[13] One study notes that the 190 modified Scud missiles that were fired by Iraq on Iranian cities between February and May 1988 caused approximately 2,000 fatalities (roughly ten deaths per missile), but 4,200 missiles launched by Germany against Britain and Belgium during World War II resulted in 11,000 casualties (3 deaths per missile).[14] Fourth, nations acquiring missiles also become less vulnerable to political maneuverings of great powers during a war-like situation. Moreover, if the proliferation remained unchecked, the armed forces of great powers are also likely to be vulnerable to attacks in different regions of the world. Fifth, because the acquisition of ballistic missiles also enhances the potential for reaching neighbors' population targets with considerable ease, countries like Israel would be more tempted to rely on their nuclear capability in order to escalate the level of deterrence vis-à-vis its Arab enemies. Sixth, it is worth noting that missile proliferation per se is not viewed as a source of disaster — rather, the fact that these missiles could be used for the delivery of chemical or even nuclear weapons. Almost all nations of the Middle East have chemical weapon capabilities at different stages of development. Moreover, Israel is known to possess nuclear weapons, and Iraq was at an advanced stage of development toward acquiring nuclear weapons before Operation Desert Storm. A number of Arab states and Iran are also known to be making progress in their possession of nuclear sophistication. (Table 7.4 contains an overview of the chemical, biological, and nuclear capabilities of a number of Middle Eastern countries.) It has also been assumed that it is only a matter of time before the chemical and nuclear know-how will be widely developed and integrated in the military arsenal of a great number of nation-states in the Middle East. When combined with nuclear or even

TABLE 7.4
Ballistic Missile, Chemical/Biological, and Nuclear Capabilities in Selected Middle Eastern Countries

Country	Ballistic Missiles	Chemical/Biological Weapons	Nuclear Weapons
Afghanistan	Yes	—	—
Algeria	Yes	Likely (cws)[a]	—
Egypt	Yes	Likely (cws)	—
Iran	Yes	Likely (cws)	Possible
Iraq[b]	Yes	Yes (cws)	Possible
		Possible (bws)[a]	—
Israel	Yes	Likely (cws)	Yes
Kuwait	Yes	—	—
Libya	Yes	Likely (cws)	Possible
Saudi Arabia	Yes	Possible (cws)	—
Syria	Yes	Likely (cws & bws)	—
Yemen	Yes	—	—

[a] cws = chemical weapons; bws = biological weapons.
[b] In the aftermath of the Gulf War of 1991, Iraq's missile capability was substantially destroyed. There have been suggestions, however, that Iraq still possesses a number of Scud missiles. Regardless of whether this is true, it is only a matter of time before Iraq starts rebuilding its missile capabilities, which have been reported to have been quite developed before this war.

Source: Extracted from Steve Fetter, "Ballistic Missiles and Weapons of Mass Destruction: What Is the Threat? What Should Be Done?" *International Security* 16 (Summer 1991).

chemical capabilities, possession of ballistic missiles tends to tremendously enhance the military might of a country.[15] Finally, and perhaps most importantly, once they are deployed, there is no effective defense against ballistic missiles.[16] Consequently, a country like Israel, whose existence has not been accepted by all the Arab states, not only remains sensitive to the escalating pace of missile proliferation among Arab states but also uses this reality to enhance its own reliance on its nuclear strike capability.

Because the proliferation of missiles throughout the Third World and, especially, in the Middle East cannot be stopped, a number of industrialized countries under U.S. leadership decided to slow down the pace, as the second best option.[17] This option, known as the "Missile Technology Control Regime" (MTCR), emerged in the form of an agreement among seven industrialized countries in 1987. Its original participants were the United States, the United Kingdom, Canada, France, Japan, Germany, and Italy. Even though the former Soviet Union agreed to cooperate with the original signatories and the PRC eventually expressed its willingness to abide by it, the MTCR became a lightning rod of numerous controversies.

CHEMICAL, BIOLOGICAL, AND NUCLEAR WEAPONS

The use of chemical weapons is not a new phenomenon in the history of warfare.[18] First use of these weapons in modern warfare took place during World War I, near Ypres, Belgium. Italy used mustard gas against the Ethiopian forces during 1935-36, Japan against Chinese military and civilians in 1939-44, and Egypt in Yemen during 1963-67. The United States admitted using riot control agents and herbicides (but not lethal chemical and biological weapons) in Vietnam.[19] More recently, Vietnam reportedly used chemical weapons in Laos and Cambodia. Ethiopia was suspected of using these weapons against the Eritrean rebels between 1980 and 1983, and the Soviet Union was accused of using chemical weapons, experimental weapons, and biological toxins against the Mujahedin in Afghanistan between 1980 and 1984.[20]

Most recently, however, the use of these weapons by Iraq against Iran and the Kurds in Halabjah, along with the growing missiles capabilities of that country, brought the dangers emanating from the use of such weapons to a new height (Table 7.4). What is even more significant in an era when the weapons of mass destruction are proliferating at an alarming speed is that Iraq had set a precedent no other Middle Eastern state could afford to ignore.

> It was Iraq that showed that creating an effective capability to wage chemical warfare cannot be an improvised side show, but must reflect a major national effort. It was also Iraq that showed that a combination of the actual effects of chemical warfare and fear of the weapon could have a catastrophic impact on an enemy, and that chemical warfare would be used against civilian targets.[21]

It is difficult to identify the countries who possess chemical weapons. Most government officials find it easier to address this issue in terms of number of chemical weapon-possessing states rather than naming them. According to one study, there is also a problem of lack of precision when it comes to defining a chemical weapon state.[22] The chief reason is the secrecy that is exercised by almost all states of the Third World on this issue. The possession of chemical weapon technology, the amount of sophistication acquired on this matter, and the status of indigenous knowledge are handled as an integral part of psychological warfare by Third World states vis-à-vis their neighbors and adversaries. For the Middle East, according to one study, Iraq was the only "known" chemical weapon state, that is, a state that either admitted to possessing such weapons or was definitely confirmed to have used them; "probable" chemical weapon states of this area are Israel, Egypt, Iran, Libya, and Syria.[23]

The chief attraction of chemical weapons for the Third World countries is that their "production is relatively inexpensive and requires little technological sophistication." From a strategic perspective, chemical weapons serve as a "force multiplier to offset the more powerful conventional forces of a rival." This is the logic or rationale (if, indeed, it could be characterized as such) underlying the quest for chemical weapons by a number of Arab states against Israel.[24] Similarly, Iraq also used it against Iran in order to repel the "human wave" attack during the Iran-Iraq War. The Middle Eastern states have also sought chemical weapons because their neighbors have reportedly acquired them. Iraqi acquisition was matched by Iran and, possibly, by Saudi Arabia. Israel reportedly possesses these weapons for the same reason, even though it also has nuclear weapons in its repertoire of weaponry.

As previously noted, the proliferation of chemical weapons in conjunction with the spread of ballistic missiles raises the destructive capabilities of all nations in the Middle East to an alarming level. The linkage of the two technologies to the strategic issues of the Middle East is quite obvious. The Arab states have been quite categorical on the issue of linkage, especially as it relates to the reduction of the threat of chemical weapons. An Arab spokesman stated, "any progress on banning chemical weapons is tied to the conclusion of a parallel ban on nuclear weapons."[25]

It is quite apparent that the Arab states are using the chemical weapons as a deterrent against an Israeli preemptive attack on their military facilities: chemical, biological, or nuclear. This linkage cannot be accepted as a "fact" without elaborating on its spurious nature, however. Chemical weapons have been utilized by Arab states against each other in the past (namely, by Egypt during the Yemeni civil war), by both Iraq and Iran against each other, and by Iraq against its Kurdish population. In this sense, these weapons have emerged as an added wrinkle to the already complicated issue of the arms race in those regions. By insisting on the above-mentioned linkage, the Arab states appear to be distracting world attention from the fact that in the Middle Eastern conflicts, the use of chemical weapons has become a routine tactic. Any potential Arab use of chemical weapons against Israel may not be very effective, because the Israelis are considerably more well-prepared than are the Iranians. Moreover, given the overall superiority of Israel in various modes of warfare, there is little doubt that they would sustain an upper hand over their Arab adversary by retaliating in kind in a potential war in which chemical weapons were freely used. If all else fails, Israel also keeps the notion of preemption alive, knowing full well that any such action will also result in a substantial loss of life within its own borders, primarily as a result of a chemical fallout.

Biological weapons as a military option have not yet achieved the level of seriousness as the proliferation of chemical weapons and ballistic missiles. They are regarded as much more dangerous than the chemical weapons because "their dispersal mechanisms are difficult to manage; a change of wind can make them as lethal to the attacker as they are to the defender"; in addition, they are more suited for mass destruction than as "precise military instruments."[26]

On the issue of biological weapons, one is struck by the abundance of speculations and unconfirmed journalistic reports on the development of these weapons by Iraq and Iran. Even one frequently cited study on the Iraqi chemical and biological capabilities relies heavily on journalistic sources; in conclusion, the author of this study notes:

> It must be concluded that none of the facilities here is known to be involved in the production of biological weapons. Indeed, it is possible that all are intended for legitimate, peaceful uses. However, even if not used to produce biological agents, these facilities do provide Iraq with the infrastructure needed to support a program to make infectious viruses and bacteria or to produce toxins.[27]

After the Gulf War of 1991, weapon capabilities developed by Iraq became history. This is not to say, however, that Iraq, with or without Saddam, would not be able to redevelop these capabilities in the long run. What is important to note here is that the present state of low level of knowledge regarding the biological weapons in Iraq (and in other states of the Middle East) might turn out to be the greatest obstacle in the way of their development as a major source of mass destruction. However, given the fast pace of proliferation of knowledge of all weapons of mass destruction, it may not be too long before one or more of these states overcome even this obstacle.

Nuclear proliferation in the Persian Gulf and the Middle East is one of the most vexing issues of the 1990s. A factor favoring nations that wish to retard the accelerated pace of proliferation is the fact that the Third World countries that are so actively seeking it find it most problematic "to acquire *all* the materials and technologies involved, and to manage the complex task of integrating them into an effective weapons systems development effort."[28] Iraq was a country that caused a lot of consternation about its prospects of acquiring the nuclear know-how, especially following the Iran-Iraq War and prior to the Gulf War of 1991. Iraqi attempts to become a nuclear power, like those of Israel, were shrouded in secrecy.[29] However, unlike Israel, which acquired nuclear technology during the 1950s and the 1960s, Iraq faced an enormous amount of export controls in the 1970s and the 1980s. These restrictions notwithstanding, that country did make noticeable progress toward the manufacture of nuclear weapons. Whatever technological knowledge it might have lacked involving the gas centrifuge enrichment program or calutron, there is no doubt that even under the prevailing regime of restrictions, Baghdad would have succeeded in overcoming the odds against mastering these issues and would have emerged as a nuclear power except for the Gulf War of 1991.[30]

Iran is also reported to have continued its progress toward the acquisition of nuclear technology at a very modest pace. Like Iraq, it is operating under a slew of international restrictions and constraints governing the transfer of technology; however, like Iraq, it is likely to continue to acquire the nuclear know-how on a piecemeal basis. Syria and Algeria also are emerging states that are likely to acquire substantial nuclear knowledge and wherewithal within the near future.[31]

The reality of the 1990s is that the proliferation of nuclear knowledge is not limited to the Western industrial states that are determined to manage, if not control, it. There is the PRC, which operates under different rules and has been more than willing to share its nuclear know-how with the states that are willing to pay (Iran, Syria, and Algeria) or states whose acquisition of nuclear technology has paralleled the strategic interests of the PRC (Pakistan).[32] Then, there is India, which has historically shown its contempt for what it perceives to be a long-standing practice of double standards and discrimination on the part of the Western industrial states (especially the United States) regarding the proliferation of nuclear and missile technologies. Consequently, it refused to be a party to the Nuclear Proliferation Treaty or to the MTCR. New Delhi has expressed an interest in exporting nuclear technology to a number of Third World countries; a noteworthy example of this policy was India's decision to sell a nuclear research reactor to Iran, and it has also signed a nuclear cooperation agreement with Syria.[33] Even though Syria is not known to possess nuclear facilities of any significance, the continued involvement of the PRC and India in the development of Syrian nuclear know-how seems bound to enhance its level of nuclear technology. France has also cooperated with Syria in the nuclear field.

THE POST-COLD WAR DYNAMICS OF THE ARMS RACE

The Persian Gulf, more so than the wider Middle East, is a region where the end of the Cold War did not appear to have brought about any appreciable lessening in interstate conflicts and arms races. This is an area that has experienced two major wars in the 1980s and in 1991. The dismantlement of Saddam's military power temporarily removed Iraq from behaving as a regional hegemony, but the internal politics of Iraq appear to be quite turbulent. A weakened regime in Baghdad has boosted the centrifugal tendencies in northern and southern Iraq. The Kurds in the north are striving to attain autonomy, and the Shi'ites in the south have escalated their own activities with increased Iranian assistance. Given the historical animosity between Baghdad and Tehran, it is quite understandable that the latter would do everything to further weaken Saddam or even topple him from power.

The same cannot be said of Turkey, however. The potential establishment of an autonomous Kurdish rule in northern Iraq is bound to escalate similar aspirations among the Kurds residing in Turkey. However, given the enthusiastic participation of the government of President Turgut Ozal against Iraq in Operation Desert Storm, Ankara and Baghdad may not be wiling to coordinate their policies on the Kurdish problem as long as Saddam remains in power. At the same time, however, given the predilection of Saddam to make deals with his enemies when he is in a weak position, one cannot categorically rule out the prospects of a rapprochement between Turkey and Iraq.

The two major actors in the Persian Gulf, Saudi Arabia and Iran, also continue to make progress in building their military muscles. Saudi Arabia already possesses an enormously sophisticated military infrastructure. The ease with which the United States could operate from Saudi Arabia during Operation Desert Storm was testimony to the high-tech–oriented nature of Saudi military infrastructure. Moreover, Riyadh continues to acquire advanced military systems, ostensibly in order to deter Iran and Iraq in the future. Between August 1990 and May 1991, it acquired $14.8 billion worth of weapons from the United States.[34]

Iran was reported to have spent $19 million purchasing military weapons in 1991 and was expected to spend $50 billion for the same purpose in the next five years.[35] Tehran, with the assistance of the PRC, Pakistan, and North Korea, is also reported to be earnestly seeking the acquisition of ballistic and nuclear technologies. The Cuban connection is being reportedly utilized by Iran in acquiring Cuban expertise in "nuclear-capable delivery systems." Cuba had acquired these capabilities as a result of the three-decade long presence in that island of the former Soviet Union. The Soviet-supplied Flogger Fs serve as "strategic aircraft" in Cuba. Iran has purchased SU-24s and MIG 23BNs, which are also capable of being utilized for delivering nuclear bombs.[36] Iran is also reported to be in the process of purchasing two or three diesel-powered kilo-class attack submarines from Russia; these submarines will be based at the Chah Bahar naval base at the opening of the Strait of Hormuz.

Under President Rafsanjani, Iran has emerged as a state that is practicing conventional diplomacy in Muslim Central Asia with a view to establishing a pan-Islamic bloc. If one were to ignore the fact that such an ambition is, at best, unrealistic, the Iranian foreign policy behavior is in marked contrast to the Shi'ite radicalism pursued by Iran under Khomeini. In the immediate vicinity of the Persian Gulf, Iran is likely to pursue actively its current two-pronged policy of emerging as a major military power and seeking political influence. In this regard, the threats of the 1980s to export the Islamic revolution to the Gulf states have been decisively abandoned.

In an attempt to boost its overall strategic objectives in North Africa, Iran under Rafsanjani has been establishing its long-term presence in Sudan. This country is likely to be utilized as a conduit to support the activities of Muslim fundamentalists in Algeria, Tunisia, and Egypt. In the Central Asian republics, Iran is also enhancing its political presence. Toward this end, the Rafsanjani government was actively mediating between Azerbaijan and Armenia in their conflict over Nagorno Karabakh. It has also been reported that Iran was seeking the purchase of nuclear weapons from Kazakhstan.[37]

The Syrian-Iranian strategic alliance is also reported to be working effectively. In the aftermath of the demise of the Soviet Union, Hafez Assad's dream of reaching strategic parity with Israel has found a new partner in Iran. Iran's eventual development of nuclear weapons might also be shared with Syria, both in the form of nuclear protection and in the transfer of technology.

The Israeli policy of sustaining its nuclear option through a long-standing posture of "nuclear ambiguity" is still intact. In fact, since the successful completion of Operation Desert Storm, there is no Arab state seriously challenging its strategic superiority. With the demise of the Soviet Union, Syria has no hope of replenishing its armaments after a potential clash with the Israelis, which, in all likelihood, is bound to repeat the crushing defeat of Syria following the Bakaa Valley skirmishes of 1982. About the only other military option Syria has at its disposal is to continue to make progress toward achieving strategic parity with the Jewish state and by utilizing the PRC, North Korea, and the Iran connections and hope that it does not have to exercise its power.

From the perspective of military preparedness, the post–Cold War years have not lowered the threat potentials in the Persian Gulf or the Middle East. The demise of the Soviet Union has only eroded the military and political positions of the Arab hard-line states regarding the Arab-Israeli conflict. This is not to say that these states were in a terribly strong position during the Cold War years, but the demise of the Soviet Union seems to have created a political and military vacuum that no state can fill. The PRC, the other remaining major non-Western military power, cannot match the military might of the United States. Presently, it also lacks the political will to confront

Washington as the USSR did during the Cold War years. These realities were also boosted by the only remaining superpower, the United States, not only dealing a crushing defeat to the most powerful hard-line state, Iraq, in 1991 but also creating a dialogue on the Palestinian question. There is no substantial progress on this issue as a result of a series of negotiations that were cosponsored by the United States and the former Soviet Union (and, after its demise, by the Confederation of Independent States). However, in the wake of the election of Yitzhak Rabin in Israel, there is hope that this reality, in conjunction with the sustained resolve of the Bush administration to continue the dialogue among major contending parties, is likely to produce an interim resolution of the Palestinian question in the form of a negotiated self-rule. If this reality were to emerge, the Persian Gulf and the Middle East will make a big leap toward the creation of further confidence and security building measures whose ultimate purposes will be to bring the rising spirals of the arms race in those regions under firm control.

CONCLUSIONS

The political history of the Middle East revolves around conflicts of different magnitude. Some of these have political origin; others have stemmed from religious, ethnic, and economic differences among inhabitants at different times. In this sense, when one thinks about the arms race in that area, one always returns to that ubiquitous question: whether arms races are facilitated by and are symptomatic of a variety of conflicts in the Middle East, or if they should be treated as just another manifestation of conflict itself. If one were to regard arms races as just another version of conflict, then one is forced to reject a frequently iterated statement that if the Arab-Israeli conflict (or the Palestinian question) were to be resolved, then the Middle East is likely to become a more serene area. But what about the Iranian-Iraqi conflict? No one can explain it away by expounding on apocryphal theories of Zionist-imperialist conspiracies, as has been done in the case of the Arab-Israeli conflict. Similarly, the conflict between Iraq and Syria over the orthodoxy of Ba'thist nationalism has survived over a long period of time. Although no one can compare the intricacy of this conflict with that related to the Palestinian question, no one can deny that the Ba'thist conflict was one of the major reasons underlying Hafez Assad's support of the Khomeini regime during the eight-year Iran-Iraq War.

The Lebanese conflict is another example of a special case. Here is a country that has been victimized by the Israeli hegemonic ambitions, the most brutal aspects of whose manifestations lasted only a few years. However, that is not to say that the future resurgence of these ambitions on the part of the Jewish state can be categorically ruled out. For now, the Israelis are content with the establishment of the so-called security zone.

Lebanon is being victimized by another hegemony, Syria, which appears to be more brutal and resilient than its former Israeli occupiers. The Lebanese case is a good example of how intensification of conflict makes it equally explosive. The arms buildup in Lebanon is only a manifestation of a larger problem that is related to the inability of a "confessional democracy" to come to terms with its own growing antagonistic tensions over the distribution of power and resources. Arms buildup has worsened these struggles among various groups.

By the same token, one can put forth a similar argument concerning the Iran-Iraq conflict. The arms race has produced an uglier and more brutal face of a larger conflict between 1980 and 1988. It is likely to surface in the future; however, the next time, the potential for use of nuclear weapons appear to be increased, given the previously mentioned resolve on the part of both Iran and Iraq to emerge as nuclear powers.

The pervasive arms race in the Middle East and the Persian Gulf appears to be raising the perceptions of the stakes or outcomes.[38] For instance, one can inferentially link Nasser's involvement in the Yemeni civil war to his strategic ambitions on the Arabian Peninsula. The recent conflicts between Iran and Iraq and between Iran and Saudi Arabia, on the contrary, appear to be directly aimed at establishing their respective strategic dominance in the region. This dominance does not have to be viewed only in terms of hegemony, even though this particular aspect could be the ulterior motives of these actors. A realistic perspective of dominance would be a nation-state's ability to influence the future dynamics of the strategic affairs of the region. This definition raises perceptions of the stakes and the outcomes of the conflict that involves Iran, Iraq, and Saudi Arabia. In this sense, arms races may be definitely viewed as phenomena of utmost significance.

However, if arms races in the Persian Gulf and the Middle East were to be viewed as instruments utilized by regional leaders to secure their interests, one comes away with a feeling that these tools are becoming increasingly inadequate. The reason for this inadequacy is the ever-increasing destructive capabilities of *all* actors in the Middle East. There was a time when one talked about the military invincibility of Israel. That country, in 1981, proved its preemptive capabilities by destroying the Iraqi nuclear facility at Osirak and, later, by bombing the Palestinian Liberation Organization headquarters in Tunisia. However, the emergence of Iraq as a military power in the late 1980s dampened this notion of invincibility. Now, of course, Iraq is out of the picture as a major military power until at least the year 2000. However, the increasing capabilities of Syria, Egypt, and Saudi Arabia to integrate missiles and chemical technologies in their warfare machineries tend to lower the potency of the Israeli deterrence capabilities with the passage of each year.

Even when one considers the capabilities of the Israelis to sustain superiority in chemical and nuclear warfare, the issue of proximity becomes increasingly significant. In any potential conflict in which Israel and Syria utilize chemical weapons, populations of both sides are destined to be victimized by chemical fallout. The Israelis might suffer fewer casualties than the Syrians, but no Israeli politician can operate on the premise of "acceptable human loss." When one thinks about the unthinkable potential use of nuclear weapons by the Israelis in future conflicts, the human sufferings on *all* sides are likely to be even more acute because of proximity between Israel and Syria.

About the only rational and acceptable choice that is left open for *all* Middle Eastern states in the post–Cold War years is to strive to lower their destructive potential on a systematic basis.

NOTES

1. Hans Maull also discusses it. See his "The Arms Trade with the Middle East," in *The Middle East and North Africa, 1991* (London: Europa Publications, 1990), pp. 117–25.

2. Adeed Dawisha, "Power, Participation, and the Dilemma of Legitimacy in the Arab World," February 11, 1986. Mimeograph.

3. For a detailed discussion of this issue, see Saeed M. Badeeb, *The Saudi-Egyptian Conflict over North Yemen, 1962–1970* (Boulder, Colo.: Westview Press, 1986).

4. *World Military Expenditures* (Washington, D.C.: United States Arms Control and Disarmament Agency, 1973), p. 3.

5. For a detailed discussion of the "military modernization and expansion," see Anthony Cordesman, *The Gulf and the Search for Strategic Stability: Saudi Arabia, Military Balance in the Gulf, and Trends in the Arab-Israeli Military Balance* (Boulder, Colo.: Westview Press, 1984), p. 55.

6. M. E. Ahrari, *OPEC — The Failing Giant* (Lexington: University Press of Kentucky, 1986).

7. The reader should be alerted to the gross discrepancy of figures reported by the Arms Control and Disarmament Agency's publication used for this analysis. For instance, the 1975 issue of *World Military Expenditures and Arms Transfers* reports the percentages of Iranian military expenditures as 9.6, 10.6, 9.6, and 13.6 for the years 1971 through 1974, respectively. The 1980 issue of the same publication reports considerably higher figures (see Table 7.2). The grossest discrepancies on these figures are on Saudi Arabian military expenditures for the same years in these issues. The point of emphasis here is that an analyst could arrive at substantially different conclusions by examining these figures.

8. Efram Karsh, "The Rise and Fall of Syria's Quest for Strategic Parity," in *Defense Year Book 1991* (London: Brassey's, 1991), pp. 197–216.

9. Anthony Cordesman notes, "Since 1990, every Gulf state has been forced to devote a steadily increasing proportion of its oil wealth to competing with the other Gulf States and/or neighboring states outside the Gulf." *The Gulf and the Search for the Strategic Stability*, p. 483.

10. Richard F. Grimmett, *Conventional Arms Transfer to the Third World, 1983–1990*, Congressional Research Service, August 2, 1991, p. CRS 20.

11. According to one estimate, both Iran and Iraq might have spent $170–200 billion for military activity. The losses in the oil sector for Iran alone were estimated to be approximately $250 billion. It would not be an exaggeration to suggest that the Iraqi losses in this sector were close to the same amount. The war-related expenditures to rebuild the infrastructures and productive systems were estimated to be about $500 billion to both belligerents. *SIPRI Yearbook 1989*, p. 165.

12. Ibid.; Anthony Cordesman, *Weapons of Mass Destruction in the Middle East* (London: Brassey's, 1991), p. 11.

13. Uzi Rubin, "How Much Does Missile Proliferation Matter," *Orbis*, Winter 1991, pp. 29–39.

14. Thomas G. Mahnken and Timothy D. Hoyt, "Missile Proliferation and American Interests," *SAIS Review*, Winter/Spring 1990, pp. 101–16.

15. W. Seth Carus, "Chemical Weapons in the Middle East," Washington Institute for Near East Policy, Research Memorandum No. 9, December 1988.

16. Seth Carus, *Ballistic Missiles in the Third World: Threat and Response* (New York: Praeger, 1990), p. 10.

17. Ibid., Chapter III. The genesis of the MTCR was the National Security Decision Directive (NSDD)-70, which was issued in November 1982. As a result of this directive, the United States initiated a series of negotiations lasting four years. The MTCR emerged as the culmination of these negotiations.

18. "Chemical warfare," as used in this chapter, includes "the use of many different types of toxic substances to inflict death or injury on an adversary." The capabilities of countries that use tear gas, riot control agents, and biological warfare agents are not included under the category of chemical weapons. For further elaboration of this point, see Gordon M. Burck and Charles C. Floweree, *International Handbook on Chemical Weapons Proliferation* (New York: Greenwood Press, 1991), pp. xi–xii.

19. James R. King, *Proliferation of Chemical Weapons and Ballistic Missiles, Risks to NATO's Southern Region* (Rome, Italy: NATO Defense College), p. 7.

20. Ibid.

21. Cordesman, *Weapons of Mass Destruction in the Middle East*, p. 36.

22. Elisa D. Harris, "Chemical Weapons Proliferation: Current Capabilities and Prospects for Control," in Aspen Strategy Group Report, *New Threats: Responding to the Proliferation of Nuclear, Chemical, and Delivery Capabilities in the Third World* (Baltimore, Md.: University Press of America, 1990), pp. 67–87.

23. Ibid., pp. 70–71.

24. Edward M. Spier, "The Role of Chemical Weapons in the Military Doctrines of the Third World Armies," in *Security Implications of a Global Chemical Weapons Ban*, ed. Joachim Krause (Boulder, Colo.: Westview Special Studies in International Security, 1991), pp. 41–62.

25. Statement of Esmet Abdel Maguid, as cited in Brad Roberts, "Security Implications for Third World Regions of a Chemical Weapons Ban," in *Security Implications of a Global Chemical Weapons Ban* (Boulder, Colo.: Westview Press, 1991), pp. 83–90.

26. Joseph S. Nye, Jr., "Arms Control after the Cold War," *Foreign Affairs* 68 (Winter 1989): 42–64.

27. Seth Carus, *The Genie Unleashed: Iraq's Chemical and Biological Weapons Production*, Policy Papers No. 14 (Washington, D.C.: The Washington Institute for Near East Policy, 1989), p. 34.

28. Cordesman, *Weapons of Mass Destruction in the Middle East*, p. 93.

29. Seymour Hersh, *The Samson Option* (New York: Random House, 1991).

30. For an overview of the Iraqi state of nuclear knowledge prior to the Gulf War of 1991, see David Albright and Mark Hibbs, "Iraq's Shop-Till-You-Drop Nuclear Program," *Bulletin of Atomic Scientists*, April 1992, pp. 27–37.

31. Leonard Spector, "Nuclear Proliferation in the Middle East," *Orbis*, Spring 1992, pp. 181–98.

32. For a prescient analysis of the PRC's arms sales policies, see John W. Lewis, Hua Di, and Xue Litai, "Beijing's Defense Establishment: Solving the Arms-Export Enigma," *International Security* 15 (Spring 1991): 87–109.

33. Spector, "Nuclear Proliferation in the Middle East," pp. 188, 189.

34. "New World Orders: U.S. Arms Transfers to the Middle East," *Arms Control Today*, March 1992, pp. 34–35.

35. Tony Banks and James Bruce, "Iran Builds Its Strength," *Jane's Defence Weekly*, February 1, 1992, pp. 158–59.

36. Yosef Bodansky, "Nuclear Weapons and Radical States Pose New Situations," *Defense and Foreign Affairs Strategic Policy*, June 1992, pp. 6–7.

37. Yossef Bodansky, "Iran Acquires Nuclear Weapons and Moves to Provide Cover to Syria," Strategic Policy Special Report, *Defense and Foreign Affairs Strategic Policy*, February 1992, pp. 1–4.

38. My thanks to Brad Roberts for raising this point.

8

The Gulf Cooperation Council: Prospects for Collective Security

Kenneth Katzman

The Gulf Cooperation Council (GCC), consisting of Saudi Arabia, Kuwait, Bahrain, Qatar, the United Arab Emirates (UAE), and Oman, is an institution that has survived the superpower rivalry, the Iran-Iraq War, and the Iraqi invasion of Kuwait. During the 1970s and 1980s, the Persian Gulf region was a major arena for East-West political and military competition.[1] In 1979, the Islamic revolution in Iran (which weakened the U.S. strategic position in the Gulf) and the Soviet invasion of Afghanistan created the perception of military and political imbalance between the superpowers in the Gulf. This led President Jimmy Carter to publicly assert that the United States would defend its interest in the region by force, if necessary. Although peace and stability represent universal U.S. interests that apply to the Gulf, securing the free flow of oil from the oil-rich Gulf region is widely considered to be one such vital U.S. interest.

The U.S. military modernization accelerated by President Ronald Reagan and the ascension of the pragmatic Mikhail Gorbachev in the USSR in 1985 began to reverse the imbalance. The strengthening U.S. position in the Gulf was reflected in the United States' reflagging and naval escort program for Kuwaiti oil tankers and the U.S. low-intensity conflict with Iran during 1987–88. The collapse in the Soviet empire in eastern Europe further changed the perceived distribution of power in the Gulf and was reflected in the Soviet Union's backing for the West against its longtime political and military client, Iraq, following the invasion of Kuwait on August 2, 1990.[2] Although the collapse of the Soviet Union has erased a superpower threat to U.S. interests in the Gulf, the Iran-Iraq War, Iraq's invasion of Kuwait, and Saddam Hussein's post–Gulf War defiance of the UN and the allied coalition have shown that the United States cannot always control regional events.

The GCC was formed primarily because of indigenous regional threats that the superpowers, partly because of their rivalry, were unwilling or unable to contain. Officially founded in May 1981 under the threat posed by the Iran-Iraq War,[3] as an institution, the GCC has not only outlasted that war among its two large and powerful neighbors but also survived armed clashes and several border disputes among its member states. For most of its first decade the GCC, although suspicious of Iraqi intentions, supported Iraq in order to protect itself from revolutionary Iran. However, Iraq, having invaded Kuwait in 1990, is now an enemy, Iran is still viewed with suspicion by many of the GCC states, and the GCC is more dependent on the protection of the United States than it was previously. Moreover, the 1991 Persian Gulf War has strengthened calls for reform and democratization within several of the Gulf states and from the United States, further testing the legitimacy and resiliency of traditional institutions and governing elites. These developments have led several of the GCC states to argue that increased military as well as political integration is needed if the GCC is to survive in the future.

It can be argued that the GCC states will depend on the United States as their ultimate security guarantor now and for the foreseeable future. The GCC states recognize that they are too militarily weak, collectively and individually, to deter or defend against a major external threat. Although the GCC states probably recognize that only the United States can ultimately guarantee their security, for domestic political reasons, none can be seen as compromising their sovereignty or Arab nationalist values for the sake of relations with the United States. As a result, the GCC states have considered forging alternate or additional collective security arrangements with several regional partners in addition to the United States. However, several of these outside security partners are considered unacceptable to at least some of the GCC states. The GCC states have also floated proposals for greater cooperation among themselves, but political differences and mistrust among the GCC states have prevented them from such significantly enhanced cooperation. Moreover, GCC diplomats admit that their military weaknesses, primarily the shortage of manpower and the lack of combat experience, suggest that even a high degree of military integration would be insufficient to meet the potential threats from Iran and/or Iraq.

COLLECTIVE SECURITY PARTNERS

The United States

Although the Iraqi invasion of Kuwait may have convinced the GCC states of the necessity of closer military ties to the United States, the approaches to the role of the United States in post–Persian Gulf War security vary among them. Some of these states, such as Kuwait, Bahrain, Oman, and Qatar, welcome close, formal, and relatively visible cooperation with the United States as a protective deterrent. Others, primarily driven by domestic concerns, have been less willing to enter into a long-term formal military relationship with the United States. Saudi Arabia and the UAE fall into this latter category. Qatar had been relatively slow to reach a formal defense pact with the United States but decided to enter into such a security pact in June 1992.[4] The UAE is still negotiating a defense pact with the United States as well, although the UAE is said to be unwilling to cede to the United States legal jurisdiction over the U.S. personnel that serve there (a Status of Forces Agreement [SOFA]). Saudi Arabia and the United States have reportedly agreed to use the 1977 Military Training Mission Treaty as the basis of an expanded security relationship, although that agreement does not provide a strong-enough basis for the type of expanded security relationship the United States envisioned after the Gulf War.[5] With the possible exception of Kuwait, virtually all the GCC states oppose a permanent U.S. troop presence on their territory but want the United States to remain directly engaged in the region, ready to intervene on their behalf should further crises develop.

The differing degrees of security relations between the United States and the Gulf states weakens collective security by creating a degree of uncertainty about the role of the United States in defending the GCC states in a future crisis. Those GCC states that have entered formal defense pacts with the United States are, at least indirectly, signaling that they do not place significant faith in the GCC itself to provide collective security. This opens the GCC to criticism by both Iran and Iraq and makes skepticism of the GCC's collective security potential a self-fulfilling prophecy. The unwillingness of some GCC states to reach pacts with the United States creates doubts about the closeness of the military relations between those states and the United States and about the U.S. commitment to their defense. Moreover, Iran and Iraq are presented with ample opportunities to drive a wedge between those GCC states militarily and politically closer to and those more distant from the United States.

Kuwait, the GCC state that was the most directly threatened by Iran during the Iran-Iraq War and then occupied by Iraq in 1990, aligned itself quickly with the United States after the Persian Gulf

War. It signed a ten-year defense pact with the United States on September 19, 1991, which even the opposition Constitutional Movement supported. Although Iraqi-Kuwaiti relations had always been tense (Iraq mobilized militarily to press its claim to Kuwait in 1961 and, during the Iran-Iraq War, tried to pressure Kuwait to yield it long-term control of Bubiyan and Warbah Islands), the Kuwaiti leadership probably did not believe Saddam would attempt to seize all of Kuwait. To this extent, Kuwait's defense assumptions were shattered to the core, leading Kuwait to drop any previous opposition to a U.S. presence in Kuwait. The U.S.–Kuwait defense pact provides for pre-positioning of some U.S. equipment, U.S. access to Kuwaiti facilities, joint exercises, and U.S. logistical support, arms sales, and training. The agreement also provides for the legal status of U.S. forces in Kuwait. The two countries held their first joint exercises in October 1991. Because of the military drawbacks to pre-positioning heavy equipment close to the potential front line, the stationing of U.S. equipment in Kuwait is limited to 58 M1A1 tanks, 58 Bradley Infantry Fighting Vehicles, artillery, and trucks.[6] The United States agreed to pre-position equipment in Kuwait primarily to demonstrate its commitment to Kuwait's defense. Over the next year, Kuwait will contribute about $215 million — about $50 million in cash and the rest as in-kind payments — to the cost of the U.S. military presence in Kuwait.[7]

The U.S.–Kuwait defense pact does not automatically provide for the United States to deploy its forces if Kuwait is attacked again, only that the two would discuss appropriate measures to defend Kuwait.[8] The pact represented a significant upgrading of previous U.S.–Kuwait security relationships; at the height of the Iran-Iraq War, Kuwait asked for and received U.S. protection for its oil tanker fleet. The tanker reflagging program represented a significant step in strengthening U.S.–Kuwait ties and implied a U.S. commitment to Kuwait's defense. Kuwait has also signed significant post-war defense pacts with the United Kingdom and France.

Bahrain also expanded its security relationship with the United States in the aftermath of the 1991 Persian Gulf War. It signed a ten-year defense pact with the United States on October 28, 1991. The Bahraini press, which generally reflects the views of the government, described it as even broader than the agreement between the United States and Kuwait. This was a possible reference to the granting to the United States of expanded basing facilities at Muharraq, about which the two countries began negotiating very shortly after the Gulf War ended.[9] Bahrain is said to be allowing the pre-positioning of some missiles and bombs under the agreement. About a month before the pact was signed, a Bahraini army spokesman publicly thanked the U.S. Defense Department for overcoming obstacles to a shipment of U.S. Stinger missiles to Bahrain.[10] The extent of the security relationship with the United States — and Bahrain's willingness to publicize its extensiveness — suggested that Bahrain believed the deterrent effect of a close relationship with the United States outweighed potential domestic criticism of the pact. (Bahrain has been the host to the U.S. Commander of Middle East Force, the forerunner of U.S. Central Command, since 1949, but this relationship has heretofore been given little publicity.)

Some observers, however, have raised questions about the utility and motivations of Bahrain's defense pact with the United States. Some believed that Bahrain's enthusiasm for military cooperation with the United States was directed at neighboring Qatar, with which it is disputing control of the Hawar Islands. Qatar's decision to sign a defense pact with the United States may have been intended to undercut the leverage Bahrain was perceived as acquiring in its pact with the United States. Moreover, U.S. military planners are said to believe that the causeway between Bahrain and Saudi Arabia could be destroyed by an attacker, cutting off access to the ground equipment stationed there.[11]

In late 1990, Oman renewed its access agreements with the United States. The agreements, first signed in 1980 and renewable every five years, have been the cornerstone of U.S.–Oman security relations, and U.S. Air Force and Naval equipment has been stationed in Oman since 1980. The key drawback to the arrangement is that Oman is too far away from Saudi Arabia or Kuwait, the likely targets of an attack by Iran or Iraq, to be effective for pre-positioning of ground assets. Oman also has a close security relationship with the United Kingdom, which trains and, in some units, such as the air force, directly commands Omani forces. However, the Omanis have been slowly phasing out the British presence in the Omani military in favor of Omani officers; the chief of staff as well as the individual service commanders are now Omanis rather than seconded British officers.

Saudi Arabia and the UAE have not yet signed defense pacts with the United States, even though the Defense Department was initially optimistic that agreements with these countries would be reached. As in the case of Kuwait, the Iraqi invasion starkly confronted Saudi Arabia and the UAE with their own security vulnerabilities. However, Saudi Arabia and the UAE are said to believe that the United States, in defense of its own interest, would return to the Gulf in force if these states are attacked again, and no extraordinary concessions are, therefore, needed. State and Defense Department officials have made several visits to these states in negotiations on proposed defense pacts, and these officials have, at several points, claimed that agreements were close at hand. The most important of all the U.S.–Gulf state defense pacts was to be between the United States and Saudi Arabia, and the failure of the two parties to agree to a formal defense pact reflects the complex relationship between the two countries. Although the U.S.–Saudi decision to use a 1977 agreement to expand military cooperation appears to represent progress toward a formal defense pact, the Saudis may use the arrangement to argue that a formal pact is no longer necessary.

In the wake of the Iraqi invasion of Kuwait, the Saudi leadership blunted domestic opposition to a U.S. troop presence in Saudi Arabia by arguing that the U.S. buildup was a specific response to a major threat and that U.S. forces would not remain in Saudi Arabia after Iraq was expelled. To the Saudis, U.S. plans to pre-position heavy equipment sufficient for one combat division — and the U.S. insistence that U.S. personnel attend that equipment — have been unacceptable. The Saudis are said to believe that such a pre-positioning arrangement might be viewed by many in and outside Saudi Arabia as a U.S. military base[12] and would open the royal family to severe domestic criticism. These considerations may have contributed to Saudi Arabia's decision to use the 1977 Military Training Mission Treaty, which is more limited in scope than the planned defense pact, as the basis of U.S.–Saudi defense cooperation.[13] Some analysts also believed the Saudis were demanding a U.S. commitment to help the Saudis modernize and expand their armed forces in return for agreeing to the U.S. position on pre-positioning.[14] In the wake of the war, the United States sent a team, led by Major General Dennis Melcor, to study Saudi Arabia's security requirements; the report was said to recommend new arms sales to Saudi Arabia, in addition to other steps.[15]

Similar concerns may account for the failure thus far of the UAE to sign defense agreements with the United States. Despite reports of progress between the UAE and the United States on a security pact, the September 1991 comments of the UAE President Zayid bin Sultan al-Nuhayyan that the UAE did not want a foreign military presence in the UAE were given prominence in the Gulf press.[16] Many observers interpreted the comments as indicating that the UAE had serious reservations about granting the United States a SOFA similar to that contained in the pacts between the United States and Kuwait and Bahrain. However, the UAE is seeking to purchase U.S. weapons, and in 1991 Congress failed to block a sale of U.S. Apache helicopters to that country.[17]

Whether because of signs of Iranian moderation or out of fear of Iran, the UAE also has tried to maintain good relations with the Islamic Republic. However, the Iranian takeover of Abu Musa island in early 1992 has seriously set back Iran's relations with the UAE and, more broadly, the GCC. Prior to the strain in relations with Iran, the UAE might have viewed security ties with Iran and the United States to be mutually exclusive, given the continued U.S.–Iran animosity and Iran's continued opposition to the U.S.

presence in the Gulf. Similarly, Qatar's relationship with Iran (it has signed several economic agreements with that country) might have accounted for that country's delay in reaching a pact with the United States. However, many analysts attributed the slow pace of negotiations with Qatar to the centralized decision making process in Qatar and the frequent distractions of the Qatari leadership from the negotiations. The role of Iran in Gulf security is discussed further below.

The "Six Plus Two" Arrangement

Since the end of the Gulf War, another security arrangement has been under discussion among the GCC states and two other Arab members of the anti-Iraq coalition, Egypt and Syria. The United States and the GCC states have said that this "six plus two" security arrangement would be complementary to, rather than incompatible with, the bilateral defense agreements forged or under discussion with the United States. However, the United States is believed to place higher priority on integrating Egypt into Gulf security than on a Syrian role. An agreement in principle among the GCC states, Egypt, and Syria to establish political, economic, and security programs — including the use of forces from those countries then deployed in Saudi Arabia and Kuwait as the nucleus of an Arab deterrent force in the Gulf — was reached on March 6, 1991, after two days of meetings in Damascus. The arrangement is known as the Damascus Declaration. In June 1991, the Damascus Declaration parties agreed to form a 26,000-person force that would consist of 10,000 Saudis, 10,000 troops from the other five GCC states, 3,000 Egyptians, and 3,000 Syrian troops to be stationed in Kuwait along the border with Iraq.[18]

The Damascus Declaration surprised most observers in the rapidity with which it was forged after the end of the Gulf War. However, to the detriment of Gulf security, the Damascus Declaration has run into major obstacles that have prevented its implementation. Shortly before the June 1991 agreement on the size and composition of the Arab deterrent force, it was publicly reported that Syria and Egypt had begun withdrawing their troops from Kuwait, contradicting previous statements that these countries would meet or increase their commitments to the force. Although the withdrawals may have been bargaining tactics in advance of the June discussions, it was reported that deep disagreements existed among the parties. The Saudis reportedly wanted the United States to continue in command of the regional forces, a condition Syria and Egypt found unacceptable, and Syria and Egypt were said to be concerned that the GCC was more interested in forging security relations with the United States than with them.[19] Many observers believed, however, that the Saudi position reflected a deep mistrust of Syria and Egypt on the part of Saudi Arabia and the other Gulf states. The GCC states feared that hosting Syrian and Egyptian forces would create the potential for Syria and Egypt to meddle in the internal politics of the Gulf states and exert influence on GCC decision making.

Financial arrangements have also apparently contributed to the difficulties in implementing the Damascus Declaration. Kuwait was said to believe that Egypt had agreed to participate primarily to receive the grant aid the GCC had offered in exchange for its cooperation. For their part, the GCC states were reportedly concerned about bearing the cost of stationing the Syrian and Egyptian troops in the Gulf, given their other concerns about the effectiveness and wisdom of the relationship.

The mistrust of Syria and Egypt was, no doubt, based on a history of difficult relations between these parties and the GCC states. Syria supported Iran during the eight-year Iran-Iraq War, and Iran was viewed as a great threat to the Gulf states during that conflict. Moreover, Syria and Iran continue to have close relations, and Iran is still distrusted by many of the GCC states, even if Iraq has now become the greater threat. In addition, in late 1991, reports began to appear that Syria was drawing closer to Iraq, possibly including the opening of some border posts for trade (which contravenes the international embargo against Iraq), reexports of Iraqi oil, and discussions on the reopening of an Iraqi oil pipeline through Syria.[20] Although both Saudi Arabia and Egypt are now considered moderate and pro-Western, misgivings between the two countries have run deep since the two took opposite sides in an internal conflict between republican and royalist forces in Yemen in 1962. Egypt was also said to be concerned that some GCC states were indicating acceptance of an Iranian role in Gulf security.[21]

Because of these differences, the Damascus Declaration has not been implemented, despite several ministerial meetings and high-level public statements of commitment to the agreement. Initially, pending an implementation agreement, the Egyptians reportedly left a token force of 5,000 troops in Kuwait and the Syrians left 1,000 troops there; these forces have since departed. A major meeting of the Declaration states to resolve the outstanding issues has been postponed several times. If the provisions of the Declaration are implemented, the parties may yet agree to form a rapidly deployable reserve force, given the differences over permanently stationed troops.[22] Syria, which has been looking to gain influence in the Gulf for many years, as well as Egypt, has been highly vocal in calling for full implementation of the Declaration, and the GCC states continue to publicly express their commitment to implementing it.

Iran as Security Partner

The most controversial potential security partner for the GCC states is undoubtedly Iran. During the Iran-Iraq War, which coincided with the height of Iranian revolutionary radicalism, Iran was the primary enemy of virtually all the Gulf states, although Oman tried to balance its relations with Iran and Iraq. Although Iraq has made itself the GCC's primary adversary with its invasion of Kuwait, most of the GCC states remain suspicious of Tehran for its actions since the Islamic revolution, especially following its takeover of Abu Musa Island, over which it had exercised shared control with the UAE on the basis of a 1971 agreement between the former shah of Iran and the amir of the emirate of Sharjah. Before the takeover, some of the GCC states believed that Iran was moderating its behavior and had a legitimate role to play in Gulf security. The GCC states that wanted to improve relations with Iran noted that President Rafsanjani indicated that he wants to improve relations with the Gulf states (Iran and Saudi Arabia have restored diplomatic relations); that Iran remained neutral in the Gulf War rather than side with Iraq; that it facilitated the release of remaining Western hostages in Lebanon; and that Iran has indicated it wants to play a constructive rather than revolutionary role in the Muslim states of the former Soviet Union. Although significant differences over the nature and extent of Iran's role in Gulf security remained, at a late November 1991 GCC foreign ministerial meeting, the six countries agreed that Gulf security arrangements should be, at the very least, acceptable to Iran.[23]

The concerns about Iran are born of a long history. One of the first major acts in the Gulf by revolutionary Iran was directed against Bahrain in December 1981. Bahraini Shi'ites belonging to the Islamic Front for the Liberation of Bahrain (IFLB), the Bahraini branch of Tehran-backed Shi'ite opposition groups throughout the Gulf, reportedly organized a coup attempt against the ruling Al Khalifa family. The coup plot was discovered and broken up by Bahraini security officials. The IFLB, headed by Hadi Modaressi,[24] is influenced by Iran through the umbrella group SAIRI (the Supreme Assembly for the Islamic Revolution in Iraq), headed the Iraqi Shi'ite leader Muhammad Baqr al-Hakim. In 1983, reports of a coup plot against the ruling Al Thani family were also linked to Iran.[25]

The next major operation came in May 1985. Kuwaiti Shi'ites apparently linked to Iran attacked the motorcade of Amir Jabir Ahmad al-Sabah. Most analysts believed the attack was an Iranian effort to intimidate Kuwait into releasing the Da'wa Party prisoners held for the attacks on the U.S. Embassy, the French Embassy, the airport, a U.S. civilian compound, an oil refinery, and the Electricity Ministry in Kuwait on December 12, 1983.[26] The amir was seriously shaken in the incident. In attempts to intimidate Kuwait into decreasing its political and financial support for Iraq, Revolutionary Guard naval elements began attacking Kuwaiti oil tankers in 1986, prompting Kuwait to ask the United States and the Soviet Union to provide protection for its tanker fleet. During the tanker reflagging operations, which began in mid-1987, Iran laid mines in the Persian Gulf, damaging escorted tankers and prompting military responses from the U.S. Navy. Iran also fired a Silkworm surface-to-surface missile at Kuwaiti's al-Ahmadi oil terminal, hitting a reflagged supertanker docked in Kuwait.

Saudi Arabia was also a major target of Iran during the 1980s. In late July 1987, Iranian pilgrims to Mecca rioted, provoking a forceful reaction by Saudi security forces. In the wake of the riots, Iran's Revolutionary Guards attacked the Saudi and Kuwaiti embassies in Tehran. Also during the period, a flotilla of Revolutionary Guard naval craft attempted to approach the Saudi coast but were driven off by Saudi aircraft.

The death of Ayatollah Khomeini in June 1989 and the ascendancy of pragmatic political leaders fostered a warming trend in Iranian–GCC relations, even before signs of Iraqi aggressiveness began to appear in early 1990. The hallmark of the improvement in ties was the restoration of Saudi-Iranian diplomatic relations, broken in 1988 in the wake of the 1987 Mecca riots, in 1991. In December 1991, Iran's ambassador to the UAE, Ali Hadi Najafabadi, was posted concurrently to Saudi Arabia.[27] The end of 1991 also witnessed the release of all U.S. hostages from Lebanon; Iran was credited with a key role in those releases. The victory of pragmatic candidates in the spring 1992 Majles (parliament) elections in Iran further contributed to the impression that Iran is curtailing its export of the revolution activities. These positive developments in Iran have helped it gain acceptance by some GCC states for its insistence that it play a role in Gulf security. (Iranian officials have said that, as a regional power, no Gulf security arrangements should be designed without Iran's participation.) In December 1991, GCC Secretary-General Abdullah Bishara was invited to Tehran — the first such invitation since the GCC was established — to discuss Gulf security. Other analysts have noted that Iran and the GCC states now have a common interest in containing Iraq, which had been the basis of Rafsanjani's efforts to improve relations with the Gulf countries.[28] However, given the continuing animosity between Iran and the United States and the Iranian move on Abu Musa, the GCC states are unlikely to choose Iran over the United States as their key Gulf security partner.

The three GCC states that had been most receptive to an Iranian role are Qatar, the UAE, and Oman. Of the three, the improvement in Iranian-Qatari relations since late 1991 has been the most significant. On November 11, 1991, the two countries signed an agreement to build four 1,800-kilometer pipelines to carry fresh water from Iran's Karun River to Qatar; the project was estimated at $13 billion. Agreements on labor, air transportation, and trade were also signed at that time.[29] It was subsequently reported that Iran may have promised Qatar support in its Hawar Islands dispute with Bahrain in exchange for the cooperation agreements. It has also been suggested that Iran also may have dropped its attempts to claim a share of Qatar's North Field natural gas development in exchange for the economic agreements.[30] The Saudis, generally opposed to giving Iran a role in Gulf security, reportedly expressed displeasure at Qatar for improving relations with Iran unilaterally. However, it is possible that Qatar was using Tehran as a counterweight to Riyadh, especially because Saudi Arabia, in early 1992, encroached on Qatar's Salwa region.[31] There was also a border clash between the two countries in late September 1992, which caused Qatar to boycott several meetings of the GCC. It is also likely that Qatar had been using its emerging relations with Tehran as a means to extract concessions from the United States in the negotiations on a U.S.–Qatar security pact.

With a large Iranian community, the UAE had always seen good relations with Tehran as essential to its security, and the UAE has been perceived as amenable to including Iran in Gulf security. This position has been the most pronounced in the emirate of Dubai, which has a large Iranian community. However, in early April 1992, Iran expelled about 60 foreign workers from the UAE side of Abu Musa Island (Iran and the emirate of Sharjah share control of the island under a 1971 agreement between Sharjah and Iran). The UAE is reportedly trying to resolve the dispute by quiet diplomacy, and it has asked Oman, which has long had close ties to Iran, to mediate in the dispute. Some analysts viewed the Iranian action as an attempt to intimidate the UAE into forging cooperation agreements with Iran similar to those undertaken by Qatar and as a signal to the GCC that it will press its claim to a role in Gulf security.[32] The effect of the move has been to alarm the GCC. Qatar has even sent its ambassador back to Baghdad, a possible indication that it would like to see a balance restored between Iraq and the newly aggressive Iran. Some of the Gulf states have also reported that Iran is building Silkworm missile sites on the island.

Saudi Arabia and Kuwait have generally been considered the most wary of Iran among the GCC states. Their cooperation with the United States lessened the possibility of their simultaneous cooperation with Iran. However, in October 1991, a senior Kuwaiti official called for closer economic and commercial ties with Iran, and Iran and Kuwait are said to have discussed plans to set up a freshwater linkage similar to that agreed upon by Iran and Qatar.[33] Iran has also returned to Kuwait civilian aircraft taken by Iraq and then flown by Iraq to Iran, dropping its previous insistence that Kuwait pay Iran maintenance fees in exchange for the return of the jets. Kuwait may have seen a more conciliatory policy toward Iran as a means to dampen Tehran's criticism of its defense pact with the United States. Kuwait may also have viewed improving relations with Iran (or the appearance of improving relations) as a tactic to ensure a continued U.S. commitment to Kuwait's defense. Beyond recognizing the need to avoid antagonizing Iran, Kuwait has not, however, advocated close cooperation with Iran on Gulf security, an action that would almost certainly jeopardize security relations with the United States. Saudi Arabia has been consistently wary about including Iran in regional security arrangements, and Iran is unlikely to gain a major role as long as Saudi Arabia is in opposition.

GCC SELF-RELIANCE

GCC Internal Dynamics

The GCC has been discussing measures it can undertake by itself as a supplement to cooperation with outside security partners. Political divisions among the GCC states have, thus far, hampered efforts to form a unified military force. However, all its member states appear committed to the GCC as an instrument of collective security, and prospects for some form of enhanced military cooperation are good.

The most significant dispute within the GCC is the conflict between Bahrain and Qatar over the Hawar Islands. The dispute flared in April 1986 when Qatari forces seized the Fasht al-Dibal reef east of Bahrain and declared an exclusion zone there. Bahrain had been improving the reef to make it into what Bahrain said was a GCC coastal observation base. Qatar claimed Bahrain was building a new coast guard station. After the clash, Bahrain reinforced its presence on the disputed Hawar Islands off the western coast of Qatar. Bahrain immediately asked Saudi Arabia and the GCC to arbitrate the dispute, and the Saudis, although unsuccessful in forging a permanent solution to the Hawar Islands dispute, were able to persuade Qatar to remove its forces and Bahrain to subsequently dismantle the improvements on the Fasht al-Dibal reef. In July 1991, Qatar, on its own, referred the dispute to the International Court of Justice (ICJ) at the Hague. Bahrain maintained that the two sides should jointly apply to the Hague to rule on the case, but a joint application has been complicated by the deep differences between the two states on the terms of the dispute. Bahrain wants the ICJ to approach the dispute comprehensively, looking at all sea and land boundaries, but Qatar wants the ruling to focus on the narrower issue of the Hawar Islands.[34] In September 1991, there was speculation about a new round of mediation efforts by both Saudi Arabia and Kuwait.[35] Since then, there have been reports of gunboat stand offs between Qatari and Bahraini naval forces. In April 1992, Bahrain vehemently rejected a Qatari decree extending its territorial waters to 12 nautical miles; Bahrain claimed the decree infringed on Bahrain's marine territorial rights.[36]

Other schisms exist within the GCC, which hamper military unity and collective security. Oman, in addition to having a border dispute with Saudi Arabia, is said to resent what it perceives as Saudi domination of the GCC. For its part, Saudi Arabia has consistently criticized Oman for its relatively independent foreign policy, such as its moderation on the Arab-Israeli dispute and its longtime ties to Iran. Even Saudi Arabia and Kuwait do not agree on every issue. The Saudis are said to oppose Kuwait's decision to hold elections in October 1992. The Saudis believe the Kuwaiti decision was the result of U.S. pressure, and King Fahd has rejected elections as part of his political reform program announced in early 1992. Both Qatar and the UAE also have border disputes with Saudi Arabia, and they have been reluctant to strengthen the GCC for fear that it will be dominated by — and, therefore, increase the influence of — Saudi Arabia.[37] It should be noted that according to Commander-in-Chief of U.S. Central Command General Joseph P. Hoar, negotiations on Saudi Arabia's border disputes with Oman, the UAE, and Qatar are said to be making progress.[38] More recently, a border dispute between Qatar and Saudi Arabia flared following a border clash between their forces at Khofous in late September 1992 (Saudi Arabia claims it was a clash between armed bedouins from the two countries). As a result of the incident, Qatar suspended its 1965 border agreement with Saudi Arabia and has been boycotting key GCC meetings. Mediation by Kuwait and other Arab states has thus far succeeded in containing the rift, and an eventual settlement is likely.

Another indication of GCC disunity is its failure to implement a June 1981 Unified Economic Agreement on a common market. The agreement provided for the elimination of some custom duties between GCC states; coordination of import, export, oil, and industrial policies; free movement of labor and capital; and the development of coordination in monetary, banking, and financial policies, including the possibility of a common currency. At a December 1991 GCC summit, the foreign and finance ministers of the GCC states agreed to consider an eight-year timetable for implementing the Unified Economic Agreement.[39]

The political and economic differences among the GCC states have spilled over into the military arena. As the Iran-Iraq War escalated in the early- to mid-1980s, the GCC states were unable to forge a joint security pact, but military cooperation did progress. In

October 1983, troops from all the GCC states participated in joint military exercises in the UAE; the exercises were termed "Peninsula Shield." The exercises involved about 6,500 troops from all the GCC states. In 1985, the Peninsula Shield was formalized into a rapid deployment force of 10,000 troops, commanded by a Saudi officer and headquartered in Saudi Arabia, and it has served as the military arm of the GCC as a whole.[40] Based in northern Saudi Arabia, the Peninsula Shield force did not react, however, when Iraq invaded Kuwait.

In the aftermath of the 1991 Gulf War, some of the GCC states have seen the strengthening of the Peninsula Shield force as the appropriate vehicle for forging GCC collective security. Saudi Arabia and Bahrain are the chief advocates of that position. They believe Peninsula Shield can be easily expanded by, for example, adding new military elements, such as air defense, to its basic structure. Saudi Arabia's support for Peninsula Shield is, at least in part, derived from its existing command of the force, an arrangement that Saudi Arabia fears might be questioned if a new security institution were established. Bahrain, which has the smallest armed force among the GCC states, probably favors bolstering Peninsula Shield because of its limited force requirements. Bahrain cannot spare the manpower for a larger GCC force, as would be required under other proposals.

In October 1991, Oman proposed a major alternative to expanding the Peninsula Shield force — the creation of an integrated GCC force of 100,000 troops. After sensing opposition among some GCC states in advance of the GCC summit in December 1991, Oman dropped its insistence on the 100,000-troop requirement but remained adamant that the proposed new force be sizeable and independent.[41] Kuwait was said to be the most opposed to the proposal, believing that its security was best guaranteed by the United States and fearful that the 100,000-person force would be stationed in Kuwait and, therefore, be in a potential position to influence internal politics in Kuwait. Kuwait also believes that even a large GCC force would be no match for a determined offensive by either Iraq or Iran. Kuwait was reported to have accepted in principle the idea of a new, independent GCC force but felt that the force envisioned in the Omani proposal was far too large. Qatar and the UAE reportedly were opposed to the force as well, probably because of their difficulty in providing large numbers of troops to so large a force. There were also concerns among the GCC states over who would command the force; these concerns were probably greatest in those states most distant politically from Saudi Arabia, the logical favorite to command the 100,000-person force. Saudi Arabia and Bahrain, as noted above, were believed to favor strengthening Peninsula Shield rather than adopting the Omani proposal.

Despite their differences over political and economic issues and enhanced military cooperation, the GCC as an institution is not threatened. As discussed earlier, military cooperation did increase throughout the 1980s, even if there are differences on the composition of a new, more integrated force. It should also be noted that, with the exception of the Bahrain-Qatar dispute, differences between the GCC states have rarely flared into armed clashes or even come close to military confrontation. Even the recent Saudi-Qatari border clash is expected to be resolved to the satisfaction of both parties. Much of the relative success in intra-GCC conflict resolution is due to the longstanding personal ties among GCC rulers and ruling families; the substantial similarities in the social compositions and political systems of the GCC states; the frequent meetings of the GCC at the technical, ministerial, and head-of-state levels; and the overarching role of Saudi Arabia in intra-GCC mediation. Because it is the richest and politically dominant GCC state, several of the other GCC countries generally coordinate their positions and consult extensively with Saudi Arabia. Saudi contributions constitute a significant portion of the budget of some of the poorer GCC states, such as Bahrain, giving Saudi Arabia substantial leverage over those states.

Indigenous Military Weaknesses

The GCC states have been driven to seek collective security, either with or without outside powers, because of the military weaknesses of the individual countries. According to most observers, in the absence of a permanent U.S. ground troop presence in the Gulf, the GCC must be able to hold off an invading force at least until the United States can bring its forces to bear on the invaders. However, the Iraqi invasion of Kuwait demonstrated that Kuwait did not have the capability or the will to slow down the invading force. The GCC states have generally acknowledged their combat ineffectiveness relative to their major adversaries, Iran and Iraq, and these states have used their military weaknesses to bolster their arms purchase requests from the United States and other suppliers. Many analysts, however, believe that sophisticated arms can only marginally improve the combat effectiveness of the GCC states and that what is needed, in addition to increased manpower, is greater professionalism and better leadership, organization, and training. The lack of these factors has been associated with poor combat performance by these states in past military engagements. A brief sketch of the military capabilities of the Gulf states follows.

The effect of the military weakness of the GCC states is to increase the dependence of the GCC on the United States for Gulf security. Even if their militaries were more unified, the GCC states will be too weak for the foreseeable future to defend against a determined threat from a rearmed Iraq. In addition to stating their willingness to defend the Gulf militarily, the United States and its coalition partners, therefore, are relying on continued economic sanctions to deny Iraq the income with which to rebuild its conventional forces and on the UN inspection regime to dismantle Iraq's weapons of mass destruction. Most observers agree that, barring an Iraqi collapse that brings Iran into southern Iraq, Iran would have significant difficulty invading any of the GCC states. However, the threat from Iran may take unconventional forms, such as sponsorship of political assassination or coup attempts, or popular uprisings from Shi'ite elements inside the Gulf states. Iran's fleet of small boats, operated by the highly ideological Revolutionary Guard, could also threaten Gulf oil terminals and shipping. The threats from subversion are countered by diligent and efficient internal security on the part of the GCC regimes themselves. To counter the waterborne threats from Iran, U.S. forces are probably needed to detect and fend off the Iranian attacks.

Saudi Arabia, the largest and most populous of the GCC states, has the most capable force among the GCC states, but it suffers from major weaknesses.[42] Most notable is a serious shortage of manpower, which allows it to field a total force of about 100,000; however, the force is divided between the 45,000-person regular army, led by Defense Minister Sultan bin Abd al Aziz, and a 55,000-member Saudi Arabian National Guard (SANG), which is commanded by Crown Prince Abdullah. The royal family has deliberately kept these two forces separate and independent as a check upon each other, but the net effect has been to undermine the combat effectiveness of the Saudi forces against external adversaries. Cooperation and interoperability between the two forces is said to be poor, especially because the more religiously conservative Abdullah has been reluctant to allow the SANG to be trained by the United States to the degree the Saudi regular army is. Moreover, the SANG is recruited primarily from the Bedouin tribes, and not all SANG soldiers serve full-time. Abdullah has also forcefully protected the tribal character of the SANG, successfully opposing Defense Minister Sultan's attempts in the early 1980s to institute conscription for the SANG.[43] The SANG also is primarily an internal security force, and much of it is deployed in defense of Saudi oil installations.[44] The regular army is drawn from the generally more progressive urban population, it is deployed in large military cities outside populated areas, and it does not have an internal security function.

The Saudi military, both regular military and SANG, also suffers from cultural and social drawbacks. Military service is not a high-prestige occupation in Saudi Arabia, as is the case in most of the Gulf states, and the armed forces are plagued by absenteeism. Both Saudi forces, but primarily the regular army, are highly dependent on foreign workers to maintain their military equipment and provide logistical support. Soldiers are said to be assigned and reassigned according to personal requests from family or powerful friends. Although the officer class is reportedly well-trained and highly motivated, the lower ranks are generally less competent and less committed. However, SANG soldiers, drawn from the fiercely independent Bedouin tribes, are generally considered braver and more able fighters than their regular army counterparts.

The bright spot in the Saudi military structure is its air force. The regime favors the air force in prestige and budgetary allocations, making an air force pilot an enviable and elite position in Saudi Arabia and enabling the force to attract competent recruits. Royal family members, who have a direct stake in the defense of the regime and the kingdom, constitute a large proportion of the air force. U.S. officers that have worked with Saudi Air Force units have noted that its squadrons represent tightly run units with a strong sense of mission and that discipline is excellent.[45] As a result, the Saudi Air Force acquitted itself relatively well in the Gulf War, whereas the Saudi ground forces were considered to have needed substantial help from their U.S. counterparts during combat.

The Kuwaiti military is in severe disarray in the wake of the Persian Gulf Crisis. Before the Iraqi invasion, Kuwait had a small force of about 16,000 troops in six brigades; the force has now been reduced to about 5,000.[46] Compounding the small size of Kuwait's military is the immeasurable damage to morale caused by its failure to offer any significant defense against the Iraqi invasion in August 1990. As the Iraqi invasion became imminent, the Kuwaiti military reportedly did not even receive orders to prepare their tanks and artillery for battle, and Defense Minister Nawaf al-Ahmad al-Jabir al Sabah fled Kuwait without leaving battle orders.[47] After the restoration of the Kuwaiti government, the Kuwaiti officer corps threatened to resign unless senior military leaders were dismissed for poor handling of the invasion[48]; targets of the letter included Chief of Staff Major General Jabir al-Sabah, Shaykhs Salim al-Sabah al-Salim al-Sabah, who was interior minister at the time of the invasion, and former Defense Minister Shaykh Nawaf. (Salim and Nawaf were given minor portfolios in the restoration cabinet, partially satisfying the officer corps.)

Since the liberation of Kuwait, there has been substantial debate about the social composition of the armed forces. Initially, the leadership vowed to recruit only Kuwaitis to a reconstituted military and not include the bidoons, Arabs from other countries who live in Kuwait but are not Kuwaiti citizens. Those officers who threatened to resign opposed efforts to purge the military of bidoons. Not only are the bidoons being recruited, there has even been talk of giving them Kuwaiti citizenship.[49] Moreover, the promotion criteria have not been altered in the wake of the Gulf Crisis; the major criterion still appears to be loyalty and personal ties to the ruling Sabah family, rather than merit.[50] Morale and leadership are said to be acceptable only in the Kuwait Air Force, which was able to extricate much of its assets ahead of the advancing Iraqi invaders. The Kuwait Air Force also expect to receive 40 new F-18 aircraft.

The armed forces of the UAE suffer from many of the same weaknesses as the other Gulf monarchies, particularly in the shortage of available manpower, a reliance on foreigners to fill its ranks, and the perception that military service is not a prestigious career or significant avenue for advancement. The federal structure of the seven-emirate UAE is an additional complication in UAE military decision making. The total force is about 40,000 troops, but it is split primarily between the two most important emirates, Abu Dhabi and Dubai. Dubai, through its independent Central Military Region command, controls about 20 percent of the total UAE force, including purchasing decisions. Abu Dhabi controls most of the remaining units of the total force, composed of forces from the other emirates. Ras al-Khaymah, headquarters of the Northern Military Region, also is said to retain some autonomy over the forces based there. Shaykh Zayid bin Sultan-al-Nuhayyan, president of the UAE and ruler of Abu Dhabi, is commander-in-chief of the armed forces, while Muhammad bin Rashid al-Maktum, brother of the current ruler of Dubai, Shaykh Maktum bin Rashid al-Maktum, is UAE minister of defense. Differences between the emirates over military policy is, therefore, magnified by the independent chains of command to the subordinate forces of the UAE military.

Military affairs are further complicated by continued political instability in the emirate of Sharjah, where the amir, Sultan bin Muhammad al-Qasimi, removed his brother Abdul Aziz al-Qasimi from the line of succession in July 1990, three years after Abdul Aziz attempted to overthrow Shaykh Sultan. There was speculation that Shaykh Zayid had backed Abdul Aziz's attempted coup, but he was overruled by the other emirates, who wanted Sultan restored in order not to legitimize seizures of power within individual emirates.

Another major problem for the UAE military is that most of its troops are foreign citizens, and about 60 percent of the total have traditionally been Omanis. Over 20 other nationalities are represented in the UAE armed forces.[51] The UAE is said to be trying to increase the involvement of its own citizens in the military, but, as in the other Gulf states, military service is not a highly regarded profession, and the government has found it easier to recruit foreigners to expand the armed forces. Like other Gulf states, the UAE is seeking to redress its weakness by purchases of sophisticated conventional weaponry, including Apache helicopters, M1A1 tanks, Bradley Fighting Vehicles, and South African self-propelled artillery. The UAE has previously relied on British military equipment.

Oman has a relatively sophisticated armed force, built largely by British advisers, some of whom still remain in the command structure.[52] Under British influence, the Omani military has long emphasized the value of training and technology and conducted major exercises with the British armed forces. This relationship has professionalized the Omani armed forces to a greater degree than those of many of the other Gulf states. The United Kingdom has also used its substantial influence with Qaboos to promote its weapons systems for the Omani military, although many senior Omanis are believed to want U.S. weapons, such as F-16 aircraft. The officer corps has also had combat experience in crushing the Dhofar rebellion, which was waged against the Omani government in the first half of the 1970s, and in several border clashes with the forces of the People's Democratic Republic of Yemen (now part of the unified Republic of Yemen). Iranian troops sent by the former shah also helped Qaboos crush the Dhofar rebellion.

Nonetheless, Oman's manpower is limited — its force consists of about 25,000 troops. Moreover, domestic pressures have influenced Qaboos to begin phasing out seconded British officers in favor of Omanis in the process of Omanization, reducing efficiency somewhat. In 1986, an Omani was made chief of the defense staff for the first time. The Sultan of Oman's Land Forces, the least technology-dependent service, has undergone the most rapid Omanization. Officer selection is also still often based on tribal affiliations and personal ties rather than on merit. Despite their relative sophistication and professionalism, Omani forces have not always performed well in their clashes with Yemeni troops.

Qatar, with only about 6,500 military personnel, can make only a limited contribution to collective security. Its dispute with Bahrain over the Hawar Islands — which stems from the expulsion of Bahrain's ruling Al Khalifa family from control of Qatar in favor of the Al Thani family in 1868 — further distracts Qatar from that collective security. Most Qataris are followers of the Wahhabi sect of Islam that is dominant in Saudi Arabia, which partly accounts for the history of close ties between those states. Qatari troops fought alongside those of Saudi Arabia against Iraq in the battle of Khafji in January 1991, although most reports attributed the victory in that battle to U.S. military advice and guidance rather than to either Saudi or Qatari military capabilities. The primary mission of the Qatari armed forces is to defend against internal threats and against Bahrain, and the U.S. State Department has said that Qatar's forces are too small and too inexperienced to effectively deter an external attack, presumably by a major power such as Iran.[53] However, Qatar is generally credited with having outperformed Bahrain forces in the 1986 clash over the Fasht al-Dibal reef.

Qatari military personnel are recruited by voluntary enlistment, mostly from Bedouin tribes that continually cross the Saudi-Qatari border. In this respect, the Qatari armed forces are similar in composition and character to those of the SANG. Much of the officer corps is derived from the ruling Al Thani family and key supporting families; the amir's son is minister of defense and commander-in-chief of the armed forces. Qatar also relies on troops from other Arab countries and Pakistan, as well as on British advice. Since the 1980s, Qatar has been purchasing primarily French military equipment, reducing its previous reliance on British equipment.

Bahrain has the smallest armed forces of the GCC states, about 2,300 troops. It, too, is preoccupied with the dispute with Qatar over the Hawar Islands. Because its defense force is too small to counter major external threats, Bahrain has generally depended on Saudi Arabia, as well as the West, for its security. Because of its vulnerability, Bahrain granted the U.S. Navy docking facilities when the British withdrew from the Gulf in 1971, and the relationship with the United States has expanded gradually since.

Bahrain is relying on the United States to upgrade its armed forces. In the late 1980s, the United States leased to Bahrain Stinger antiaircraft missiles and, in 1990, delivered 12 F-16s to the Bahrain Air Force. Bahrain also has ordered eight Apache helicopters, the Patriot antimissile system, and M1A2 tanks from the United States. Bahrain also has built a $100 million air base in the south of the main island of Bahrain, with U.S. assistance.[54] Although Bahrain has signed a defense pact with the United States in the aftermath of the 1991 Gulf War, Bahrain has recently become the first GCC state to call for improved relations with Iraq.[55] This position is likely to complicate Bahrain's relations with Saudi Arabia and Kuwait, as well as the United States. Bahrain's prime minister had sent greetings to Saddam Hussein at the end of the Muslim holy month of Ramadan, and there reportedly were contacts between the two countries at the margins of the Earth Summit in Rio de Janeiro in June 1992.[56] Just as several of the GCC states are forging closer relations with Iran, it is likely that other GCC states will eventually follow Bahrain's lead and call for better relations with Iraq and that the Gulf states' longstanding policy of attempting to balance Iran and Iraq will reemerge.

Rapprochement between some of the GCC states and Iraq will likely set back U.S. efforts to forge durable collective security arrangements in the Gulf. Barring a change of regime in Baghdad, Saudi Arabia and Kuwait are certain to strongly oppose any such rapprochement, and the Bahraini overture to Iraq has already strained Bahrain's relations with those two states. The resulting additional splits among the GCC states on this issue will also disrupt the unified front the GCC has tried to forge to balance out Iraq. Perhaps most important, the United States is likely to view GCC states' rapprochement with Iraq as a betrayal of the men and women who risked their lives to save the Gulf states from Iraqi aggression. The U.S. commitment to GCC defense is, therefore, likely to weaken.

CONCLUSION

Although the collapse of the Soviet Union has not proved sufficient, by itself, to stabilize the Persian Gulf, the collapse did make the 1990–91 Gulf Crisis manageable for the United States and its coalition partners. Paradoxically, although the Soviet military supplies that helped make Iraq a conventional power have ended, Russian arms sales to Iran may create a future imbalance in favor of that country.[57] Soviet aid notwithstanding, both Iran and Iraq have been clever and able in threatening U.S. interests in the Gulf, even if neither is a match for the United States militarily. Moreover, although the Iraqi invasion caused several of the GCC states to drop objections to formal military relations with the United States, the GCC states have still not found common ground on forming a more unified military, either among themselves or in concert with other Arab states. Many observers believe the Iraqi invasion also has not yet motivated the GCC states to undertake major military reforms that would improve their combat effectiveness, but rather to rely on the United States ever more heavily for their security. This reliance, in turn, may undermine the legitimacy of the Gulf regimes in the face of nationalist and radical Islamic domestic opposition, possibly leading the GCC states to subsequently distance themselves from the United States. Such distance would then leave the GCC states more vulnerable to future threat from Iran and Iraq, a result exactly opposite to the goals of the GCC in their enhanced security cooperation with the United States.

With the weakening of Saddam Hussein's Iraq at the hands of the coalition, the Gulf balance was again upset, and Iran's aggression on Abu Musa is one manifestation of that imbalance. Iran may feel it now has a free hand to dominate the Persian Gulf, yet, its actions have been sufficiently measured so as not to provoke U.S. involvement against Iran. Iran's resurgence has led some GCC states, such as Bahrain, to speculate about renewed ties to Iraq and led Qatar to return its ambassador to Baghdad. These Gulf state actions demonstrate that, no matter their hatred for Saddam and his invasion of Kuwait, Iraq may be a useful element in restoring a balance vis-à-vis a resurgent Iran. U.S. relations with both Iran and Iraq are still severely strained, meaning that the options for maintaining a balance in the Gulf are limited to containing both Iraq and Iran politically and militarily. This, in turn, increases the likelihood that the United States may again have to act militarily in the Gulf to protect its interests.

NOTES

1. For a further discussion of the superpower rivalries in the Gulf, see Adeed Dawisha and Karen Dawisha, eds., *The Soviet Union in the Middle East* (New York: Holmes and Meier, 1982).
2. For further discussion of the strategic relations in the post-war Gulf, see "The Twilight of Peace in the Persian Gulf," *Harvard International Review* 13 (Winter 1990–91).
3. The Iran-Iraq War will be referred to as such, but "Persian Gulf War" or "Gulf War" will refer to the 1991 coalition war against Iraq.
4. "Qatar Agrees to Defense Pact with United States," *Reuters*, June 4, 1992.
5. "U.S., Saudis Agree to Use Old Military Pact for Expanding Cooperation," Washington *Post*, May 31, 1992, p. A10; text of 1977 agreement in Department of State, United States Treaties and Other International Agreements, Vol. 28, Part 2, 1976–77, pp. 2409–24.
6. "Fractured Cooperation May Dash Gulf Security," *Defense News*, March 16, 1992, p. 6.
7. "Kuwait to Pay $215 Million for U.S. Presence," *Defense News*, June 15, 1992, p. 26.
8. "Kuwait Journal: The Runaway Army Is Back but Standing at Ease," New York *Times*, January 14, 1992, p. A4. The administration generally tries to avoid providing a formal security guarantee, because doing so would raise the agreement to the level of a formal treaty, which would need ratification by the Senate.
9. *Middle East Economic Digest*, April 26, 1991, p. 11.
10. *Middle East Today*, September 4, 1991.
11. "Fractured Cooperation May Dash Gulf Security," p. 6.
12. "U.S., Saudis at Odds over Arms Cache," Washington *Post*, October 20, 1991, p. A1. For similar reasons, the pre-positioned equipment in Kuwait is being guarded and maintained by civilian contractors, not U.S. military personnel. Presumably, this formulation was being considered in the Saudi case, although the grater volume and sophistication of the equipment to be stationed in Saudi Arabia may preclude the use of contract personnel.
13. In concert with the U.S.–Saudi agreement to use the 1977 treaty to expand their security relations, Defense Secretary Richard Cheney directed the U.S. Army to set aside 200 M1A1 tanks and 200 Bradley Fighting Vehicles for eventual pre-positioning in Saudi Arabia. This was about one-third less equipment than the United States originally hoped to pre-position there. "U.S., Saudis Agree to Use Old Military Pact for Expanding Cooperation," May 31, 1992, p. A10.
14. Ibid.
15. Ibid. In August 1990, the United States sold Saudi Arabia an emergency arms package of about $2.231 billion in defense articles and services in the wake of the Iraqi invasion of Kuwait. The following month the administration planned to sell Saudi Arabia an additional $21 billion in defense equipment; however, largely because of opposition in Congress, the unprecedented package was broken down into smaller packages that would be considered separately. In late September 1990 the administration submitted for congressional review the first phase of the overall package, valued at over $7.3 billion, consisting of defense articles and services deemed most critical to Saudi defense requirements in the Gulf Crisis.

Congress did not block the sales. However, in January 1991, the administration announced that it was postponing the second phase of the large package, citing the need to assess Saudi requirements. In late 1991, the United States sold Saudi Arabia four additional batteries of Patriot antimissile systems; the sale incurred little opposition in Congress, in large part because of the defensive nature of the Patriot system. However, in early 1992, the Saudis were said to be requesting 72 F-15 fighter jets to upgrade its air force, a proposed sale that has incurred significant opposition in Congress. See U.S. Library of Congress, Congressional Research Service, "Arms Sales to Saudi Arabia: Current Status," *CRS Issue Brief IB91007*, updated November 6, 1991, p. 8.

16. *Middle East Today*, September 10, 1991.

17. Some in Congress argued that the sale conflicted with U.S. efforts to establish a multilateral arms transfer control regime for the Middle East. Such an arms control initiative was formally proposed by President Bush in May 1991 and has resulted in several meetings among the five permanent members of the UN Security Council (also the five large arms providers) in an attempt to establish an arms transfer control regime.

18. U.S. Library of Congress, Congressional Research Service, "U.S.–Syrian Relations Since the Iraqi Invasion of Kuwait: A Chronology," *CRS Report 91-895 F*, December 18, 1991, p. 16.

19. "Arabs Fail to Agree on Kuwait Defence," London *Financial Times*, July 17, 1991, p. 6.

20. "Iraq Oil Exports Reported," New York *Times*, November 25, 1991, p. A14.

21. *Middle East Today*, April 23, 1992.

22. "Arabs Fail to Agree on Kuwait Defence," p. 6.

23. *Middle East Today*, November 28, 1991.

24. "Bahrain," in *Defense and Foreign Affairs Handbook* (Alexandria: International Media, 1991), pp. 69–70. His brother is Mohammad Taqi Modaressi, head of the Iraqi opposition group Islamic Amal, which has also been linked to SAIRI.

25. "Qatar," in *Defense and Foreign Affairs Handbook* (Alexandria: International Media, 1991), pp. 810–13.

26. The Da'wa (Call) Party is a Shi'ite opposition group with branches in Iraq and several of the Gulf states. The Da'wa is believed to be less receptive to Iranian influence than is SAIRI, and the issue of Iranian control was probably responsible for a further split in the Iraqi opposition movement in the early 1980s. Other acts of terrorism, such as the hijacking of a Kuwaiti airliner to Tehran and the holding of Western hostages in Lebanon, also represented, in part, attempts to free the Da'wa prisoners. One of the Da'wa captives was a relative of Imad Mughniyah, one of the key captors of Western hostages that were held in Lebanon (two German hostages remain). The Da'wa prisoners escaped from their jails in Kuwait during the Iraqi invasion of Kuwait. See also U.S. Library of Congress, Congressional Research Service, "Lebanon: The Remaining U.S. Hostages," *Issue Brief No. IB85183*, updated November 1, 1991, p. 9. For a further discussion of the Shi'ite opposition movements of Iraq, see Amatzia Baram, "From Radicalism to Radical Pragmatism: The Shi'ite Fundamentalist Movements of Iraq," in *Islamic Fundamentalisms and the Gulf Crisis*, ed. James Piscatori (Chicago, Ill.: Fundamentalism Project, American Academy of Sciences, 1991), pp. 28–51.

27. *Middle East Today*, October 28, 1991.

28. R. K. Ramazani, "Iran's Foreign Policy: Both North and South," *Middle East Journal* 46 (Summer 1992): 393–412.

29. *Middle East Today*, November 11, 1991.

30. "Iran Presses Gulf States to Ensure Cooperation," *Reuters*, April 29, 1992.

31. *Middle East Today*, April 10, 1992.

32. "Iran Presses Gulf States to Ensure Cooperation," April 29, 1992.
33. *Middle East Today*, December 10, 1991.
34. "Bahrain Rebutts Qatari Case at World Court," *Reuters*, June 17, 1992.
35. *Middle East Today*, September 12, 1991.
36. "Qatari Decree on Territorial Waters Disputed," Paris Monte Carlo Radio in Arabic, April 17, 1992.
37. "Fractured Cooperation May Dash Gulf Security," p. 6.
38. Excerpts from General Hoar's March 5, 1992, testimony before the Senate Armed Services Committee, reprinted in "Complex Factors Defy Predicting Middle East's Future," *Officer* 68 (May 1992): 38–42.
39. *Middle East Today*, December 23, 1991.
40. "Fractured Cooperation May Dash Gulf Security," p. 6.
41. *Middle East Today*, December 4, 1991.
42. For a further analysis of the capabilities of the Saudi armed forces, see Anthony Cordesman, *The Gulf and the Search for Strategic Stability: Saudi Arabia, the Military Balance in the Gulf, and Trends in the Arab-Israeli Military Balance* (Boulder, Colo.: Westview Press, 1984).
43. Nadiv Safran, *Saudi Arabia: The Ceaseless Quest for Security* (Ithaca, N.Y.: Cornell University Press, 1988), p. 339.
44. David Lamb, *The Arabs: Journeys Beyond the Mirage* (New York: Vintage Books, 1991), p. 271.
45. *Aviation Week and Space Technology*, May 23, 1983.
46. "Kuwait Journal: The Runaway Army Is Back But Standing at Ease," p. A4.
47. Ibid.
48. "Kuwaiti Officers Threaten to Resign," London *Financial Times*, June 21, 1991.
49. "Defense Minister on Nationalities in Army," *FBIS*, July 9, 1991, p. 25.
50. "Kuwait Journal: The Runaway Army Is Back But Standing at Ease," p. A4.
51. "United Arab Emirates," in *Defense and Foreign Affairs Handbook* (Alexandria: International Media, 1991), pp. 1020–23.
52. "Oman," in *Defense and Foreign Affairs Handbook* (Alexandria: International Media, 1991), pp. 744–46.
53. "Qatar," pp. 810–13.
54. "Bahrain," pp. 69–73.
55. "Bahrain Breaks Ranks and Urges Closer Ties with Iraq," *Financial Times*, June 22, 1992, p. 12.
56. Ibid.
57. "Iran Said to Commit $7 Billion to Secret Arms Plan," New York *Times*, August 8, 1991, p. 3.

Conclusion: Regional Outlook

M. E. Ahrari and James H. Noyes

As the chapters in this volume underscore, the politics of the Persian Gulf continue to follow the statement of the nineteenth-century French journalist Alphonse Karr: "The more things change the more they remain the same." There are some changes, to be sure; however, by and large, the strategic affairs of this area have not experienced the magnitude of mutations that have taken place in other parts of the globe. The acute political rivalry between Iran and Iraq, which led to a long and bloody war between 1980 and 1988, has subsided because of the Iraqi defeat and the dismantlement of its military power in 1991. However, the competition for strategic dominance between Iran and Saudi Arabia is accelerating. Largely because of the role it played in destroying the military power of Saddam Hussein and in forcing him out of Kuwait, the Saudi monarchy envisions a definite military role for itself in the post–Cold War Persian Gulf. The pro–status quo-oriented Saudi role in this war did not appear to have assuaged the fears and concerns of smaller Peninsular states regarding the growing strategic clout of Riyadh. No evidence reflects their fears more vividly than the willingness of a number of them to sign security agreements with the United States. Saudi Arabia is not a part of this trend, its own preference being an "over-the-horizon" U.S. presence. That kingdom had preferred this policy throughout the 1980s, when it perceived Khomeini's Iran as a threat to its security.

This trend toward relying on the United States for security underscores a sad reality of the Middle East. Arab states in the 1990s continue to suffer from a deep mistrust of each other. The so-called Damascus agreement was the most recent and visible victim of this suspicion. Saudi Arabia and Kuwait, whose sovereignty and territorial integrity were to be protected under this agreement, did not want the presence of "Arab" security forces on their soil. They were afraid that Egypt and Syria would utilize their presence to interfere in their domestic politics. Egypt and Syria, the two main participants in this security arrangement, were fantasizing about an unending flow of hard currency from the rich oil states. This capital would bankroll their economic development and purchase weapons. Egypt and Syria continued to spend an inordinate amount of their precious and scarce resources in buying weapons. When they realized that the Peninsular states were either unwilling or unable to fulfill their expectations, Cairo and Damascus lost a major incentive to participate. Egypt was also unhappy, because the smaller Peninsular states were interested in pursuing a dialogue with Iran for future security arrangements. Such a potential Iranian participation meant that the significance of the Egyptian military presence in the Gulf would be diminished The continued rivalry between Tehran and Cairo undoubtedly also weighed in the eventual refusal of the former to participate in the Damascus agreement. Iran was reportedly financing the growing activism of the Islamic forces in Sudan and Egypt, and in any event, Tehran's consistent postrevolution efforts to destabilize Arab governments made it an unlikely guarantor of Gulf security.

The political economy of oil in the Persian Gulf appears to be undergoing a major change in the post–Cold War, post–Gulf War world of the 1990s. The latter event itself was the first intra-Arab armed conflict in which oil played an important role. The outcome of this war might have also changed oil affairs, if not permanently, at least for a long time. Because the bullying of Kuwait by Iraq resulted in a severe punishment of that bully, the oil states are not likely to think of military action in future oil-related conflicts. This is a notable change and, indeed, an important development when one considers the growing competition between Saudi Arabia and Iran. Oil is also an important source of disagreement between them.

As a dollar-surplus state that also has a small population, Saudi Arabia does not have financial needs that are as acute and as immediate as those of Iran. Saudi megainvestments in buying sophisticated armaments necessitate large finances; however, there is no comparison between the needs of this country and those of Iran. The war-ravaged economy of the Islamic Republic must be rebuilt in the shortest possible period of time, which requires enormous sums of capital. Then, there are military aspirations of that country that also necessitate equally large financial investments. Oil becomes the only source of bankrolling the economic and defense needs of these countries. Even though their need for capital is a common variable, how to go about utilizing oil is an issue on which Tehran and Riyadh are a world apart. As a dollar-needy state, Iran opts for exploiting the oil market for all it is worth and on a short-term basis. As a dollar-surplus state,[1] as a country that has huge oil reserves, and as a country with enormous investments in the industrial world's economies, Saudi Arabia must pursue a policy of price moderation.

Moreover, Saudi Arabia, as an important aspect of its portfolio diversification strategy, has been quite active in vertical integration in the industrial consuming countries. As such, Riyadh must establish its credentials as a reliable supplier of oil. It means that the Saudis can no longer remain loyal to production programming that has been advocated by the Iranians. The intent underlying this strategy is to create artificial production shortfalls in order to firm up prices. Thus, on the issue of oil, Saudi Arabia and Iran are likely to remain on opposite sides despite their membership in the Organization of Petroleum Exporting Countries throughout the 1990s.

The significance of Iran in the Persian Gulf appears to be on the rise in the 1990s. That country is in the process of bouncing back from the ravages of the eight-year war with Iraq that ended in 1988. Although the domestic debate over its international role is far from settled, President Rafsanjani has already decided to bring his country back to the fold of the international community. Therefore, the Iran of the 1990s is less zealous in its foreign policy behavior than it was during the previous decade. The primacy of the Islamic variable is still quite visible; however, a de facto predilection for pragmatism is also equally apparent. At the same time, Iranian activism in Central Asia and North Africa is likely to be closely watched by the Gulf countries as well as the United States.

Even though Saudi Arabia continues its policy of keeping Iran from participating in the Gulf Cooperation Council (GCC), or in another security agreement that is likely to emerge in the future, it would be difficult to stabilize that region by excluding Iran. The Saudi rulers know it only too well.

The continuing arms race in the Persian Gulf is an issue no major arms supplier appears to tackle seriously. An earnest plan for its de-escalation must come from one or more of the major suppliers. No Persian Gulf state is likely to take any serious steps in this direction. In a world now without superpowr competition, military power in general is seeking new roles and new purposes, and the political economy of arms races has acquired a heightened significance. In the industrial world and former Soviet societies, the military sectors are desperately trying to survive drastic budget cutbacks that are being implemented by their respective governments. China and North Korea also place urgent priorities on arms sales. Defense industries in all these societies are in dire need of hard cash. Under these circumstances, the Persian Gulf remains a place where conflicts remain active, if not intense. At the same time, efforts to resolve them still favor techniques that were a sine qua non of the Cold War years, when militarism was rampant and reliance on military confrontation and arms buildup was very much in vogue. Almost all states of the Persian Gulf are also capable of paying cash for their weapons needs. Consequently, in response to their needs for keeping their weapons industries alive and competitive, major arms suppliers are largely paying lip service to curtailing the arms race. Their high economic stakes keep them from putting their actions where their mouths are.

A good starting point is to resuscitate endeavors that the major arms producers took since the Gulf War of 1991 to curb arms races in the Middle East and elsewhere. Perhaps President Bill Clinton would take the lead in this regard. It should be noted, however, that Clinton is presiding over an economy in which the defense industry badly needs dollars to sustain its present level of employment. An earnest U.S. endeavor for the curtailment of the arms race would only result in further shrinking of the U.S. defense industry. Would a U.S. president who made economic growth his top priority adopt a policy that would increase unemployment in the defense sector? Would he also be prepared to confront the essential issue of Israel's nuclear and missile arsenal, which is directly linked to the Gulf's arms control problem? Perhaps not. However, how would one go about bringing this seemingly unstoppable arms race under control? There are no simple solutions. Major arms suppliers have to bite the bullet, negotiate multilateral plans aimed at reducing arms sales, and develop measures to minimize chances of cheating by one or more participants.

The exportability of Islamic revolution to the Peninsular states is no longer a valid threat in the post–Cold War Persian Gulf. That is not to say, however, that this threat was based upon a realistic assessment of the political capabilities of the Khomeini revolution in the 1980s. As a religious phenomenon, this revolution was not exportable, because it was the product of a Shi'ite Iran. As such, it was not likely to become an overwhelming force in the Sunni polities of the Arabian Peninsula, but nonetheless, it was a potent force in the largely Shi'ite eastern province of Saudi Arabia and in those GCC states like Bahrain with substantial Shi'ite populations. From the political perspective, this revolution appeared exportable, because of the similarity of the processes of governance in Iran and the Peninsular states. The latter entities were monarchies, like the imperial Iran. In the Peninsular societies, the political process was exclusivistic and elite oriented, as Iran was under the shah. In the Gulf sheikhdoms, there were no mechanisms for the expression of political dissent, like Iran under the Pahlavi rule. It was the similarity of these political variables that had created considerable consternation among the sheikhdoms of the Gulf that their rule might also abruptly end, as did that of the shah. In the 1990s, this threat appears less imminent.

Sunni Islam is not a threat to political order in the Peninsular states, for all of them have maintained a sufficient amount of commitment to Islam. Moreover, all these countries also make sure that the religious establishments within their polities continue to put their stamp of legitimacy on their rule. Such precautions are likely to provide political stability for these sheikhdoms, at least through the 1990s, despite troubling evidence in Saudi Arabia of activist dissent among some religious teachers.[2]

What about the prospect of democracy in the Persian Gulf in the 1990s? The evidence in this regard is quite mixed. Popular elections that were held in Kuwait in October 1992 provided a reasonable semblance of democracy. However, the chances of repetition of this experiment elsewhere on the Peninsula are minimal, at best. King Fahd is already on record discarding such a possibility for Saudi Arabia. A serious blow was dealt to the prospects of introduction of democracy a little distance from the Persian Gulf, in Algeria. In the aftermath of the decision taken by the military dictators to steal the elections from the Islamic Front, Algeria appears to be teetering at the brink of political instability and, indeed, potential disaster. The Arab sheikhdoms are likely to tighten their grip on power in the wake of growing political turbulence in Algeria. However, as the worldwide clamor for democracy rises, it is only a matter of time before military dictators, absolute rulers, and their anachronistic mode of ruling will be swept away. Islam is likely to become the basis for such a political change, for it provides no theological basis for absolute or authoritarian rule.

The dynamics of great power involvement have undergone some of the most dramatic changes in the post–Cold War Gulf. The old and familiar U.S.–Soviet rivalry of the Cold War years became a thing of the past. In its place, a new competition is emerging between the gradually unifying western Europe and the United States. The latter, although remaining the only superpower, no longer dominates the globe in the realm of economics. On economic affairs, the pendulum of advantage in the Persian Gulf might be swinging more in favor of a united western Europe and Japan. Such an eventuality appears to be in the making in the 1990s but remains far from imminent, because western European countries are running into a number of stumbling blocks in their attempts to emerge as an economic union. On security affairs, the United States remains a dominant actor, especially after its military victory over Iraq.

Can the United States utilize this victory to make (or remake) the Persian Gulf to its liking? An answer to this question cannot be given without elaborating on the specifics of this question. What exactly is meant by "remaking the Persian Gulf to its liking"? If the United

States prefers a stable Gulf, that reality is at hand for now, although issues dividing Iran and Iraq have yet to be addressed, let alone those between Kuwait and Iraq. The long-range future of stability in this region is dependent upon the impetuous dynamics of a number of issues.

The first and foremost problem is the future dynamics of the disparity between the rich and poor states of the Persian Gulf and the Middle East. This is a conflict that, like cancer, is slowly eating away the governing capability of rulers in a number of "have-not" societies. The United States can be of limited assistance on this issue. It can facilitate a dialogue or extend its good offices for negotiating mechanisms of aid and trade among rich and poor Arab states. Western Europe and Japan may also figure prominently. However, any dominant role for Washington in providing economic assistance to the have-not states in the Arab world is out of the question. In the 1990s, the United States is largely going to practice the old adage of "charity begins at home." Perhaps one can better comprehend this phenomenon by recalling the popularity of "America firstism" in the 1992 presidential elections. Clinton was only one of the prominent proponents of this view, although his rhetoric was not as shrill as the one propounded by President George Bush's arch critic in this campaign, Pat Buchanan.

Second, controlling the arms race is an issue that is definitely a part of the U.S. wish list for the Persian Gulf and the Middle East, but in this, Washington is part of the problem as well as its potential solution. It can play a crucial role in curbing the arms race, but at the same time, it has played an equally important role in escalating it. As President Bill Clinton enters the White House, the important questions remain whether his administration would curb this race and absorb the resultant loss of billions of dollars of business for the defense industry and whether the cooperation of other weapons suppliers could be had. The chances of such a happenstance remain very low. Therefore, on this issue, what the United States wants and what sacrifices it is willing to make to attain its objectives are two different things.

Third, regarding the Palestinian question, Washington undoubtedly wishes to see it resolved. Its continued activism on this issue also remains of utmost significance. At the same time, the willingness of Israel and Palestine to compromise on this obdurate issue is of similar importance. The United States under the Clinton presidency must proceed to revive momentum. Within Israel, the government of Prime Minister Yitzhak Rabin is operating on the basis of a fragile parliamentary compromise. The growing activism of Hamas — the Islamic extremist group — in the occupied territories is a development that should be watched with concern by all forces for peace.

Fourth, the United States cannot decide how to deal with Iran. The United States' major ally, Saudi Arabia, also suffers from the same symptoms. Some of the smaller Peninsular states have no problem reaching a rapprochement with Iran. In fact, almost all of them are finding ways to cooperate with their larger neighbor, although the lower Gulf states regard Iran with an underlying fear that parallels the continuing apprehension felt by Kuwait and the upper GCC countries toward Iraq. Iraq lags in the military competition for now. Even after the ousting of Saddam Hussein from power, Iraq will confront international restraints on rebuilding its military power enjoyed prior to the Gulf War of 1991. However, as the long period of sanctions has shown, these restraints can prove porous. In the post–Cold War years, the Saudi-Iranian competition is likely to harden on military and diplomatic issues both in and around the Persian Gulf.

Militarily, Iran is emerging as a major regional power. Despite their sustained efforts to match the Iranian military strength, Saudis will lag in overall capability while excelling in air defense. Iran has the population base. It is rebuilding its industrial and military infrastructures. In the field of technology, Iran leads Saudi Arabia. In the 1990s, it has to reconstruct its prerevolutionary technical know-how, a process that is well under way.

On the diplomatic front, Iran remains active in North Africa. As such, it is causing considerable concerns for Husni Mubarak. Iran already has a major presence in Sudan, from where it is reportedly providing political and economic assistance to the radical Islamic elements in the Maghreb.

Iran also remains quite active in Muslim Central Asia, competing with Turkey and Saudi Arabia. Given the Sunni nature of all Central Asian Muslim states, except for Azerbaijan, Saudi Arabia may have a slight advantage over Iran. However, given the fact that the Iranians' perspective of Islam is proactive and revolutionary, it might serve as a tough source of competition for the conservative and status quo-oriented Saudi perspective of Islam.

The United States has adopted a policy of watchful neglect toward Iran. The "watchful" part of this foreign policy forces Washington to keep an eye on Iran, because it is perceived as a state that sustains an adversarial posture toward the U.S. strategic interests.[3] Therefore, the United States cannot afford to ignore the Iranian activism. The "neglect" aspect of U.S. foreign policy toward Iran emerges in the continued refusal of the former to do business with the latter, although U.S. oil companies now purchase Iranian crude. In the Persian Gulf, the United States is continuing to supply the Saudis with sophisticated weapons, hoping that the GCC would eventually emerge as an entity that at least could produce a tripwire defense of the Persian Gulf in the event of a crisis. Even then, the U.S.

commitment to defend the political status quo in that area has to last at least through the 1990s, if not for a longer period.

In North Africa, Washington is hoping that the government of Husni Mubarak will survive the growing challenge from the Islamic forces. It should be noted, tangentially, that the growing activism of the Islamic challenge in Egypt has a lot to do with the acute nature of the economic deprivation and disparity that prevails in that society. Egypt continues to blame Iran for the increased activism of the Islamic extremists. There may be an element of truth to these charges. It should be pointed out, however, that extremism of all sorts sprouts under conditions of acute economic disparity. In this sense, the intractable economic problems faced by the Mubarak government are substantially responsible for the escalating activities of the Islamic extremists.

In Central Asia, the United States has been promoting the Turkish secular model and hoping that the Iranian Islamic model would be rejected by the newly independent countries.

After the turbulent decade of the 1980s, the Persian Gulf was rocked once again during the Gulf War of 1991. Following Saddam Hussein's defeat in that war, that area appears comparatively serene. However, there are a number of issues, covered by various contributors in this book, still simmering that might lead to more bloody conflicts. Saddam, the brute who caused so much bloodshed, turbulence, and economic calamity for his own people, for the Iranians, and for the Kuwaitis, is still in power. The maddening arms race between Iran and Saudi Arabia continues to remind the world that Saddam does not have monopoly on insanity. Major Gulf suppliers are also active participants in this collective act of madness.

The urgent need of the post–Cold War decade is to end this arms race. The Persian Gulf states equally urgently need a system of collective security that involves all major and minor actors. After the end of Saddam's rule, such a system should also, with dispatch, include Iraq. Only by creating ample stakes for all major actors in a collective arrangement can the United States and other great powers begin to build a peaceful and stable Persian Gulf. Alternatively, the proverbial Armageddon is being approached with the active participation of a number of regional and great powers — authoritarian states as well as democracies.

NOTES

1. One should not take this term literally. Even though Saudi Arabia has incurred a considerable deficit related to the Gulf War of 1991 and has borrowed large sums of money to finance its economic- and military-related expenditures, it remains a dollar-surplus country (or potentially so) in comparison with Iran.

2. All Arab regimes, on occasion, have used subtle and even not-so-subtle pressure on the religious establishment to endorse their policies. Most recently, King Fahd was reported to have used the same tactic when he "retired" a number of Saudi *Ulamas* (religious scholars) who refused to endorse his policies. See Youssef M. Ibrahim, "Saudi King Ousts 7 Senior Clerics for Acts of Criticism by Omission," New York *Times*, December 15, 1992.

3. It should be noted that such a perception is a two-way street.

Appendixes

APPENDIX A
The Proliferation of Chemical Weapons in the Middle East and Its Implications

Egypt	Used chemical weapons during the civil war in North Yemen during 1963–67; reported to have supplied the technology to Iraq and Syria.
Syria	May use chemical weapons technology against Israel in future conflicts to offset Israel's conventional military superiority; reported to have supplied the technology to Iran and Libya.
Iraq	Used chemical weapons against Iran and the Kurdish population in the 1980s; may use them against Iran, Israel, or Saudi Arabia in future conflicts.
Libya	May use chemical weapons against Egypt in future conflicts in an attempt to offset Egyptian conventional military superiority.
Israel	Reported to have supplied chemical weapons technology to Taiwan and South Africa; may use chemical weapons technology against Syria and Iraq in future conflicts, especially if Israel decides to forego its nuclear retaliatory option
Iran	Used chemical weapons against Iraq in the 1980s; may use them against Iraq or Saudi Arabia in future conflicts.
Saudi Arabia	Reported to have acquired chemical weapons technology; may use it against Iraq or Iran in future conflicts.

APPENDIX B
The Proliferation of Ballistic Missiles in Selected Middle Eastern Countries

Country	System	Range/Payload (kilometers/kilograms)	Type	Source	Status
Algeria	Frog-4	50/250	BM	Soviet Union	R
	Frog-7	65/450	BM	Soviet Union	O
Egypt	Frog-5	50/450	BM	Soviet Union	R
	Frog-7	65/450	BM	Soviet Union	O/U
	Scud-B	300/1,000	BM	Soviet Union	O/U
	Scud-100	600/500	BM	North Korea/Egypt	D
Iran	Shahin-2	60/180	BM	Iran	O/U
	Nazeat	120/180	BM	Iran/China	O/U
	Mushak-160	160/N.A.	BM	Iran/China	O/U (?)
	Iran-200	200/N.A.	BM	Iran/China	O/U (?)
	Scud-B	300/1,000	BM	China/North Korea	O/U
	Scud-C	600/700	BM	North Korea	O
Israel	Lance	130/275	BM	United States	O
	Jericho I	650/500	BM	Israel/France	O
	Jericho II	1,500/650	BM	Israel/France	T/O
	Jericho IIb	1,300/700	BM	Israel	T/O (?)
	Shavit	2,500/750	SLV	Israel/France	O/U
Kuwait	Frog-7	65/450	BM	Soviet Union	R
Libya	Frog-7	65/450	BM	Soviet Union	O
	SS-21 (?)	120/450	BM	Soviet Union	O
	Scud-B	300/1,000	BM	Soviet Union	O/U
	Otrag	480/N.A.	BM	Libya/Germany	D/C (?)
	Al-Fateh	500/N.A.	BM	Libya/Germany	D
	Ittisalt	700/N.A.	BM	Libya/Germany	D
Saudi Arabia	CSS-2	2,000/2,000	BM	China	O
Syria	Frog-7	65/450	BM	Soviet Union	O/U
	SS-21	120/450	BM	Soviet Union	O
	Scud-B	300/1,000	BM	Soviet Union	O
	Scud-C	600/700	BM	North Korea	O (?)

Note: BM = ballistic missile; R = removed from service; O = operational; U = used in attacks; D = in development; N.A. - not available; T = tested; SLV = space launch vehicle; C = cancelled.

Source: *Arms Control Today*, April 1992.

Selected Bibliography

Adelman, M. A., "Oil Fallacies," *Foreign Policy*, February 1991, pp. 3–16.
Ahrari, M. E., *OPEC — The Failing Giant* (Lexington: University Press of Kentucky, 1986).
___, "Conflict Management of OPEC States," *Mediterranean Quarterly*, Summer 1991, pp. 86–109.
___, ed., *The Gulf and International Security: The 1980s and Beyond* (London: Macmillan, 1989).
Alnasrawi, Abbas and Cheryl A. Rubenberg, eds., *Consistency of U.S. Foreign Policy: The Gulf War and the Iran-Contra Affair* (Belmont, Mass.: Association of Arab-American University Graduates, 1989).
Bina, Cyrus, "Limits of OPEC Pricing: OPEC Profits and the Nature of Global Oil Accumulation, *OPEC Review*, Spring 1990, pp. 55–74.
Bohi, Douglas R., "Evolution of the Oil Market and Energy Security Policy," *Contemporary Policy Issues*, July 1987, pp. 20–33.
Burck, Gordon M. and Charles C. Floweree, *International Handbook on Chemical Weapons Proliferation* (New York: Greenwood Press, 1991).
Cordesman, Anthony, *Weapons of Mass Destruction in the Middle East* (London: Brassy's, 1991).
Doran, Charles F. and Stephen W. Buck, eds., *The Gulf, Energy and Global Security: Political and Economic Issues* (Boulder, Colo.: Lynne Reinner, 1991).
Efrat, Moshe and Jacob Bercovitch, eds., *Superpowers and Client States in the Middle East: The Imbalance of Influence* (New York: Routledge, 1991).
Fuller, Graham, "Respecting Regional Realities," *Foreign Policy*, Summer 1991, pp. 39–46.
Goodby, James, "Transparency in the Middle East," *Arms Control Today*, May 1991, pp. 8–11.
Graham, David, "Explaining Middle Eastern Alignments During the Gulf War," *Jerusalem Journal of International Relations*, September 1991, pp. 63–83.
Grimmett, Richard F., *Conventional Arms Transfer to the Third World 1983–1990* (Washington, D.C.: U.S. Government Printing Office, Congressional Research Service, 1991).

Harrison, Abby, "The Haves and Have-Nots of the Middle East Revisited," *SAIS Review*, Summer–Fall 1991, pp. 149–64.
Hersh, Seymour, *The Sampson Option* (New York: Random House, 1991).
Hunter, Robert E., *The United States and the New Middle East: Strategic Perspectives After the Persian Gulf War* (Washington, D.C.: Center for Strategic & International Studies, 1992).
Hunter, Shirin, *Iran After Khomeini* (Westport, Conn.: Praeger, 1992).
Lenczowski, George, *American Presidents and the Middle East* (Durham, N.C.: Duke University Press, 1990).
Looney, Robert E., "World Oil Market Outlook: Implications for Stability in the Gulf States," *Middle East Review*, Winter 1989–90, pp. 30–39.
Mead, Walter J., "The OPEC Cartel Thesis Reexamined: Price Constraints from Oil Substitutes," *Journal of Energy and Development*, Spring 1986, pp. 239–42.
Norton, Augustus R., "Breaking Through the Wall of Fear in the Arab World," *Current History*, January 1992, pp. 37–41.
Olorunfemi, Michael and Maria Knoble, "OPEC's Experience in the 1980s: Shaping Its Strategies for the 1990s," *OPEC Review*, Spring 1991, pp. 1–13.
Quandt, William, *Saudi Arabia in the 1980s: Foreign Policy, Security and Oil* (Washington, D.C.: Brookings Institution, 1981).
Roberts, John, *A War for Oil: Energy Issues and the Gulf War of 1991* (Boulder, Colo.: International Research Center for Energy and Economic Development, Occasional Papers, No. 13, 1991).
Safran, Nadav, *Saudi Arabia: The Ceaseless Quest for Security* (Cambridge, Mass.: Harvard University Press, 1985).
Sandwick, John A., *The Gulf Cooperation Council: Moderation and Stability in an Interdependent World* (Boulder, Colo.: Westview Press and Washington, D.C.: American-Arab Affairs Council, 1987).
Tussing, Arlon, "An OPEC Obituary," *Public Interest*, Winter 1983, pp. 3–21.
Twinam, Joseph Wright, *The Gulf, Cooperation and the Council: An American Perspective* (Washington, D.C.: Middle East Policy Council, 1992).

Index

Abu Musa island, 83
Afghan War, 24
Algiers Accord of 1975, 11
Al-Hakim, Baqir, 110, 205
Al-Nuhayyan, President Zayid bin Sultan, 202
Al-Sadr, Ayatollah Muhammad, 39
Al-Turabi, Hassan, 94
"America firstism," 226
Arab Cooperation Council, 37
Arab-Israeli conflict, 10
Arab-Israeli War of 1948, 174
Arab-Israeli War of 1967, 4, 7
Arab-Israeli War of 1973, 7
Arab oil embargo, 8–9, 10, 130
Arms proliferation (missile proliferation), 13
Assad, Hafez, 11, 37, 38, 180
Aswan Dam, 7

Baghdad Pact (also CENTO), 3, 4
Baker, James, 43
Balance of power in the Persian Gulf, 12
Battle of Khafji, 215
Berlin Wall, 1, 2
Blagovolin, Sergei, 32
British withdrawal from the Persian Gulf (1968–1970), 4–5, 11, 12
Buchanan, Pat, 226
Bush, President George, 2, 134, 139

Cadillac-like military establishment, 128
Camp David Agreement, 8, 52
Carter, Jimmy, 9, 197
Carter Doctrine, 86, 103
Central Treaty Organization (CENTO), 3, 4
Cheney, Dick, 139
China's arms sales to Iran, 43
Clinton, President Bill, 96, 224, 226
Clinton administration's continuation of Bush's policies, 57–58
Commonwealth of Independent States (CIS), 1, 9, 22
Comparison of Soviet actions in South Yemen (PDYR) and in Afghanistan, 24
Competitive superciliosity of Iran and Saudi Arabia, 87
Conference on Security and Cooperation in the Mediterranean (CSCM), 69–70
Conflict within the GCC, 208–10
Conflict between Nasserites and monarchists, 174–75
Cost of Desert Storm, 22–23
Cost of Iran-Iraq War, 22

Damascus Declaration, 38, 114, 134, 203–4
Desert Storm coalition, 25, 35, 38, 39

238 / Index

Dhofar rebellion, 215
Dollar surplus states, 222
Dulles, John Foster, 3

Egypt's role in the Iran-Iraq War, 28
Eisenhower, Dwight, 3
Euro-America discussed, 60
European Economic Community (EEC), 9, 10, 11
Explanation of the price decline of 1986, 152–53
Exportability of the Islamic revolution, 85
Exportability of the Iranian revolution, 104

Factors contributing to the emergence of Iraq as a regional power in the Persian Gulf, 103–4
Fahd, King, 139
Faisal, King, 126, 131
Fez summit, 132
Front-line Arab states, 175

GCC plus two agreement, 89. *See also* Damascus Declaration
General Agreement on Tariffs and Trade (GATT), 63
Geo-economics vs. geopolitics, 57–58
Gorbachev, Mikhail, 2, 9, 25, 86, 197
Greater and Lesser Tumbs, 83
Great Satan, 84
Green peril discussed, 60–61
Gulf Cooperation Council (GCC), 1, 11, 14, 22, 23, 37, 38, 102, 125, 133, 135, 136, 143, 179

Hard-line Arab states, 9
Hawkish Iranian oil policy (1970s), 83
Hussein, Saddam, 11

Implications of the disintegration of the USSR, 29
International Monetary Fund's role in Egypt's economy, 27–28
Iranian activities in Sudan, Egypt and Lebanon, 40–41
Iranian hostage crisis, 6
Iranian interactions with the Gulf sheikhdoms, 41–42
Iranian military build-up, 162
Iranian military purchases, 190
Iranian overtures toward the USSR in the late 1980s, 24

Iranian revolution, 5
Iran-Iraq War, 6–7, 11
Iran's acquisition of nuclear technology, 14
Iran's attitude regarding the Iraqi invasion of Kuwait, 115–16
Iran's hyperactive foreign policy in north Africa and Central Asia, 81–82
Iran's ties with small Gulf states, 206–7
Iraqi coup of 1958, 7
Iraqi invasion of Kuwait, 12
Iraqi-Soviet ties, 114
Islamic Front for the Liberation of Bahrain (IFLB), 205
Islamic resurgence in the Persian Gulf, 13
Islamic Salvation Front (Algeria), 94
Islamistan, 60
Israeli nuclear capability, 13–14
Israeli policy nuclear ambiguity, 191
Israel's nuclear policy, 44

Jami'at Islamiya (Egypt), 95

Karr, Alphonse, 221
Khalid, King, 126
Khomeini, Ayatollah Rouhollah, 3, 5, 6, 7, 38, 40, 84, 103, 104, 106, 110, 116, 138, 206, 221, 224
Khrushchev, Nikita, 7
Kissinger, Henry, 8
Kozyrev, Andrey, 36
Kurdish insurrection in Iraq, 110
Kurdish problem, 12
Kurdish rebellion in Iran, 39

Legitimacy of the Middle Eastern governments explained, 172–73
Linkage between arms race in the Persian Gulf and OPEC's cohesion, 161–62

Missile Technology Control Regime (MTCR), 185, 189
Mubarak, President Husni, 132, 139

Najafabadi, Ali Hadi, 206
Nasser, Gamal Abdel, 4, 7, 131, 173, 145, 193
Nasserism, 27, 138
New political thinking, 2
New Saudi Arabia, 134
Nixon, President Richard M., 4, 83

Nixon Doctrine, 4, 5, 82
North Atlantic Treaty Organization (NATO), 53, 55, 58, 64, 173

One-and-a-half pillar policy, 83
Operation Desert Storm (Gulf War of 1991), 11, 12, 125, 135, 138, 139, 141, 144, 184
Operation Staunch, 6
Organization for Economic Cooperation and Development (OECD), 153
Organization of Arab Petroleum Exporting Countries (OAPEC), 8, 84
Organization of Petroleum Exporting Countries (OPEC), 8, 34, 84, 107, 127, 128, 130, 177
Ozal, President Turgut, 119

Pahlavi, Shah Mohammad Reza, 4, 5, 81, 181
Palestine Liberation Organization (PLO), 8, 22, 52, 95, 131, 142, 193
Palestinian Question, 8, 226
Pan Arabism, 4
Pax Americana, 60, 61, 62
Peninsula Shield, 210
Perestroika, 2
Persian Gulf as a new arena of competition between U.S. and Europe, 49–50
Post–Desert Storm U.S. policies in the Persian Gulf, 42–43

Qassem, Karim, 3, 4, 7

Rabin, Prime Minister Yitzhak, 192, 226
Rafsanjani, Ali Hashemi, 68, 88, 94, 115, 190, 191
Rapid Deployment Joint Task Force, 5
Reagan, Ronald, 5
Rejectionist states (Libya, Syria, and Iraq), 8
Relations between Iraq and Turkey, 119
Responses of the oil market in the 1980s, 151–52
Revitalization of NATO, 49
Revolutionary Guards, 118
Role of the "center" in Iraqi politics, 111–12
Russian submarine sale to Iran, 35
Russian ties with Iran, 35–36
Russian ties with Saudi Arabia, 34–35

Rutskoi, Alexander, 30, 32

Sadat, Anwar, 7, 8
Saleh, General Zubair M., 94
Saud, King Abd al Aziz, 126
Saudi foreign policy of the Faisal-Fahd era, 130
Saudi-Iranian relations, 206
Saudi oil policy in the 1990s, 165
Security Council Resolutions (SCRs) 660, 661, 678, 107–8
Shakrai, Sergei, 33
Shi'ite rebellion in Iraq, 39–40
Sobor described, 33
Socialism in one country, 7
Soviet arms supplies to Iran, 9
Soviet invasion of Afghanistan (1979), 5
Stalin, Joseph, 7
Sterligov, Alexander, 32
Structural factors contributing to the marginalization of Iraq, 101–2
Suez crisis, 3

Tarasenko, Sergei, 33
Thatcher, Margaret, 55
Tripolarity of the international political system, 10
Truman, President Harry S, 82
Truman Doctrine, 51
Turkish significance in post–Cold War years, 67
Twin Pillars policy, 5, 178

USCENTCOM (1983), 5, 6
U.S.–European tensions over out of area entanglements, 59
U.S. policies in the Persian Gulf, 42
U.S. reflagging of Kuwaiti vessels, 23

Variables enhancing Iran's strategic significance in the Persian Gulf (1990s), 117
Venice Declaration, 52

Wahhabism, 137
Waning influence of the USSR in the Gulf War of 1991, 25
Watchful Neglect defined, 82, 227
Western European Union (WEU), 51, 54, 58, 59

Yelogin, Vyacheslav, 36
Yeltsin, President Boris, 136

About the Editors and Contributors

M. E. Ahrari is Professor of Middle East and West Asian Affairs at the Air War College. He is a specialist in U.S. policy process, with interests in foreign and defense policies, superpower relations in the Middle East, and the political economy of oil. His books include *The Gulf and International Security* (1989); *Ethnic Groups and U.S. Foreign Policy* (Greenwood, 1987); *OPEC — The Failing Giant* (1986); and *The Dynamics of Oil Diplomacy: Conflict and Consensus* (1980). He has also published extensively in professional journals in the United States, the United Kingdom, and Asia.

Leon T. Hadar teaches at the American University School of International Service and serves as an Adjunct Scholar at the CATO Institute. His recent book is *Quagmire: America in the Middle East* (1992).

Ahmad Hashim is a consultant on the Middle East, specializing in Iraq. His recent writings include an article in *Current History*.

Kenneth Katzman is a Middle East specialist at the Congressional Research Service in Washington, D.C. His most recent book is *The Warriors of Islam: Iran's Revolutionary Guard*.

Robert E. Looney is Professor of National Security Affairs at the Naval Postgraduate School in Monterey, California.

James H. Noyes has been a Research Fellow at the Hoover Institution since 1985. He served as Deputy Assistant Secretary of Defense for Near Eastern, African, and South Asian Affairs in the Nixon and

Ford administrations. He has written *The Clouded Lens: Persian Gulf Security and U.S. Policy* (1979; rev. 1981), and his most recent publications have appeared in *American-Arab Affairs* and in M. E. Ahrari, ed., *The Gulf and International Security* (1989). Since 1984 he has served as editor of the Middle East section of the *Yearbook on International Communist Affairs*.

Joseph Twinam is John C. West Professor at The Citadel. He is a former Deputy Assistant Secretary of State for Near Eastern and South Asian Affairs under the Carter and Reagan administrations.

David Winterford is a member of the faculty of the National Security Affairs Department, Naval Postgraduate School, Monterey, California. Currently, he is writing a book on the strategic impact of changing economic relations in the Middle East and Far East.